JUDAISM'S PROMISE,
MEETING THE CHALLENGE
OF MODERNITY

PETER LANG
New York • Bern • Frankfurt • Berlin
Brussels • Vienna • Oxford • Warsaw

www.ingramcontent.com/pod-product-compliance
Lightning Source LLC
Chambersburg PA
CBHW052143300426
44115CB00011B/1501

SEYMOUR W. ITZKOFF

JUDAISM'S PROMISE, MEETING THE CHALLENGE OF MODERNITY

PETER LANG
New York • Bern • Frankfurt • Berlin
Brussels • Vienna • Oxford • Warsaw

Library of Congress Cataloging-in-Publication Data
Itzkoff, Seymour W.
Judaism's promise: meeting the challenge of modernity / Seymour W. Itzkoff.
p. cm.
Includes bibliographical references and index.
1. Judaism—21st century. 2. Judaism—Essence, genius, nature.
3. Judaism—History. 4. Jews—History. I. Title.
BM565.I89   296.09'051—dc23   2012012647
ISBN 978-1-4331-2006-0 (hardcover)
ISBN 978-1-4331-2626-0 (paperback)
ISBN 978-1-4539-0871-6 (e-book)

Bibliographic information published by **Die Deutsche Nationalbibliothek**.
Die Deutsche Nationalbibliothek lists this publication in the "Deutsche
Nationalbibliografie"; detailed bibliographic data are available
on the Internet at http://dnb.d-nb.de/.

Cover illustration by Jules Itzkoff

© 2014, 2015 Peter Lang Publishing, Inc., New York
29 Broadway, 18th floor, New York, NY 10006
www.peterlang.com

All rights reserved.
Reprint or reproduction, even partially, in all forms such as microfilm,
xerography, microfiche, microcard, and offset strictly prohibited.

Moses Mendelssohn (1729–1786); Hermann Cohen (1842–1918); Mordecai Kaplan (1881–1983)

—Judaic Visions of Modernity

BOOKS BY SEYMOUR W. ITZKOFF
Smith College, Emeritus Professor

Cultural Pluralism and American Education	1969
Ernst Cassirer: Scientific Knowledge and the Concept of Man	1971, 1997 (2nd edition)
A New Public Education	1976
Ernst Cassirer, Philosopher of Culture	1977
Emanuel Feuermann, Virtuoso	1979, 1995 (2nd edition)
The Evolution of Human Intelligence	
1 *The Form of Man, The Evolutionary Origins of Human Intelligence*	1983
2 *Triumph of the Intelligent, The Creation of Homo sapiens sapiens*	1985
3 *Why Humans Vary in Intelligence*	1987
4 *The Making of the Civilized Mind*	1990
How We Learn to Read	1986
Human Intelligence and National Power	1991
The Road to Equality, Evolution and Social Reality	1992
The Decline of Intelligence in America, A Strategy for National Renewal	1994
Children Learning to Read, A Guide for Parents and Teachers	1996
The Human Prospect	
1 *The Inevitable Domination by Man, An Evolutionary Detective Story*	2000
2 *2050: The Collapse of the Global Techno-Economy*	2003
3 *Intellectual Capital in Twenty-First-Century Politics*	2003
4 *Rebuilding Western Civilization, Beyond the Twenty-First-Century Collapse*	2005
Who Are the Jews?	
1 *Soul of the Israelites*	2004
2 *A Nation of Philosophers*	2004
3 *Fatal Gift, Jewish Intelligence and Western Civilization*	2006
The World Energy Crisis and the Task of Retrenchment	2008
The End of Economic Growth: What Does It Mean for American Society?	2009

Table of Contents

Introduction ix
Chapter 1: The Future of the Jews? 1
Chapter 2: Sources for the Religious 11
Chapter 3: Torah/Law 27
Chapter 4: Scriptures 45
Chapter 5: Talmudic Republic 63
Chapter 6: Haskalah: Crisis 83
Chapter 7: Our Judaic Heritage 101
Chapter 8: *Holocaust:* A Message for the Jews 117
Chapter 9: Israel, Judaism: Our Contemporary World Malaise 131
Chapter 10: Understanding Historical Judaism 147
Chapter 11: Judaism Reconstituted 169
Chapter 12: Values and the Future 187
Notes 201
Index 213

Introduction

Our Concern

Judaism and the Jews are gradually disappearing. Take a look at the comparative numbers of Jews and other religionists and you will understand my meaning. Few Jews even whisper about this looming demographic and civilizational disaster. Why? Simply, fatalism.

What you will read in the pages and chapters that follow is an argument by a dissident Jew who does not accept this fatalism. In front of everyone's eyes, the message is that Judaism is an ancient fossilized tradition, irrelevant to the world except for a nation, Israel. This is wrong. Israel does profess to be a Jewish state, modern and progressive. But Israel itself at the least faces the same demographic tidal wave that may efface Diaspora Judaism. Demography is not necessarily destiny. I here want to argue against this dismal determinism.

Much of this book delves into the historic achievements of the Jews. In order to explore the possibilities for the renewal of Judaism you must understand its past, and why it has for so long survived so much malignant opposition. This is important because the truly heroic adaptability to change amidst the threats inherent in these events is hidden to students of Jewish history. Why, because of the control of Jewish education by those who want to preserve their powers of domination, the doorkeepers of contemporary Judaism. These consecrated ones are destroying Judaism today.

If you can truly absorb the meaning of the radical alterations made by Jews to adapt our faith to the ever-new of history, you will understand that it is still possible for a new Jewish leadership to go forth and educate the world to rise up to a higher level of intellectual and moral values. As part of this enlightened understanding of Judaism's path through many thousands of years of destiny, you will also begin to understand the contemporary power structures within our faith and heritage.

The current waning of Judaism as a religion and culture is due to the fact that its surface institutional representations are petrified. They might have been appropriate in the 16th century given the anti-Semitic hatred and persecutions that Jews suffered under the thumb both of Islam as well as Christianity, but since then the challenges have been different. The seductions of assimilation and toleration have seen millions of Jews flee the synagogue to evaporate into the woodwork of secularism or Christianity. As a result the synagogue has convulsed into successive splinterings in its attempt to hold on to its congregants and bring them back.

Isn't it ironic that the one Judaic group that is flourishing in numbers and media recognition today is the *Haredim*, the ultra-orthodox pious, garbed in their 15th-century uniforms. But, of course, few dare to engage in public discussion of their views on personal immortality, the *Messiah*, the role of women in their congregations and family life, their responsibilities in defending their homeland, either the United States or Israel, their commitment to do a day's work for self-support. Sadly they are the window dressing of today's Judaism.

This concern for the existence and future of a modern and relevant Judaism is the message of "Judaism's Promise." The challenge to Judaism in its ability to survive the 21st century should constitute one of the most important lessons for the entire world, both for Jews and non-Jews. This importance of Judaism lies in the deeper core, one might say the metaphysical assumptions rooted in a pure monotheism as it relates to the moral behavior of humans, here originally set forth in the Ten Commandments. The documents that thence issued from the Israelites and the Jews over the millennia symbolize this striving to preserve these truths. These were and are an education for Western civilization. The contemporary crisis is thus not merely a Judaic one, but in reality echoes a deeper and universal malaise. A modernized Judaism, still true to its fundamental intellectual and moral commitments, could do much to reverse this downward trend. A moment of opportunity? We ought not waste it.

The present book is thus written to establish the intellectual ground for a new generation of Jews to make this heritage again relevant both to the Jewish people and to those non-Jews who might want to become one with Judaism. The ancient rituals and traditions do have a deeper and universal meaning, and we need to explore their significance. Most important, the primal monotheistic vision of the founding Levites, priests, prophets presented humankind with a new vision for our species, humbling in the face of those ever-unknown powers in the universe.

This understanding was and is critically important to the founding of the faith, the social disciplines and the belief in the existence of the deep roots of the moral law. From this irresistible set of convictions came the Torah, the Holy Scriptures, and the Talmud. We need to tend to these historic visions, but always, go beyond.

It is to the young that these concerns are devoted more as an invitation to enrich and supplement the good of the past than as any *dictat* from "on high." This book sets forth a personal search for meaning, but the issues are universally relevant. The conclusions are simply that our Judaic vision can be saved and reinvigorated. Much of the argument in the following chapters constitutes a contextual underlining of the true historical meaning of Judaism's contributions to our civilization. Most important, the inherent rational secularity, the moral intellectuality of these thousands of years of persistent struggle to obey the law can be reinvigorated, but not by any rigid set of edicts from the mythological past. To the young Jew: do it your way, invigorate the heritage.

Most rabbinical texts treat Judaism as a tradition of whole cloth, a unified vision of which the rabbinate is today the singular purveyor. But, there is in fact no unified Judaic heritage. Rather this heritage is more a series of revolutions in which many well-ensconced leadership traditions have been abandoned. New sets of leaders and ideas have successively come to fruition to allow Jews and Judaism to survive history's always new challenges. That is our argument for the future. From a secular, scholarly standpoint in this book, we identify four revolutionary traditions, thus to argue for our fifth.

Cutting the Chains of Rabbinism

Here is a fifteen-hundred-year-old heritage, certainly evolved over time. Much in the ritual traditions of Judaism today will never be effaced. But should they encompass more than a few percentage points of the substance of Jewishness? As the reader will find from the historical chapters in this book, the rabbinic tradition itself constituted a revolutionary turn from an ancient historic vision, the written Torah, the law.

The Talmud, the core of rabbinical Judaism, grew out of the pharisaic revolution's Oral Torah. Here the words of *Jehovah* were supposedly given to Moses who transmitted them at a distance of over a millennium to the Pharisees to modify, override, re-interpret the written Torah, in the context of modernity, then, Hellenistic civilization. What started as early as the sixth century BCE as an interpretation of the Pentateuch to the ignorant survivors of the Babylonian captivity (by Ezra and Nehemiah), grew over the centuries into the Oral Torah, a way of fending off the modernistic rationalism and culture of Hellenism.

Here in the spirit of Plato was a 'lie of words,' meant to guide the *am ha arez*, the people of the land, into moral and public behavior more congruent with modernity. The priestly Sadducees of the Temple would at that time accept nothing as Holy Writ beyond the Torah. They scoffed at the Pharisees as "Greek" intellectuals, and then they themselves immersed themselves in the wealth-producing rituals of the Second Temple and the cultural institutions of the Greeks. The Samaritans, in old Israel, wanted only the Five Books as holy guidance. 'But they essentially were Assyrian immigrants, not true Judeans.'

What is critical, as I demonstrate in this book, is that after the Sadducees disappeared, with the obliteration of the Second Temple, the victorious Pharisees themselves did not recreate the Oral Torah teachings into a permanent written document. Instead, at the end of the first century, they created the Holy Bible of the Jews, the Pentateuch, the Prophetic and the Wisdom writings, *TaNaK*. This in a sense was testimony to the intellectual power of Hellenism. The Holy Scriptures were part of the Jewish response.

The Mishnah and then the Talmudic setting down of the traditions of the Oral Law came, at the earliest, one hundred and fifty years later, an interpreted way of life in the then-established *modernity* of Roman and oncoming Christian challenges, the Jews ever more, a people apart.

The Holy Scriptures, the various Talmuds are all rich in wisdom and guidance. They remain a deep and precious heritage of the Jews. But they served a world that no longer exists. We need another Talmud, a new guide to the future, a future now devoid of the supernaturalism that, at least among modern Jews, gains no adherence over their real beliefs and behaviors.

"Judaism's Promise," then, should be seen as a prolegomenon to a new, progressive Judaism. It will value Torah, Scriptures, and Talmud, together with the accumulated writings of ancient and modern intellectual and moral minds, Jews and Gentiles. It will put this wisdom into a form that will discipline a widening community of Jews with the defensive fiber to allow Judaism to flourish humanely for another three thousand years.

Writer's Perspective

This book is written by a Jew, a secular Jew educated in the Yiddish schools of the Workmen's Circle (*Arbiter Ring*), but also in the New York City Public Schools. An American citizen first, a Jew second. The human mind can love pluralistically. My parents were immigrants from Czarist Russia. They had a deep love for

America, their adopted nation. Putting me in semi-socialist Yiddish schools was a nod to our heritage. At the same time they were totally committed to the full Americanization of their children, their commitment diminished not at all by their Jewish heritage. Their allegiance to this nation and mine lay in the fact that our nation still cherishes the privacy of community histories and beliefs. All humans need the amalgam of a national plus an ethnic heritage. The great test comes in the balancing of the two.

When asked why they did not attend a synagogue, this after my first initiation to a Bar Mitzvah party of a friend's elder brother, both my parents spoke out strongly—"hypocrites." Their Judaism demanded more of themselves. And that was the end of the discussion. Neither of my parents had a high school education. But culture, music, literature, was their passion. Even after twelve to eighteen hours of slaving away, my mother, a dressmaker in the garment district, my father chained to his candy store, all I heard in our cramped apartment was the Metropolitan Opera. It nearly drove me crazy. I wanted to hear the "Yankees."

I write about this to contrast the orthodox way of Judaism with my family's views on the synagogue. My parents viewed synagogue Judaism as a philistine institution under the thumb of very materialistic and amoral people, who called themselves Jews. Whenever my sister and I would talk about the books that we obtained from the public library, they would ask whether the authors were Jews. To them the highest mark of a Jew was whether he was a Sholem Aleichem, a Fritz Kreisler, or a Richard Tucker.

Such opinions about synagogue Judaism were not mine alone. The masses who have left Judaism testify to the aridity of the institution and the present crisis it represents for this richest of religious traditions. Note that Moses Mendelssohn, the great 18th-century Enlightenment Jew who wanted all his brethren to breathe the free air of Emancipation, saw all of his children convert to Christianity, Felix, his composer grandson included. Yet, it should be known, Felix still considered himself a Jew.

Both of my parents lost many dear ones in the *Holocaust*. I remember looking into my father's drawn face when I pointed with childish energy to the *New York Times* map showing the Nazi divisions closing in on his small railroad town, then inhabited by his mother, sisters, brother, their children. The *Panzer* divisions were surging toward Moscow, this in late 1941. I will never forget the silence of his eyes. The Germans came too fast. Much of his family and my mother's in the Ukraine were consequently destroyed.

One of the wonderful aspects of historic Judaism is that people like myself as well as the most reactionary *Haredim* are inclusively part of the Jewish community. So we can all talk together about what it means to be a Jew, and what the future might bring. I remember asking my father why as a semi-socialist he voted for

FDR, the 'savior' of capitalism, rather than Norman Thomas. He winked. I guess he meant that his socialism was a big tent.

Rabbinical Riches

The rabbinic tradition is rich. The term "rabbi" is Aramaic, not Hebrew, and translates as "teacher." We Jews have been taught by many fine "teachers": Baruch Spinoza, Solomon Maimon, Moses Mendelssohn, Karl Marx, Sigmund Freud, Ernst Cassirer, Albert Einstein. Not all of them were educated in seminaries. Many fine American minds have emanated from the Jewish Theological Seminary in New York City and Hebrew Union College in Cincinnati, both institutions devoted to the training of rabbis. In a variety of books on the Judaic heritage one finds illuminating and unself-conscious truths that are a credit to these rabbinical authors.

For example, Rabbi Shaye Cohen, in his study of the "The Beginning of Jewishness," admits to the conventionality of the matrilineal rabbinical law that has caused so much anguish when Jewish men fall in love and want to marry women who don't happen to be born into a Jewish family. It is in the Mishnah, the prolegomenon to the Talmuds that one finds the exclusion of children of non-Jewish mothers married to Jewish fathers from claiming a Judaic heritage [Cohen, S. 1999. *The Beginnings of Jewishness*, Berkeley: Univ. of California Press, pp. 263.] It was a third-century adoption from Roman law. The Romans had their own reasons, and the scholars of the Mishnah had theirs. The Rabbis obeyed, and some Jews meekly followed. Many others left Judaism.

Also, Rabbi Joel Kraemer in his biographical study of Moses Maimonides (d. 1204 CE), admits to the probable factuality of the oft-stated rumor that Maimonides and his family converted to Islam under the press of the Almohads, while many Spanish and North African Jews did not, and were *not* killed by these Islamic fundamentalists. [Kraemer, J. 2008. *Maimonides*. New York: Doubleday, pp. 123-4.]. The Maimon family had their reasons, probably economic, for so doing, as they migrated from Cordoba in Spain to Fez in Morocco. Later, Moses Maimon moved first to Crusader Palestine (Acre), where he seemingly reclaimed his Judaic heritage, then migrated to Muslim Egypt where he doctored Saladin's harem and now flourished in his Judaic intellectualism.

Revolutionary Judaism

In *Judaism's Promise* I describe the four revolutionary stages of Judaism. The point is, why not another revolution? We desperately need to reexamine what Judaism stands for.

The first great revolutionary transformation took from the Mosaic stragglers to the Holy Land the concept of one abstract if personal God, demanding a unity of these always chaotic fighting tribes. Yahweh had chosen them instead: of all others to adhere to a higher moral law, to come together as a people who celebrate their human weakness under the disciplines of the Ten Commandments. It took hundreds of years to spell out the *concretia* of life lived under the law, Torah, and always we are educated to the human fallings away from these disciplines. The complete writing down of the Five Books only became tangible when the holy temple in Jerusalem was destroyed and the Jews as a nation lost their homelands.

The second revolution was also a rising up to the challenge of national disaster, then the destruction of the Second Temple by all-powerful Rome and the need to solidify the faith in a richness that went beyond the ancient books of the Pentateuch. Thus, in Yavneh, c.90 CE, the Pharisaic leadership synthesized into Holy Scripture the Pentateuch, the Prophetic and historical writings, plus the growing literature of the wisdom teachers such as Job. Here was a full response to Greek intellectualism, a faith, a portable vision of life that as with the written Torah needed no political nationality to preserve this searchlight into the mind and the soul of humanity.

The third revolution came hundreds of years later, as Christianity was beginning to challenge Judaism as the true faith. The Jews no longer could hope for national redemption. The Talmuds of Palestine and Babylon assembled the "Oral Law." Then, the Holy Scriptures were literally superseded in interpretation and obligation. The Talmuds were a running encyclopedia of an evolving faith now accommodated to the changes of supernatural modernity. And in the great medieval debates between Christianity, Islam, and Judaism, they proved second to none in this articulation with their daughter faiths.

The Enlightenment was the next and fourth great challenge. It trumpeted emancipation and egress from both the physical as well as the mental ghetto of the Jews. Thence from the mid-eighteenth century to our time, the synagogue has struggled with the meaning of science, rationality, and community. Clearly it has failed. Jews in the millions have abandoned their identity. In the twentieth century two significant events have occurred to underline the crisis of our religion. The first was the *Holocaust*. The true meaning of this terrible event has never been bravely faced by Jew or Gentile alike. The second was the gesture of absolution by the Christian world, the establishment of Israel as a Jewish state in the ancient homeland. In successive chapters we will discuss the deeper significance for today of these two events.

The fifth revolution is yet to come. It must be born with the coming of new generations of Jews who see their heritage from the standpoint of an enlightened scientific education to which they all have now been subject. It must open Judaism to the fresh breeze of universality instead of exclusivity. It must teach Jews and Gentiles the moral and intellectual lessons that were created in the ghettos of the Talmudic era. Then, a people lived in classless, defensive poverty, but yet immersed themselves in an intellectual and literate commitment to the law. This evolving faith must above all be a defender of reason and morality, an ever-modernizing scriptural and Talmudic dialectic good for the future.

Chapter Summaries

The first two chapters are (a) preliminary statements of the problem of survival facing Judaism, and then (b) a secular perspective on religion, its human origins and the inevitable challenge of severing the ever-modern religious form of thought and life from rank, primitive supernaturalism.

Following are four chapters devoted to delineating the evidence for these great turning points in the evolution of Judaism. One has to make the case. For the revolutionary character of these shifts in perspective requires the delving into the documentary research itself. These cumulative movements are revealed in both the writings of the Jews as well as their historic encounter with nations and peoples surrounding them. But there are also schismatic historic traditions which have had their own rationales for the faith. And there are also reasons why these were left in the dust.

Chapter Seven leaves the contextual historical analysis for a perspective on those revolutionary turns in Judaism. What is their meaning for today? Our forbears could make these sharp turns in the face of the challenge to survival. Why can't we?

Chapters Eight and Nine more explicitly address the current challenges to the survival of Judaism and the Jews. Chapter Eight develops an analysis of the *Holocaust*, perhaps the most traumatic and convulsive event that has ever scarred the odyssey of Judaism in civilized history. The claim developed here is that while much of the realities, the facts of this event in history, have been fairly expounded, the real meaning of the *Holocaust* has been largely avoided by Jew and non-Jew alike.

The Jews did not fall victim to the supposedly pseudoideology of eugenics as promoted by the Nazis and their followers. Rather, the Jews of Europe were the explicit victims of a millennial dysgenic event that attempted to rid Germany and Europe of Christian Europe's most "challenging" enemy, those so-called poisonous Jews. Why were they so defamed? Why was it so easy for Christian Europe to eradicate them? The answer! They were too intelligent, too productive, too successful in contributing to and assimilating into Christian Europe's high civilization.

Chapter Nine addresses the world as we find it today, and those challenges that are placing and will place the Jews in ever-greater danger. The explosion of impoverished humans of diverse religious backgrounds, especially Islam and Christianity in the undeveloped world, the growing anti-Semitism, and an Israel under threat, are the themes of this chapter. One solution is to expand Jewish demography through a policy of inclusive recruitment reminiscent of the pharisaic recruitment of Jews throughout the Roman world, "god-fearers" (Chapter Four). Today the Jews are middle class wherever they can be found. The State of Israel prospers in its secular democratic and scientific commitments, a model for humanity. But it is surrounded by an Islamic demographic time bomb of hate and envy.

In Chapter Ten we examine the unique contributions of the Jews in their vision of a people "chosen," chosen to be holy, moral, to bear the burden of history. Monotheism, circumcision, *kashrut* and the Sabbath regulations are dealt with from a historical point of view. How can they be interpreted from the secular standpoint of our century with full appreciation of their function for Israelite and Judaic survival? In addition, the critical exclusionary matrilineal principle, a directive that has mortally wounded the faith, used by the rabbis to enforce their powers to decide who is a Jew is historically analyzed. Finally, this chapter argues for the historic contributions of the Talmudic tradition in its creation of the powerful intellectualism within the post-medieval Jewish community.

The modern significance of these historic Jewish ritualistic, moral, and institutional traditions is raised. Why are they important and why should they be retained in a modern reconstitution, now without the need for supernatural obeisance. In Chapter Eleven, this reconstituted Judaism is given substantive character. What has Judaism given to the modern world? There is historic significance even in the institution of the synagogue and the function of the rabbi. However, at the heart of the Judaic metaphysics is the monotheistic principle shorn of its ancient anthropomorphisms that sometimes have marred its powerful significance, here a people committed to live under a higher law than momentary human convenience. Why have the Jews survived? *The law*. The world needs Judaism.

The final Chapter, Twelve, entitled, "Values and the Future," presents a concrete model of a modern, moral, secular vision of Jewish religiosity as it might be developed in response to the challenges of modernity. One of the most important issues raised with regard to the criteria for being a Jew is the moral/materialistic problem. Poor for so long among wealthy and powerful Gentiles, Jews in the West today are emancipated and middle class, some very wealthy. For a people who have undergone the *Holocaust*, because they were Jews, most of these poor East European Jews, we need to raise the question as to whether it is seemly for Jews to surround themselves with personal wealth.

The nature of the synagogue is again central to the question of modernity and relevance. In its original function in the days of Philo and the Pharisees, it was a gathering place for intellectual and moral discussions (Chapter Four). What is its use now? We also need to reexamine the role of a paid, professional rabbi. A final set of principles is presented as a discussion model for a Judaism of the future, a religion with a promise to welcome many more intellectually and morally committed communicants, here and now, a faith in law and reason.

CHAPTER ONE

The Future of the Jews?

Contemporary Context

The role of the Jews in the modern world relates to a pungent and relevant statistic. In a review of the demography of the religions of the world, the 2007 edition of the *Encyclopedia Britannica* gives us the following "membership" numbers as of 2006: Bahai, 7,800,000; Buddhist, 382,542,000; Christian, 2,173,184,000; Hindu, 871,982,000; Judaism, 15,118,000; Muslim, 1,335,964,000; Zoroastrian, 180,300.

It is clear that the Jews constitute but a small percentage of religious adherents in our world. In 1930, with a world population of 2+ billion, there were about 16 million Jews in our world. The *Holocaust* destroyed over one third of these. Naturally, there has been an increase since then to the current figure of just over 15 million worldwide. But also since 1930, the population of the world has more than tripled, to over 7 billion.

It is well to recall that in the days of Persian hegemony, c. 500 BCE to 500 CE, Zoroastrianism was a thriving, relatively gentle monotheistic competitor of the Jewish religion. Persia was overrun by Muslim invaders shortly after this time frame. Islam was forcibly inscribed onto the Persian nation and its many adherents throughout the Middle East. Today Zoroastrianism is a remnant religious memory.

Is this to be the fate of Judaism if we consider it within the contemporary dynamics of history? We can argue that Hinduism is a national religion of India. It is likely, because of its liberal pluralistic embodiments to remain, in some form, as an identifying characteristic of Indian nationalism. Buddhism is more complex. It was the once-dominant religion of China, Korea, and Japan. Today it is difficult to describe the depths of allegiance to its tenets by the vast majority of these populations. It certainly remains strong among Tibetan ethnics, also in Cambodia and Laos, and to some extent in Myanmar (once Burma).

The religions that might be called the offspring of Judaism, Christianity and Islam, especially the latter, show signs of vigor and expansion. This is particularly true in the world's poorer nations and communities. In Europe, Christianity suffers from the same malaise as that affecting Judaism, a falling away from orthodoxy into secularism. Here both religions have formed an ethnic and political base as cultural religions. The state of Israel is an exemplar for the Jews.

Islam, on the other hand, has fallen from its centrality of power in the medieval period to a new florescence of passionate adherence and vigor, partially subsidized by petroleum, but also from the depths of its now political/historical resentment of the West for the latter's centuries-old power and wealth. Little worldly benefit reaches the Muslim masses from those Muslim nations and cliques that control the oil output. One must add that a modern, relatively wealthy and militarily powerful Israel is a further goad to Islamic resentment and militancy.

For Judaism and the Jewish people, now a mere drop in an ocean of believers, the picture is not promising. The state of Israel, while Jewish in culture and heritage, is a secular society with a large and growing Muslim minority. The truly religiously observant minority of Jews is politically and socially powerful, but heavily dependent for its economic survival on the will of the secular Jewish majority. How long the economic subsidization of the anti-political religious minority can continue is questionable.

In general the proportion of Jews in the United States, reckoned at about five million, has increasingly shrunk. Most of the categorized Jews are secular, the intermarriage rate now approaching 50%, the children of these religious "hybrids" being lost to the community of Judaism by rabbinical preemption. Some secular Jews would argue, 'well, so what?' No law in human history mandates that after 5,000 years of existence Judaism and the Jews should survive as a group indefinitely into the future. Take the current fate of above-mentioned Zoroastrians. Or, consider the Hellenism of the ancient Greeks, which in no way is reflected in the current culture and religion of the contemporary Greek-speaking people. That once glorious civilizational vision, one of the roots of the modern West, has vanished forever!

The Case for Judaism

We do not argue here that the fate of the Jews is to irrevocably resemble the fate of Zoroastrianism. However if one makes a statistical analysis as to how many Jews crossed the threshold of a synagogue, sponsored by any of the contemporary Judaic sects, and in any one year, the probability is that the population of Jews in this world would be reduced by half. Further, if one would calculate the demography of Jews on the basis of serious and continuous worship either at home or within the confines of a synagogue or other religious sanctuary, the number of Jews on this planet would again be cut by a large percentage. This is true to a certain extent in Christianity and to a lesser extent in Islam. But these religions are much plumper in their demographic measurements and can afford the losses as they are offset by their gains. Judaism is on the brink.

The argument to be presented here is that Judaism and the Jews need not be a historic relic. There is much in both the historical reach of the Jewish experience as well as its religious, political, and moral confrontations that rises to make of Judaism a potent factor in the future of the human race. The problem lies in the current leadership, the supposed leadership, one might correct. Judaism is today ensconced in the past. The only route for a thinking Jew seems to be secularism, with a nod toward the heritage, cultural, linguistic, even philosophic.

Indeed, in the United States, two recent movements within rabbinic Judaism have added an emancipatory element to the dialogue. In the movement of Reconstructionism, articulated by a Lithuanian-born Orthodox/Conservative Rabbi Mordicai Kaplan, an attempt was made, and in some intellectual depth, to modernize such religious conceptions of God, salvation, rituals, the Sabbath, holidays, and the synagogue itself. Kaplan intuited the problem, but as a devout Jew and long a member of the faculty of the Jewish Theological Seminary (once orthodox, more recently a conservative trainer of rabbis), he could move only so far. Because of Kaplan's intellectual integrity, his teaching institution was forced to keep him on as a valued member of the Seminary and despite the vociferous objections of his rabbinical faculty colleagues. Kaplan threw out the entire megillah. "Judaism without a theoric God" was his theme. Rabbinic Judaism was maintained, but in the metaphorical interpretation à la Philo of Alexandria, Egypt, c. 50 CE.

To answer the limited radicalism of Reconstructionism's overhaul of Judaic theology was Rabbi Sherwin Wine's Jewish Humanism, Wine was trained in secular philosophy as well as in Reformed Judaism at the Hebrew Union College in Cincinnati. Wine's major opus was entitled "Judaism Beyond God." His thought was to shift Judaism away from formal belief, for example in the supernatural veracity of the Torah heretofore believed to be the teachings of Yahweh as given to Moses. His perspectives were close to Kaplan's view of "Judaism as a Civilization." However, Wine made no attempt to retain any portion of the above conceptual and linguistic traditions of Judaism, albeit even in a metaphorical dressing. Rabbi Wine's humanistic Judaism sought to celebrate the traditional cultural and intellectual traditions only now cloaked in a modern distinctly secular political liberalism.

Both leaders have won a following. They created new synagogue congregations which have commemorated the leadership of the founding rabbis as well as promoting in Judaism new moral and institutional directions. Rabbi Kaplan died in 1983 at the age of 101. Rabbi Wine was mysteriously killed in 2007, in an automobile accident in Morocco at the age of 78. The expected revolution in Judaic belief and practice did not occur. Somehow the need for new forms of synagogue Judaism, reconstructionist of the ancient theological formulas, or the embracing of a completely secular reinterpretation of Judaism within a synagogue setting, by means of liberal sociopolitical values, have not reignited a surge of proselytes converting to either vision.

Most Jewish descendants both in Israel and the United States of any current generation value the appellation, Jew. Sadly, a large proportion of their descendants subsequently disappear from the Judaic manifold. Most often they are the products of marriages *prima facie* unacceptable to the rabbinate, except Reform, Reconstructionist, and Humanist congregations. If their parents were so disinterested in synagogue Judaism that they would marry outside the faith (especially a Jewish male to a non-Jewish female), it is highly doubtful that rabbinical Judaism would be interested in welcoming them into the fold.

Part of the withering process is due to the liberal emancipatory settings within which Ashkenazi Jews have lived since the 18th century. More and more humans in the developed world can live without religion. Indeed the gap is painful for many who must search for meaning in their lives through a commitment to a form of religion. Over a billion Chinese have abandoned Buddhism and Christianity. Still, many Chinese would return to a form of religious commitment if they could. South Korea is an example of a nation whose peoples are able to take or leave religion. Many of these have rejected their ancient roots in Buddhism and turned to various forms of Christianity. Today there are more Christian South Koreans than Buddhist, 26% to 23%. The majority proclaims no religious affiliation.

The *Holocaust* should have sharpened the Jews' awareness of their heritage and the importance of reinforcing this ancient commitment in the face of unimaginable hatred by ostensibly Christian Europeans during World War II. Sadly, the establishment of Israel as a political home for the remnants, and Israel's consequent struggle to survive again against a tide of unrelieved hatred, war, and terrorism, has diverted Jewish analysis from the broader issue of survival in the *galut*.

It will be the argument in this book that indeed there is a case to be made not merely for the survival of Judaism and the Jewish people, a continuity that is congruent with the maintenance of Western civilization. But also, a case can be made beyond the two most recent attempts by Rabbis Kaplan and Wine for a Judaism that can flourish into a new era, one beyond the Reform Judaism that was German Jews' response in the mid-nineteenth century in their coming to terms with the Enlightenment, science and secularism, and the consequent political and sociological emancipation.

Judaism and the Jews are under siege. In the United States there is liberal acceptance and then in consequence a surge to economic and social dominance. A tacit pact has been made by observant and non-observant Jews to quiet any dialogue. To gain status, power, and economic wealth it is now necessary to keep one's Jewish mouth sealed. In Europe, it is the same, except that since WW II a new factor has emerged. True, the Europeans in general are in a sanitary process of paying official penance for the 20th-century horrors. At the same time they have opened their doors to massive Islamic immigration and consequent underclass internal demographic expansion. Certainly in France, for example, the Jews are once more under physical siege by Muslim hatred. We have stated above and will discuss below the situation in Israel which down the line two or so decades from now may face an internal crisis, notwithstanding possible annihilation by a united external Islamic jihad.

Judaism must be strengthened. But it will not happen by the mere continuation of the present paralysis of both thought and action. We need to create powerful centripetal forces of attraction to a Judaism that is in concert with tomorrow as well as yesterday. Certainly this Judaism must be in harmony with what the most progressive and contributing Jews of the last several centuries have set out as their pathway, again similar to the great Jewish movements of the past. At the same time Judaism cannot divest itself of the inner religiosity and moral scrutiny which is at the core of this 3,000-year-old civilizational tradition. If we cannot go as far as Rabbi Kaplan in his use of traditional vocabulary, we need not throw out the baby with the bathwater as has Rabbi Wine.

The example of South Korea with the large-scale adoption of Christianity in its various permutations should give us pause as to the "why" of the continued attractiveness of religion to modern populations. Naturally, the South Koreans could not be blamed for their sense of hostility to the long occupation by the Japanese and the latter's nationalistic variety of Buddhism, Shintoism. Christianity could be seen as a rejection of the religious outlook of the occupiers. Yet the seeming coherence of Christian beliefs with a completely modernistic view of such issues as abortion, contraception, stem-cell research, cloning, all those bio/social innovations that worry fundamentalist Protestant and Catholic Americans, requires a deeper understanding of religious belief as held by these Asiatic citizens.

The above reality of South Korea, and indeed the United States where external allegiance to religious affiliation can still coexist with modern scientific secular decision making about life and law reflects the need for deeper connections with fellow humans and history to order one's life commitments. Seemingly there are not enough intrinsic human fulfillments in just being modern, scientific in outlook, even democratic in political organization. Reflected here is a need to have a higher belief system, a moral structure made coherent in the institutional ritual and heritage of church or temple. There needs to be an accompanying literature of humility and guidance along with a nonprofessional ministry to lead a people forward in a behaviorally ambiguous world.

As we will develop in the next chapter, the religious impulse in a setting of community social belief goes beyond the surface material associations of modern dynamic materialism. Who we are as humans cannot be defined alone in sociopolitical national terms. There needs to be in every human being an awareness of the fragility of all life that ultimately transcends political associations.

Here the experiences of the Jews stands high in solution to this pantheon of human weakness. Moses railed against the "stiff-necked" ragged runaways from Egypt, and their perennial fall into every pathology that human existence can present. The Jews as a historic people have taught the world much about survival, the sustenance that a defensive moral vision of life opens up for us, now and into the future.

Religion beyond the Political

Our 21st-century world is especially dangerous for the Jews. A tiny contributing people to the functioning of the modern West, they are now doubly endangered by the crisis under which this self-same West is presently experiencing. The chaos, violence, and counterrationality that we see in contemporary Islam is merely the beginning of what may turn out be a new shift in world culture away from science and democracy, away from secularism and rationality, to wars of religion and ideology, one against the other.

This issue that will be further developed in later chapters must at least be mentioned here. The *Holocaust* may be only a horrific reminder of what is in store for mankind as we go from the barely two billion people on earth early in the twentieth century to the 6.2 billion at the beginning of the 21st century and the expected 9–10 billion humans by mid-21st century. The economic collapse of 2008–2009 was essentially precipitated by the relative shortage of oil and the consequent spike in its cost. Oil and the other crucial fossil energies have made possible the abundant food, medical, and industrial/technological advances of the past one hundred years. It is here where we must place the point of origin of this spectacular growth in human populations. The concern is not only that so few Jews have participated in this demographic ebullience. More to the point, it is potentially tragic for civilization that the true lesson of the perdurance and even flourishing of Jewish creativity and moral integrity has not found its way in greater measure into the larger domains of humanity.

And it is in this looming specter of vast shortages of the essentials of material middle-class life, no less basic survival that will define the meanings of human experience as we wend our way deeper into this 21st century. We must be prepared for potential horrors of conflict precipitated by semireligious and ideological demonologies seeking scapegoats and victims. The Jewish people and their remaining institutions of belief and culture have profited as we entered this new century. But we have already experienced the acts of irrationality linked to powerful technological capabilities, death machines. Two world wars should have taught the leadership of the secular West something about ideological and religious irrationality. Continuing genocides of innocents along with the Jews' own destruction should teach us what can happen under such circumstances. Indeed, the cataclysm of the *Holocaust* itself occurred in a time of growing prosperity and knowledge. What might happen in a time of desperation? How should the Jewish people prepare?

Understanding is the precursor to protective action. Religions can be allied with power and autocracy, and of course persecution and genocide. The medieval church, the Inquisition, the current alliance of mullahs and the state in Iran, indeed throughout the Islamic world, exemplify a contemporary alliance of political power and the religious thwarting of free thought and the institutions of liberty. The most egregious failure of religion was of course the disregard by the Catholic Church and most of the Protestant denominations in Europe for the plight of the Jews. This conscious industrial and bureaucratic destruction of the Jews should have been an enduring lesson for Christian Europe. This implicit residual hatred and disdain should be a contemporary lesson for the Jews—not merely, "never again," which are mere words, nor even the armed defense of Jewishness as exemplified in Israel's brave determination. Rather, what is needed is a call to enter, to join the Jewish community for all the human good that Israel and the Jews as a people represent, in the past and potentially into the future.

The ancient Jews' series of military defeats ironically represents one of its most important contributions to human decency. This was the series of wars the Jews waged from 67 to 135 CE throughout the Roman world against Roman imperial might and the Roman pretensions to world hegemony. The three wars: in Judea,

67–70 CE; in Cyrenaica, Cyprus, Egypt, Mesopotamia, 115–118 CE; finally the war in Palestine of Bar Kokbah, 132–135 CE, were all losing ventures in the Jews' attempt to maintain their political and religious independence. None of these wars served to bring about the final victory of a holy Israel, and the impending resurrection of its holy dead. In this failure, and the subsequent Jewish expulsion from the political mainstream, once again a people alone in an alien world, the Jews prepared the ground for a new and further undermining of Rome.

This was the Jewish sect of Christianity. These Christian dissidents from Israel learned well the lesson of Roman power. They intuited that while the political and military power of Rome was for the moment invincible in terms of opposition from within, they could unleash another dimension of dissidence. Here, they absorbed the mystery teachings of the Judaic Pharisees, lessons resonant of the deeper elements in the human psyche, those emotional mysteries that can never for long be managed by mere material power. Thus Christianity gradually undermined the very meaning of Roman suzerainty. Eventually Rome dissolved as a civilizational entity. The material institutions that had to be entertained were filled with a new infusion of red corpuscles of belief and commitment. Roman power died and Christian religious power supplanted it as a new and universal reality.

The point here is not to glory in the petrifaction of the Roman arteries of domination that were translated into a new *imperium*, Papal Christianity. Rather it is to note that the Jewish revolts against Roman autocracy opened the door to a more gradual and insidious undermining of Rome. The religious temper separated itself from the political structure to become a new revolutionary stage in the defining of civilization. Jewish religious and then political and military dissidence was the provocative and necessary precondition. We ought not disdain the religious form of human thought and behavior. Under conditions of great political and economic stress the human psyche will make religion and ideology manifest.

Secular Analysis

The symbols and discourse of religion echo to a deeper strand of thinking: emotional, personal, non-sensitive to factual and material realities. Yet religious movements often garb themselves in the vestments of political and material institutions of power so as to further their ends. Our lesson should be that the forces of human nature that embody such power in turn can seldom be countered by the secular hand, no less the secular mind. Thus while fine Judaic minds such as Mordecai Kaplan or Sherwin Wine may have an impact in their thinking, writing, and proselytizing to segments of the Jewish community, the traditionally orthodox or the ultraorthodox *Haredim/Chabad* will not be in any way touched by their analyses and of course the secular evidence that motivates their institutional efforts. Traditionalist beliefs and orthodox behaviors are motivated by extrarationalist, extrascientific secular research and evidence.

The great changes in religious allegiance and belief in the past several centuries testify to the power of secular life over supernatural systems of belief and the entire sociological and economic power structure that once made them viable. Judaism was once a powerful and international presence in the modern world, the Greco-Roman world. Its leadership made a critical error in going to war against Rome. Three times its secular pretensions were smashed. It then withdrew, the Christian leadership sensed an alternate road to eventual power and dominance.

There is no reason why Judaism cannot once more attract allegiance and identification with the modern world, this time to exert the significance of rationality, intellectuality, moral discipline and humility. This it can do while retaining its perennial vision of the law and the moral principles that undergird it. To fight against disintegration and oblivion necessitates sharp reconsideration as to what Judaism has meant throughout its 3,000 years of history. It has redefined itself in the past. It can do so once more. Rabbinical parochialism, sectarianism, and an exclusionary synagogue culture predict a future of permanent decline for Judaism. Here we mean more than numbers, rather the influence of Judaism on the destiny of our species.

This essay will be a secular analysis of the religious, historical, and cultural dimensions of Judaism and the Jews. The intent is to examine whether a truly vibrant and expansive Judaism is now and in the future possible, given our knowledge of the historic experiences of this people.

Think of Judaism as an ancient tree. It has many calcified remembrances of ancient limbs. At the top are old and withering branches. These are the now traditional sects, orthodox, conservative, reform. Several new branches have attempted to replace the veterans. They are rather mangy newcomers; not much future here. Toward the bottom of the tree is a branch that has emerged from one of the calloused remnants. It is vigorous but grows downward. Here are the ultraorthodox with their romantic evocations of the past. This branch has a wooden support, the gardener/state is attempting to keep it upright. However, for the tree to have an independent future, it needs the fertilization of fine minds, energetic hands in tune with the science of horticulture. New branches are desperately needed.

It is important to reiterate that because one studies from the standpoint of history or science, a conception of deity, whether of Yahweh, Christ, or Mohammed, one does not thereby intend to or in actuality mean to degrade these symbols. Nor does one seek to undercut the religious emotions of need which powers the fidelity of billions. Without becoming a devotional adherent of a religious communion one can respectfully view these traditions as allegorical truths but still objectively analyze this vision of reality without sarcasm and disdain.

Religiosity Digs Deep

In the next chapter we shall preview our analysis of Judaism's great historical confrontation with humankind's sense of weakness and vulnerability, the need, also, to understand and explain. The religious form of human thought was created out of our unique biosocial structure, a mind that perceives but yet cannot reach the ultimate understanding. It then creates out of its own spontaneity, a symbolic structure of meaning. Hopefully this understanding will translate into human behavior that will work instrumentally.

The achievement of Judaism is that while it confronted this weakness of humans, the need to understand, the evolving faith was created far enough along in history so that it was able to take and reject. The resultant monotheistic moral vision of Deity became a powerful challenge throughout subsequent history, and indeed for the daughter branches that sprang from the original oak. Even today, as we will point out, the symbolic evocations of ritual meant to symbolically hold these people together in defensive discipline have their modern counterparts.

What we need will be a new instrumental revivification of these ancient and essential perceptions of human nature. What we will also learn is that the religious forms of human thought and humility digs deep into our essence as moral beings, the necessity to choose what we are and how we act.

CHAPTER TWO

Sources for the Religious

The triviality of man, both in his physical being and in his temporal aspirations, is in sharp contrast to the vastness about him. It is tempting to escape from responsibility as an instrument of Divine purpose through the illusion that the immensity of the universe and his own physical insignificance are a measure of relative value. Yet in view of the proverbial prodigality of nature no consideration could be more preposterous. Flowers produce millions of pollen grains, so that one may find its way to an ovule; trees bear fruit without number, so that the species may survive through a few. That galaxies and supergalaxies, numbering many millions and containing millions of suns, should derive meaning from the evolution of a minor planet in one of the less important systems of a sentient creature, knowing good and evil, is far from inconsistent with the usual procedures of Creation. If it be true of all the conglomerations of atoms, man alone has the power to be like God, in his ability to choose his path, fulfilling or resisting the Will of his Maker, he is indeed the ultimate triumph of Creation. The universe as a whole proceeds according to its inexorable laws, in man God has created a being which can obey, because it can also defy, which can obtain perfection, not through a process beyond its control, but through one which it itself directs.

Aware of the possibility that he has this unique role in existence, man will find its rejection for the sake of trifling advantages of power and luxury difficult indeed. To know God metaphysically may be consistent with rebellion against Him; but to know him religiously is not.[1]

The above quotation is by a distinguished rabbinical leader and scholar, Louis Finkelstein, identified with the Conservative movement in Judaism as represented by the Jewish Theological Seminary, in New York City. He traditionally posits the weakness and insignificance of humans in our universe which has of necessity required the existence of a higher power, both to rationalize mankind's need to obey as well as its willful postulation of free will. No, indeed, this very ability to choose a destiny requires that humans come to terms with this higher religious power to free and believe. Any other alternative implies disaster.

The Long Road Upward

Merely to accept and rationalize the dominance of institutional religion over the history of humans will not clarify our problems with institutional Judaism and its contemporary crisis. To attempt to understand the origin and meaning of this universal recognition of the power of religion, you have to go very far back in the experience of our species, to the misty origins of humans. This anterior story needs to be told, and from the standpoint of the secular mind, the empirical mind. No traditional bow to religion here.

We are anthropoids. Our nearest relatives are chimpanzees, gorillas, and orangutans. But we separated, tens of millions of years ago. We have long been alone on our special path into sapiency, with a big brain that exuded culture and sometimes civilization. And indeed, it is this unique brain which produced the varied forms of the religious experience. Indeed religion too is part of our naturalistic heritage.

Judaism, as with most modern religions, arises out of this basic predicament of human existence—the growth of the high cortical human brain. This human brain is an evolutionary product of an ortho-selective process. That is, its growth and selective evolution was not constrained by traditional close adaptive/selective discipline. The latter process happens often in evolution. It usually leads to premature structural or behavioral specialization and ultimately extinction. The natural conditions for dominance ever change; high intelligence gave its bearers plenty of adaptive leeway. In terms of behavior, humans have only the human brain to guide them in making proper adaptive choices, but no close guiding instinct. This is why we can choose to obey a god or not. Our only specialization is language, then the subsequent invention of writing and literacy.

But how can we rationally guide ourselves through the aegis of the thinking power of our cortex? Our emotional allo-cortex and limbic system have also exploded in size and behavioral dominance. We have the capacity for "time binding," the ability to look forward at possible consequences and solutions for the events of the moment. But we also have these torrents of emotion which in our fears and intrinsic human weakness demand that we momentarily pray to the gods to save and forgive us.

That of course is the great mystery. How did our anthropoid relatives wind up living predigested behavioral lives, while humans strode down another evolutionary path into the perplexing mix of cultures, albeit dominance? The task of explanation is long and complex.[2] But there is a relatively short answer that can throw light on our perennial need for some kind of religious obeisance. The path upward from ordinary, smart, tiny, defensive "apeness" to tall, aggressive, dominating humanness has been a long one. Yet in one sense the path has been consistent with an ancient animal adaptation, braininess. Basically a large brain served the adaptive purpose to keep the animal running, staying out of the way, allowing it to reproduce and raise its young to reproductive maturity. This adaptation of animal life goes back at least half a billion years.

The ancestors of humans were the mammal/anthropoid line chosen by chance to follow this path. Whales, rats, starlings represent other animal pathways in evolution. These adaptive solutions allowed for their intelligence to give them a survival advantage. For the whales it was tough that they had to run into humans who wanted their sperm oil and blubber. Humans happen to be at the leading edge of ground dwelling, versatile avoiders of pain. Over the eons, this brain of movement and time binding worked. The world and the external environment, ever changeable, constantly presented new challenges. Increasingly, the brain became the efficient means for survival.

It happened a long time ago that we were upright, walking and running animals, better to look into the distance and see danger, better to peep above the tall grass to hear danger. And so the brain grew ever more powerful. This successful pathway into the present became ever more adaptively and selectively useful. How did this come about? Certainly success did not result because our ancestors wished survival into being. And regretfully, no gods decided that we were to be number one, some 20 million years down the evolutionary time line. There is an ancient tradition in the dialogue between genetic structure and external challenges to follow the path of least resistance. By probability, those genes whose directional mutations were preserved selectively had a predictable tendency to mutate again in the same direction. The glory of it was that in an ever-changing world this genetic tack worked.

Nature/evolution through strictly mechanical dynamics has discovered for living things, that, in an ever-changing environment on our planet Earth, those creatures with genetic structure adapted to change, as contrasted with snails and amoeba, tend to mutate more often. Another way to put it is that those lines of life whose genetic structure is more unstable will travel down a constant mutating program of adaptation and natural selection. But not all successful mutational dynamics will work out constantly, or forever. The Irish elk and the saber-toothed tiger are recent examples of animals whose long success finally got them into trouble. *Hypertropism* eventually interfered with their reproductive success, thence they became extinct.

Our great brain is an example of evolution in a straight line, here until this suddenly gigantic head of ours began to challenge the more ancient and modest birth canal of the human female. The brain grew not because of any specialization, perhaps with the exception of our linguistic abilities, which certainly helped survival communication in the early stages of *Homo sapiens* drive upwards. As we are discovering there were many human experiments that survived into modern times, from about five million years ago. No doubt the great success of baby-faced, balloon-brain *Homo sapiens sapiens* as compared with big, primitive-brained, thick-boned competitors such as Neanderthal was due to this unique protuberance which gave *Hss* an unspecialized behavioral advantage over other human experiments which have disappeared into the sunset.

This advantage with the exceptional specialization for spoken language led to better communication in hunting, planning out the life of the band or tribe over the changing seasons, especially in the cold latitudes of the Pleistocene ice ages, from 1.9 million years ago to about 10,000 BCE. The creatures who emerged victorious from this very precarious pathway of survival were the Cro-Magnon peoples of Europe and West Asia, with some peripheral humans living throughout the continents with the exception of the Americas and Antarctica.

The Neanderthals, heavy-boned and cold-adapted peoples of Europe and West Asia, experienced the invasion of their territories by Cro-Magnons from about 45,000 years before the present. The last Neanderthal seems to have disappeared about 27,000 years ago. Since there is no fossil or other cultural evidence of war and killings between these two people, it is assumed that, as the Neanderthals were outclassed for good living and hunting grounds, their reproductive dynamic became increasingly paralyzed in depression and panic, and they disappeared like many another once-dominant line of living creatures.

Inner Rules

Cro-Magnon culture was shaped over a large area from Russia to central Spain by the ecological and climatic conditions of this period, certainly alternating between very cold millennia and more benign climatic periods. Their brain and thus their behavior had been in the making for millions of years, reaching this unique climax sometime between 200,000 and 100,000 years ago. From thence they had to unconsciously apply this new brain to the experience of interacting with a world external to their bodies. Their crutch for survival was generalized thinking, the "g" of modern psychometric general intelligence. This vast new homeland into which they had wandered and now had them settling down away from their unknown northern "Garden of Eden," was filled with rich valleys, rivers, plains, all wealthy in sustenance. Herein, over a period of 35,000 years they multiplied and prospered.

The hunting was good. They learned to make fire and how to fabricate animal pelts into clothes. Very soon something else began to be released from their minds, the manufacture of beautiful artifacts of the hunt, jewelry from a variety bones, ivory, stone, and soon art and perhaps religion. While they lived in caves, they expressed their unanticipated vision of the beautiful, the reverential not necessarily in their home places, but rather in caves that they visited, no question but the earliest church/mosque/synagogue like refuges. Often high on a ridge above their homesites near rivers, they painted and told us at a distance of many thousands of years what was important to their minds. Clearly, their material wealth, perfected in their thoughtfully derived hunting, fishing and gathering techniques, liberated them in leisure to pursue these mysterious urgings.

In the pitch darkness, deep inside these caves they fabricated "lanterns" made of hollowed-out stone receptacles within which were laid down animal fat and a plant wick which would burn slowly in the dark. Here they painted their magnificent panoramic esthetic/religious evocations of the beasts which provided them with abundance. The paints were a variety of ground-up vegetable matter, certainly the product of much experimentation. The settings, the murals, evoke the dark of the Sistine Chapel, a sacred place where the men would gather to inform themselves and their kin, and us from afar, what was now bubbling outward from this as yet naïve and unchallenged mind.

In several cases we note human figures as part of their self-expression. In one case a man is bent over, perhaps in dance, antlers attached to his head, a tail dragging behind him. The Australian aboriginal people, and others, too, have expressed this sense of unity with the animal kingdom which provides for sustenance and life, in dance and symbolic imitation. And this ancient reflection of a celebration, a ritual evocation hints even dimly what is going on in their minds, their culture.

At all times in the evolution of our species it was the thinking brain that was key to survival. This is the case with the placental mammals that have risen to dominance over the past 60 million years. And within the placentals, it is very often the brainier exemplifiers of a particular adaptive line which have pushed forward for their glimpse of the sun and the stars. Mammals are emotional animals—the key to their protection of their relatively vulnerable young. Humans have carried this emotional valence along with the growth of the thinking brain. The linkage of the genes for quiet cortical intelligence has pulled along the concomitant growth of the allo-cortex, the emotional brain.

No longer does instinct work to link these two elements of mammalian adaptation and natural selection. Nature decided in its inexorable wisdom to exchange the rigid rules of instinct, and rooted adaptation with the more dynamic use of brain analysis in times of voluptuous change. Instead of the steadying adaptive rules of instinct passed down from generation to generation, the growth of the cortex necessitates its assertion during times of environmental change. The concomitant failure of instinct to meet such challenges over the past sixty million years of the mammal placentals testifies to the extinction of so many of these lines. It fell to the anthropoids to be the most powerful represented group of cortical forms of adaptation to lead the way into modernity and sapiency. The growth of this surging brain inside a ballooning skull went unchallenged until it met its morphological limits in the human female birthing process. The fossil remains of Cro-Magnon reveal many barely adolescent female graves, often with the vestigial remains of a human infant.

This relative disappearance of a given set of behaviors heretofore ruled omnipotently by prescribed genetic guidance has left humans alone in the biological world. The vestiges of the animal and anthropoid past yet are evident in our now roaring set of emotional energies, sexual, aggressive, and thus often violent. Out of this new neurological equation, practical survivalist thinking overlain by emotional passions, has evolved forms of thought and behavior which now under-gird civilization: painting, music, the dance, jewelry and clothing design, plastic arts, religion, literature, poetry, love, war, ethnicity, and patriotism, the panoply of mysterious cultural expressions which define our human nature.

Bereft of automatic instinctual behaviors we are left with choice. But what are the criteria for choosing? The 20th-century existentialists hit on it. Essentially, we are alone in the universe. Just think: for over a billion years nature has been balancing the adventure of biological evolution between stability and change. The neurological carriage which ended up being a brain responded selectively to the change factor in our earthly environment. Heretofore the relatively protected genetic potencies of sexual reproduction have opted for stability, maintaining an adaptive stasis within placid environments. Many animal and plant types have existed within their steady instinctual restraints on behavioral and structural change for over a billion years. The other guys prospered as the earth turned and the conditions for life constantly changed. For an evolutionary moment human fecundity in its powers, has exploded over our planet. Which line will win out in the end?

Discovering Ourselves

The problem of religion is rooted in this fact that we have a human nature that went beyond the traditional instinctual bonds of animal behavior. Our universe of choice is not closely guided by our behavioral genes. But of course, in the most general way, they must be. This guidance is over such a broad spectrum of behavioral variabilities that we are essentially left alone to choose, bereft of the sureties that guide wolves or chimpanzees in their natural realm. But note, the wolves and chimps for all their calm regularities of life patterns are now vulnerable to a change which their genes had not planned on, i.e., man's recent aggressive predatory expansion and his powers to dominate and destroy.

The challenge comes down to this. We humans have to discover who and what we are. Not only do we have to act out our human nature as did the Cro-Magnons spontaneously and unselfconsciously. But we have to discover this human nature within a physico/biological environment ever more of our own making: urbanism, technology, the destruction of our ecology (species), climate change, etc.

Consider the time line we have earlier proposed. The final eruption of the Cro-Magnon brain and morphology, giving due consideration to the human fossil record, was probably completed some time between 200,000 and 100,000 years ago. We here date the European invasion of the Cro-Magnons, who were of light skin and hair, as well as gracile in bone structure, to c. 45,000 BP (before the present). Their fossils give no evidence for specialized ice-age type of adaptations, bone and body, as do the Neanderthals, who were of light skin and hair, but heavy-boned, cold-adapted humans.

The earliest cultural remains of Cro-Magnon are to be found in East Europe and West Asia at about 45,000 years ago. Their demography kept on moving West without vacating their eastern territories and thus we find a thriving West European Aurignacian culture, similar to the earlier Russian, at about 35,000 years. These are fully formed social/cultural units in their technology, their use of a variety of fabricating materials, jewelry, clothing, art, painting and sculpting. In their effusive expression of symbolic re-creations of their physical environment, this search for meaning had to have embodied religious, mythic elements of belief and expressive devotion.

Consider, it took at least 50,000 years for these unusual human types, proto-Cro-Magnons to (1) rid themselves of retrogressive intelligent types as they picked out soul mates of similar competence under extremely harsh environmental and ecological conditions. (2) Their conjoint competence had to eventually allow them to bring as many fragile neonates into reproductive maturity as could create a cultural unit, band or tribe. (3) Then, living together, surviving together they had to create a culture of practical survival techniques plus the creation within their culture ambience of the symbolic emotional glue so as to survive as social units. (4) At a certain point their numbers began to tell on their ecological resources and they started moving, migrating.

One probability is that that these Cro-Magnons originated in a moderate climate. Their bleached skin and light-colored hair would argue for a northern latitude. Their lack of a cold-adapted morphology would hint at this moderate climatic environment. A rough guess: the West Asian Caucasus. Then, with the technical fabricating and organizational skills to hunt, fish, gather fruits and berries, and do art, they moved both north and west into Europe proper as the climate allowed, meeting all along the way the then-ensconced aboriginals, the Neanderthals, to the latter's ultimate regret.

Think again about this 50,000-year period, at least, within which these Cro-Magnon ancestors of ours had to discover their inner competencies and passions so as to live out this Upper Paleolithic scenario. This way of life, while there were cultural changes which anthropologists have duly accounted for, still maintained its basic formulas. The technology changed a bit. The hunting varied in terms of what was available. The art evolved also. What of their religious, mythopoeic visions and ideals? It was a 35,000-year-long tradition that finally fell apart only after the glaciers withdrew to the north. A wholly new climatic and ecological set of circumstances had literally dissolved this far flung stone-age proto-civilization.

We 21st-century humans have had about 12,000 years beyond the Stone Age to create a modern sociopolitical version of our mysterious human nature. Few would be brave enough today, to argue that we understand this human nature. One cannot say that the struggle to find material security is the key to understanding the dynamics of human evolutionary or literate history. Even the basics of procuring food for oneself and family, clothing, shelter, security from want or war is overlain by much complicating symbolic static. Take for example, the research of Alexander Marshack, a magazine editor turned anthropological researcher.[3] He put together a wide variety of seemingly random inscribed stone implements, ivory and bone plaques. Although there were different styles of incisions on these materials, there seemed to be patterns, similar to what a hunter would do to the stock of his spear or gun to denote the kills. But these objects were not weapons, and the conclusion was that the lines and swirls of markings were too regular to be doodles. In fact the agreement by scholars was that they were likely marks to denote the segmentation of time, a mark for each day, in the cycles of the moon, or a female menses, or perhaps the movement of the sun, its settings at different times of the year, or the migration of fish up the river or animals to a highland grazing ground.

Once the daily or weekly grind of providing for life sustenance was completed, the human mind wanted to understand the patterns that were being spontaneously recognized. Certainly, even the act of hunting was accompanied by a search for significance, in the symbolic rituals of dancing in the dress of an important animal, or painting or carving a mural of the animal and human life surrounding the community. This brain of humans was picking up sensory information which did not trigger instinctive survivalistic responses. This human brain was turning those basic five sensory inputs into a search for organization to structure causal relationships of events—results, clouds=snow or rain, etc. The cognitive brain and the emotional mammalian dynamo underneath throbbed with energy, a spontaneous inquiry into all of life's inner and outer experience, to try to understand, order, find meaning. Religious or mythic envisionments would come naturally in this attempt to understand the order of things, the powerful hum of their emotional energies as they sought to find a protective sustenance of belief.

We understand these effusions of mental energy transformed into objective reality as symbols. The symbols that humans use to express meaning are radically different signs, organized perceptions, as compared to the signal behavior of animals. Animal perceptions are turned into signals which trigger automatic behaviors, instinct. Humans take in these perceptions and turn them into thought/emotion-induced symbolic meanings. They are conventional which means they have no fixed or permanent meaning. Humans can constantly redefine the same perceptions into new meanings, new symbolic complexes. These can take the form of artistic, mythic, political, or religious forms of belief and behavior.

In one moment we can create and pray to a religious symbol; it could be a cross or a tree. The next moment, we could change our mind and spit on it, or cut it down. The same fluidity of meaning exists for politics and the flag. In the symbolic forms of the visual arts, we can believe in the tradition which begins with Giotto and even absorb a Warhol into the esthetic pantheon. Others can call this modern incarnation a scam. Since symbols of meaning are cortically initiated we can hold these meanings over time in our mind. Our time-binding abilities, memories within structures of meaning, allow us to create the social institutions and interpersonal moral values which define human culture. In this way institutional religions began to take form out of this limbic system/allocortical expressive passion and the cortical grey matter reification of emotion into meaning and then into physical reality, priests, rabbis, temples, synagogues, and eventually a storefront.

The Form of the Religious

The form of the religious will always be the basic and primeval modality of symbolic thought. It should and does always reflect the dawning awareness in humans of their aloneness in the universe. And with that unique sense of being apart, comes the realization, buttressed by constant experience, of the vulnerability of humans. Not withstanding the power of the human brain over animal and plant life, humans are still weak. Bereft of blind instinctual defenses to fall back on, they are forced to symbolically confront the implacable forces of nature. Oh, to be a chimp happily and nonchalantly munching on a fruit high up a tropical tree.

We may as did the Cro-Magnons in their moments of leisure try to fathom those regularities of the seasons, our bodily functions, the rhythms of plant and animal life. To cut notches is one thing. To objectify in terms of a predictive rule is another. More often it probably moved them to bend down in conjoint prayer or song, hoping that their expedition to hunt will result in a kill, and food for the season. At the same time they no doubt clasped those sexual totems, the hand-sized nude Venuses which as delicious symbols they had carved out of ivory. You may wear a crucifix or a Star of David on a chain around your neck; they carried such pornographic talismans for good fortune and the dream of warm sex once they returned from the hunt.

In the beginnings of the postglacial period c. 12,000 years ago, migratory as well as more sedentary agriculturists objectified this search for understanding of their fears, vulnerabilities, joys, and the emotions of survival, by reifying this inchoate psychological angst into objectified entities. These now-defined religious practices involved human and animal sacrifice, totems of value, sacred objects, sacred animals, and sacred places on high. There were negative values also, taboos and prohibitions, sinful human actions, contaminated places, foods, animals, and objects. Here we find, universally among all peoples at the dawn of history and among the unsophisticated of our own time, sacral objectifications of signification that seem practically irrelevant to our own sophisticated secular, scientific eyes. Yet, a lightning bolt, a split tree, drinkable water discovered coming from a hillside, a bird hovering over a dying animal, all symbols of meaning for life and survival, could precipitate wonder, and that question, *why*, what does it mean for our destiny?

Evidence from the primitive tribal world of subsistence hunting and gathering hints at the existence of an emotional world of mythic and religious feeling. These emotions are pervasive and overpowering. There is hardly any dimension of life that does not pulsate with the emotional rhythms of the religious sensibility. The philosopher Ernst Cassirer studied this primordial human emotional search for meaning and predictability and identified it as the earliest stratum of mankind's search for understanding: "The primary mythical fact is a man divided and torn by manifold outward impressions, each bearing a magical-mythical character, each laying claim to the whole of human consciousness and drawing it into its sphere, each imprinting its own color and mood. At first the ego has nothing to oppose to this impression and is unable to change it but can only accept it and in the act of acceptance become its prisoner. It is tossed this way and that by the expressive factors of the various phenomena, which assault it suddenly and irresistibly. These factors follow one another without fixed order and without transition; unpredictably, the various formations change their mythical 'face.' Without transition, an impression of the homelike, familiar, sheltering, and protective can shift into its opposite, the inaccessible, terrifying, monstrous, and gruesome."[4]

Amid the confusing passions of fear and hope, the relentless pouring into the senses of energy-laden perception that need to be explained ordered, there is another world of more mundane meaning. This is the daily grind. High intelligence does impose the need to order these impressions, if only to bring home sustenance. And as the success of the day momentarily calms the emotions of the night, humans began to mentally and physically order events to transform the inchoate questions about reality which once convulsed the human mind into a constantly changing mélange of mythic, magical, and religious feelings.

No longer were there to be casual celebrations of the seasons, of the crops, or even sexuality on high. Here, an edifice, a building, sometimes a shelter from the forces of nature, a Temple. Along with power, the ability to turn inanimate material into monuments, there is still a need to plea to the higher forces, gods, to side with this people, this community, to endow them with power, luck, goodness, survival. The sense of wonder and the weakness of humans in the face of remorseless nature conjure up fears of perpetual personal weakness, the need not to dissolve unstated but still deeply felt moral laws.

The ever-recurring iniquities in human behavior require expiation. There comes a need to appease the possible anger of the gods. In primitive annals of tribal survival, it led to the sacrifice of the eldest male. "Take your son, your only son, Isaac, whom you {Abraham} love, and go to the land of Moriah {temple mount in Jerusalem}, and offer him there as a burnt offering on one of the mountains that I shall show you." {Genesis 22: 2}

The result among the settled, on a hilltop, the ziggurat or pyramid rising from the plain, artificial mountains were built to be close to the sun, stars, moon. In England and elsewhere in Europe, Stonehenge–like monuments were built, celebrations of human power, reflecting the search for the meaning of the regularities of nature, and 21st-century humans still build on high signifying an admission of the need to appeal to the mysterious powers of the heavens, forces over which humans still have little control. Those early monuments to the religious form of thought thus were special places in the human search for meaning.

While it is not clear what religious patterns of control or celebration, "totem and taboo" existed for these c. 35,000 years of proto-civilizational living within a largely hunter-gatherer economy, the settling of the descendants of the Cro-Magnons in the river valleys of the south allowed for the development of rich agricultural surpluses, the domestication of animals for food and clothing, and the beginnings of complex variegated urban life patterns and specialization.

Yet even in the early urbanization of the Sumerians at the confluence of the Euphrates and Tigris rivers in Mesopotamia much of the ancient mythico-religious patterns of behavior persisted, still, oriented towards a more sophisticated cultural existence. The city of Uruk, 4000–3000 BCE: "In the spiritual sphere, the torrents, twists, and turns of mythopoeic thinking in symbols embedded in reality are surmounted, if not straightened out, by application of universal principles and rules. The world perceived as a unity in diversity is accordingly organized into a social whole. The natural variability of communities, in most cases linked principally by the factor of co-residence and accompanied by industrial sites and service holdings is interspersed by groupings that see themselves as manifestations of divine will, communities divided among elites and commoners is constantly leveled."[5]

We must remember that this organization of our mental faculties, the placing of religion within a pantheon of diverse symbolic/psychological vectors-interests of humans that occurred in the Sumerian cities was epitomized in this great and early urban center, Uruk, c. 4000–3000 BCE. These dates reveal a beginning of organized religious institutions almost 2000 years before the first religious writings in Canaan by precursor Israelite and Judean tribes. These holy ancient tales were later marshaled into the J and E versions of the Torah, the first five books of the Holy Bible.

The early Sumerian tradition was solidified by the perfection of writing in syllabic cuneiform script. While writing beyond the pictographic state was a powerful modernizing and abstractive element in the economic and technological power of the city states, its impact was also religious, as much of the taxes, contracts, law documents, and hereditary grants, were deposited within holy grounds to be protected by priests. The power over the human mind of this written world was supernatural in nature. How else could it be understood rationally?

The gradual amplification of the economic and social structure of life did much to transition humans from raw mythic symbols of meaning, blatantly emotional, to structured pantheons. There can be no question that the rush of symbolic energies which in the beginning created a mélange of mythic *foci*, now reflected an important intellectual evolution in human behavior. Unquestionably, the evolution towards more philosophical religious structures reflected the intellectual powers within the respective cultures which themselves advanced the socioeconomic zone of life. Religion here now symbolizes the weakness and the ignorance of humans, the need to order, make functional, the universe of change and danger within which they live. As the human economy now produced sustenance in such abundance as to release the expression of the other symbolic forms of culture it could create a true civilization, the arts, technology, law, even common law and a written democratic constitution. This was first expressed in early Sumerian urbanism.

> A famous episode found in the first two tablets of the Epic of Gilgamesh, c. 2700 BCE.... In it is explained how Enkidu, the wild man of the steppe, hairy and barbarous, only intimate with animals and living a life like them, becomes a man in the full sense of the word: ... a civilized man, a city man who eats bread, drinks beer, and grooms and dresses himself. This transformation is the work of a courtesan from Uruk who came to look for him in the steppe and who introduced him to love; hence not simple intercourse with a female, but love with a real human. Thus, human and refined love, *i.e.*, free love.

Once he had discovered it and had acquired a taste for it, Enkidu could only follow his teacher to the city, where she taught him to eat, drink, and dress, and where she completed his transformation. Thus free love is presented as being the point of access to a life that is truly cultural and human. It is difficult to better indicate its worth and its importance.[6]

This Sumerian epic, so similar to the much later Iliad in its heroic and so often secular interaction of humans and gods, was written down in the Sumerian language, then copied into later Semitic versions. It is almost 2,000 years older than the first writings down of the traditions of the Yahwist and Elohist traditions in Canaan and the respective tribal areas, Aram in the north, the Midian, in the south, and Edom east of the Jordan.

As we will develop in the next chapter, the transition from the magical mythic, totemistic levels of religious worship was a gradual one, having a variable dynamic in different parts of the precivilizational world. But with the coming of literate political and social institutions, a more modern invocation of mankind's primordial sense of weakness, vulnerability, ignorance, began to take on modernistic tonalities.

Religiosity Evolves

In the beginning of most religious traditions the gods were everywhere. And in most religious traditions animal and sometimes human sacrifice were the norm. Regressions such as the introduction of human sacrifice into the Sumerian monarchical tradition, 2600 BCE, often heralded the specialized decline of a cultural tradition, the Semitic Akkadian conquest of the Sumerian cities c. 2400 BCE, being an example. The attempted, and probably real sacrifice of Isaac by his father Abraham exemplifies the pre-Mosaic tradition among the Habiru or Soshu tribes of Canaan and the desert.

Certainly the Greeks moved beyond animal sacrifice into a complex theophany of gods and powers, a civic tradition that was not embarrassed at their sacral borrowing from other peoples, mostly from the Asiatics at the eastern end of the Mediterranean littoral. Yet even during their most glorious day of philosophical and scientific enquiry, the mid-fifth century BCE, the Athenians banished a visiting philosopher, Protagoras, for skeptical and agnostic pronunciation over the real existence of their many and blatantly mortal gods.

The same ethnic locus for polytheism can be seen in the Hindu tradition. Here animal worship and sacrifice have not been abandoned by the most fundamentalist and anti-modernist groups, rural and urban. Great poetic and mythic themes have been injected into Hindu life by the introduction of literacy. Here is a religion that still lives by way of its ethnic and geographical integrity, the great sub-continent that is India.

What the invention of literacy has done for the evolution of religion is to deepen its own self-awareness of belief and thus lend an ever greater cognitive discipline to such ideas. At the same time the literary element began to reflect other symbolic dimensions of human ideation. It is no accident that the *Iliad*, c. 750 BCE or the earlier J and E versions of the Pentateuch add rich esthetic, poetic, dramatic, and moral elements to the actions of the gods and their human subjects. Indeed the small town of Eridu, one of the earliest cities of Sumer, and well before its subsequent literacy revolution, already had a large shrine stretching skyward, dating to c. 4500 BCE.[7]

The Egyptian step pyramids owe their creation to visiting Sumerian traders and engineers who brought writing as well as engineering and architecture into the Egyptian system of worship. In all these articulations of the institutional dimension of the religious we see other human symbolic intentionalities being expressed. In Egypt, c. 2700 BCE we can see the kernel of a culture being transformed into a civilization. Religion may open up the human mind so as to express its inner potency for questioning beyond the gross practicalities of surviving, reproducing, nurturing the young to reproductive maturity. But as the mind discovers ever new cognitive powers, these seem to further release those mysterious creative juices which give almost infinite dynamic to civilizational change and growth. Religion essentially evolves to find new sources of meaning in that mystery that is human nature.

Perhaps the most subtle development within the religious sensibility is the transformation of supernaturalism in most religions into the ethicism of Buddhism and Taoism/Confucianism. Certainly the latter two are closely linked to Chinese ethnicity, nationalism, and history. While admitting to the special holiness of the Buddha, the founding holy man's deep moral insights, and his ascetic way of life still did not become the means to reify him into a god.

Indeed, in our own time, late 19th-century secularly minded American Jews, under the leadership of Felix Adler, separated themselves from very liberal Reform Judaism, itself recently born in Germany, mid-19th century, here to form the Ethical Culture Society. This movement soon attracted numerous non-Jews to its communitarian and secular outlook on a very modern scientific world. But the fact that it has remained a relatively small communitarian enclave of discussion testifies to the need for other deeper elements that traditionally root religion into the hearts of humans.

Judaism

The problems of contemporary Judaism reflect the wider evolution of religiosity in our modern world. The communist war against traditional religious beliefs,

Protestantism, Catholicism, Budhism, and Taoism had an epic impact on these religions in the domains where communists ruled politically. In the post-communist era of Europe, religion has made a small comeback. But it also has had to suffer the challenge of middle-class secular education, which in Western Europe has seriously debilitated the traditional religious dynamic; the churches are empty.

Organized religions today seem to perdure in those nations and cultures of the majority poor. The Jews today throughout the world are overwhelmingly middle class. Supernatural belief is not on the menu, even in the most ultraorthodox venues. What does exist here in the orthodoxy is the veneration of the literature of the past, the attempt to live lives consonant with an ancient verisimilitude of traditional belief, and under the aegis of a charismatic leader.

As we will point out in subsequent chapters Judaism is the most primed of the ancient orthodoxies to have the possibility of redefining itself in the modern era, without losing the cultural, ethnic, historical and literary tradition which has formed it. It can exist without the metaphysical supernaturalism, in contrast to the view of Rabbi Louis Finkelstein, quoted at the beginning of this chapter. Judaism has within its historical evolution of over 3000 years of civilizational history undergone numerous and revolutionary changes in its institutional character, even in its most basic metaphysical and theological beliefs.

The exact nature of the Judaic coming to terms with secular science while retaining what is most deep in its history, in terms of its reflecting on the human condition and its quest for the understanding of *Homo sapiens'* place in the universe, cannot be known in advance. A new and modern Judaism will arise at the urgings of educated young, interested and involved Jews, who want to drive to the essence of this religions's value framework and create new and modern institutions which can serve in expanding the demography of Jews as well as contributing to the sustenance of the civilized world.

Prelude to Torah

The search for understanding is perennial. Those ancient tribal elements which came together to form the Israelite federation at the end of the second millennium, BCE, did so because they were under threat by advancing foreign powers in the lands surrounding them.

They felt inchoately the need to create a centripetal cultural force that would bring them together in strength against these ever more powerful forces of modernity. These others were arming themselves with iron and were mustering new social disciplines in their urban agricultural settlements. The arrival of Moses' wanderers from Egypt and his vision of one God, Yahweh, became a powerful vision for these nomadic groupings, a means for rooting tribal unity in an all powerful God setting forth His binding laws. The energizing purity of this theonomous vision, no idols, fertility or nature gods, was intellectually tantalizing.

The Commandments were the binding force of this powerful God, Yahweh. In obedience these people, His people, would be chosen, a nation of priests devoted to the heavy burden of fulfilling these demands. With this visionary moral power they would now be victorious over their enemies, would surmount the dangers of life itself in a world that seemed beyond comprehension.

To put these laws of Yahweh into service for his people however, was a difficult discipline for a wild, undisciplined, nomadic people. Thus the search for the concrete embodiment of the Law, now became an overriding social necessity. It required new intellectual powers and new intellectual leaders. In the end a Torah had to be created, written and applied with the force of God. Only then could these "chosen" survive the chaos of the world around them.

CHAPTER THREE

Torah/Law

Defined

In the Old Testament books of Genesis and Exodus, the Hebrew plural of *torah*, *torot*, is usually linked with phrases such as "my commandments, my laws, my *torot*" {*Genesis 26:5, J*}, also {*Exodus 16:28, P*}. In *Leviticus* and *Numbers* the word torah denotes specific ceremonial rules for priests {*Leviticus* 6:1, 11:46–47, all *P*, *Numbers* 19:2, P}. In Deuteronomy, historically the last addition to the Pentateuch, the term *torah* is more generally applied to the laws, rules, narratives, curses, blessings, and speeches of the Pentateuch: "this book of the Torah" {Deuteronomy 29:20, D-1; 30:10 D-2}.[1]

These five books have retained their modern titles as they were adapted from the Hebrew, which usually titled these writings from the first words of each section of the intended unified whole. The Greek transliteration adapted in the Christian Vulgate now constitutes orthodox usage. From a 1965 edition of the orthodox Jewish Masoretic text, the contemporary titles of these books are used here.

Thus the Pentateuch (the five), "... is a collection of several groups of laws and commandments that were given to the people of Israel, set in a framework of stories that explain the special status of the people before God."[2] It is important to emphasize that these texts, in addition to the Decalogue, the Ten Commandments, in its various forms within the Pentateuch are to be considered, the word of Yahweh as given to the prophet Moses, and then to be taught by himself and his successors to the people of Israel. "The Torah of the Lord which he gave by the hand of Moses" {Ezra 7:10; Nehemiah, 8:1, 9:3, 10: 30}.

The Torah, Prophets, Writings, which constitute the holy books, Tanakh, are also holy to Christianity, and to a lesser extent to Islam. For many centuries these writings have been literally accepted as the preexisting, (creation) word of God, as given to Moses and as laterally written down for the Israelites. To the extent that these successor religions of Judaism accept the Old Testament, to that extent they followed the laws and the preachments therein.

Sources

As early as the Middle Ages, in Spain, Jewish scholars and Rabbis were beginning to question some of the inconsistencies in the Pentateuch, not merely the different styles of Hebrew writing, but also puzzling issues such as the third person voice of Moses, descriptions of his death, which certainly could not have been written by him, as well as events, tribes, and persons who could not have existed in the time frame that the life of Moses implied, historically.

Philosophers such as Thomas Hobbes and Baruch Spinoza, the latter excommunicated from the Jewish community in Amsterdam, pointed out serious inconsistencies, especially in Deuteronomy, which clearly revealed another writer's hand. Finally, in the 19th-century modern scholarly analysis began to break up the five books of Moses into component writings which seemed to have been edited together to form the whole of the Torah. A Scottish scholar, William Robertson Smith, a contributor to the *Encyclopedia Britannica* lost his professorship by pointing out that evidence clearly revealed the multi-authorship of these five books, thus probably excluding the holy attribution to the prophet.

Smith was instrumental in inducing a young German Protestant theologian, Julius Wellhausen, to contribute the results of his scholarly integration of all the recent studies revealing the nature of the written contributions to this corpus. In an 1879 edition of the *Encyclopedia Britannica*, the 9th, Wellhausen wrote a lengthy article, "Israel," which brought full light to what is now called the "Documentary" analysis of the sources for the writing of the Pentateuch. Today, even the Catholic Church accepts the reality and persuasiveness of this scholarship in the understanding of the nature of authorship of the Pentateuch. This universal acceptance of the main thrust of the "Documentary" interpretation is still rejected by the orthodox rabbinical tradition.

Today, scholars identify five different writing traditions in the Pentateuch: J to the time of Solomon, tenth century, latest to his son, Rehoboam, early ninth century in Judah; E is considered to have been written in the Northern Kingdom, Israel, sometime during the ninth to the eighth century. Both J and E have much older material, written and oral, added to the texts. P is controversial, scholars divided as to whether its main components, in addition to the inclusion of more ancient materials, were written in the era of Hezekiah, King of Judah, toward the end of the eighth century. Else, it was written in exile in Chaldean-Babylonia, or shortly after, on the return to Judah (Yehud), now part of the Persian Empire, in the mid-sixth century. (Possibly both views are reconcilable). Deuteronomy through 2 Kings, although consisting of much original and relatively old documentation and tradition, was probably written in Judah in the time of Josiah, latter seventh century, with numerous addenda; Deuteronomy 2, completed in the early sixth century, either in Babylonian exile or after the return to Jerusalem after 539 BCE is exemplified in descriptions of the destruction of Jerusalem and the First Temple, clearly written after Deuteronomy 1.[3]

Both J and E, were written down long after a literary tradition was initiated in this part of the world, alphabetic writing has been found in the Sinai dating back to 1500 BCE. The stories in Judges clearly go back to a pre-monarchical era, probably part of an oral and literary tradition in Canaan that was not to be included in the Torah, see for example, {Judges 8:15–16}. Also the much later Chronicles harking back historically to this earlier period discusses the scribal families of non-Israelite tribes {1 Chronicles 2:55}.

Such early written documentation is acknowledged in the Pentateuch, for example: Book of Wars of the Lord, {Numbers 21:14}; Book of Jashar (of the Just), {Joshua 10:13, 2 Samuel, 1:18}; The Song of the Well, {Numbers 21:17, 18}; Song of Sihon and Moab, {Numbers 21:27–30}; Song of Lamech, {Genesis 4:23, 24}; and Song of Moses, {Exodus, 15:1–22}.[4]

Also, The Book of the "Annals of the Kings of Israel" and "Annals of the Kings of Judah" is mentioned over a dozen times by the Deuteronomist Historians, first written in the days of the King of Judah, Josiah, c. 630 BCE. Also, Chronicles, 5th–4th century BCE uses records of the Prophets, "Nathan, Shemaiah, Iddo" to construct its parallel history of the Israelites.[5]

Certainly the earliest authors, J and E, either as individuals or a group of individuals reveal important differences in style and content. J, from the Judean Yahweh desert experience is more piquant, even colloquial in his treatment of the tradition. E, God is Elohim from the Israelite north, reflects a more northern traditional Mesopotamian/Syrian heritage, that of their god El, as in Beth-el, Peni-el Israel. The tribes themselves as they appear in Genesis appear to have two sources of origin. Except for Reuben, Simeon, Levi, and Judah, associated with Yahwist themes, the others invoke the god Elohim. And indeed it is these ten tribes who split off into the kingdom of Israel; oddly Benjamin remains with Judah.

In fact, in Genesis, Jacob's original name is changed in the town of Beth-el to Israel, recognition that this northern Mesopotamian name (Jacob) has now been joined into a new people, the Israelites of Canaan. A reflection of the diverse integration of these two tribal groups is the fact that the first king of the united monarchy, Saul, from Gibeah in Benjamin, a northern tribe to be later joined to the southern monarchy, Judah, except for his son Jonathan, gave his other sons non-Yahwistic, Baalistic names.

What we learn from Wellhausen's documentary approach is that the editing of the original traditions and then their written nationalistic historical and religious program, reveals many hands to have here been at work. While the language and vision of the priestly tradition (P) is clear in the first four books of the Pentateuch, other editorial minds are also evident. What Richard Friedman calls the Redactor, is today mostly attributed to the hand of Ezra, foremost, and then Nehemiah and other priestly shapers of the final form of the Torah. And this occurred well after the building of the 2nd Temple, c. 500–400 BCE.

And while one would expect that the division into two rival kingdoms, Judah in King David's capital of Jerusalem, now led by Solomon's son, Rehoboam, and then the secession by Jeroboam, head of the Josephite tribal corvée under Solomon, first headquartered variously in Shechem, Penuel, Bethel and Dan, would reveal in the J and E versions, probably set down at the beginning of the respective reigns of their conjoint history, a deep animosity. A close reading shows that this is not true. There are many passages where one sees preferences insinuated by the respective versions. But then again there are others in which the J writer is sympathetic to a northern Israelite figure or incident, and vice versa. It is clear that these authors were not as yet under the thumb of the reigning politico-military regime. They were writers, poets, artists, and deep believers in their holy consecration. The accession of Solomon's Rehoboam and then the immediate breakup into Judah and Israel, 925 BCE, exactly 100 years after the crowning of Saul, set into reality an entirely new set of religious dynamics.[6]

With regard to the priestly writer(s), the majority view today presents a time frame within the reign of the Judean king Hezekiah, 715–682 BCE. There is an interregnum of about 200 years between the setting down of the religious and political history of the Israelites in J and E, and the additions of P, the priestly writer(s). But during this time of political separation, it is quite likely that the chaotic political and military destinies of these two kingdoms gave to the Levitical and priestly cadres in each kingdom much freedom of action. The subsequent reforms of centralization by Hezekiah argue for this earlier decentralization and relative freedom for literary and historical reconsiderations.

J and E were joined at some point during this long period of political separation. P entered powerful additions to the books of Genesis, Exodus, and Numbers.

The book of Leviticus, the third in the canon was almost wholly a priestly addition, except for some later redactions, concerned with ritual orthodoxies. The very strong sacramental orientation of P throughout the Torah is believed to be due to the forced centralization of worship, sacrifice and the required donations to the Jerusalem Temple, initiated under Hezekiah.

The final book, Deuteronomy, is a compilation of two sources. One derives from the explicit admission by the Deuteronomistic historian, that King Josiah, 639–609 BCE, had been informed by his scribe Shaphan, c. 622 BCE, that the priest Hilkiah had found a "scroll of the *torah*" in the temple of Yahweh in Jerusalem.[7] Richard Friedman associates this earlier stratum with the priests at Shiloh and argues that the new centralization which King Josiah sought to bring about was not to be at Jerusalem but at this older northern or E-centered holy city. He also associates D1 with the prophet Jeremiah who was a young contemporary of the King.

D2 is today associated with the return of the exiles to Jerusalem after 539 BCE now under the protection of the Persian kings. Deuteronomy, in its entirety which attempts to duplicate the historical and sacramental character and narrative of the earlier covenantal books, is thought to have been associated with the early books of the so-called Deuteronomistic histories, Joshua, Judges and 1 Kings, now included in the Biblical corpus along with the prophets. However, at some point, this agreed upon by most scholars, Deuteronomy was redacted such that it became a supplement and conclusion, "the song of Moses," an ancient blessing here attributed to Moses. Central to Deuteronomy is a code of law ostensibly preached by Moses to the Israelites which sums up the divinely authorized social order of the Israelites in their current c. 620–450 BCE historical status as a people.

While much of Deuteronomy 2 may have been written in exile, 586–539 BCE it is believed that the prophet Ezra, who returned to Jerusalem from Babylon c. 450 BCE had a hand in the final redaction and integration of the Torah. It is written in Nehemiah, himself a Jewish official assigned by the Persians c. 440 BCE, to be governor of Judea, that Ezra assembled the people of Jerusalem. "They told the scribe Ezra to bring the book of the Law of Moses, which the Lord had given to Israel" {Nehemiah 8:1}.

The implication here is that the Torah had by now reached its final and complete form and needed to be orally read to this relatively unsophisticated and unknowing people, this the text of their ancient and holy laws: "So they read from the book, from the law of God, with interpretation. They ("Ezra and Levites") gave the sense so that the people understood the reading" {Nehemiah 8:8}.

An analysis of the Samaritan version of the Pentateuch, here written in Old Hebrew, and also in substantial agreement with the more recent Septuagint version, that, translated from the Hebrew to the Greek for the Alexandrian Jewish community in c. 280–260 BCE almost two hundred years earlier than the Samaritan edition, reveals few differences with our modern Masoretic and New Standard Revised versions. Those few differences in the Samaritan text, in *Exodus*, *Numbers*, and *Deuteronomy* are attributed to redactions later made by the prophet Ezra in the more universal text. This would put an almost complete version of the Torah as existing antecedent to Ezra and possibly linked to the exilic community in Babylon or on early return, 550–500 BCE.[8]

Contexts

Built on a long-existing written record of events, stretching back several hundred years from the time of Moses' entry in Canaan, hypothetically in the 1200–1100 BCE time frame the Pentateuch itself was the product of a four-hundred-year process of development and accretion, c. 900–500 BCE. This occurred during the split of the United Kingdom, the formation of the two kingdoms and then the destruction of the polity of both Israel and Judah. Of course the final event was the forced exile of the Judean elite, 597–582.

It is this elite group of priests, scribes, Levites, longing for the homeland in spite of their relatively prosperous circumstances along the Euphrates River at Nippur who made further emendations and additions to existing historical and holy documents, and who on their return to Jerusalem, after 539 BCE completed the Torah as we know it today. Even in the context of an era of relatively slowly moving cultural and historical events this integration had to have been influenced by the evolving perspective, political, religious, intellectual, that this document now gives us.

For one, both J and E present a picture of the religious, political, and economic character of the ancient Near East that reveals the changing urban, agricultural, and Bedouin-like wanderings of peoples struggling to preserve life and limb. One reads through Genesis, Exodus, and Numbers, and it is quite clear that Yahweh and Elohim fit the ancient picture of nature gods endowed with magical powers, the ability to create destructive events as in the inflictions by Yahweh on the Egyptian pharaoh, and a variety of sacral injunctions that reflect the anxieties, fears, and emotional desires for sustenance and revenge that these untamed and vulnerable humans emoted day by day, moment by moment.

An example of this is given in the J story of Adam and Eve in Genesis, the role of the snake/serpent in the Garden of Eden. "Now the serpent was more crafty than any other wild animal that Lord God had made" {Genesis 3:1-J}. The theme here is fear of wild animal power and the weak and gullible human, in the face of transcendental evil.[9] It is an ancient human theme, first expressed and written down over 1500 years earlier in the Sumerian epic of *Gilgamesh*.

The serpent appears again in an Elohistic story in Numbers, when the people rise up against Moses and God, who then sends fiery snakes to bite and kill the Israelites. They repent and the Lord orders Moses to create a bronze serpent to be put on a pole. Thence whenever an Israelite is bitten by a snake "they would look at the serpent and live" {Numbers 21:6–9, E}. This fear of snakes/serpents is again echoed in {Deuteronomy 8:15} and in {Isaiah 30:6}. Max Weber notes the universality of the metaphor of the power and fearfulness of humans towards the snake in the Phoenician god of healing whose symbol was the snake.[10] In the Sinai desert of Midian such an actual bronze artifact was found dating to the era of this ancient tribe of Yahweh into whom Moses had married.

By the time we get to the era of the priestly additions and emendations to the Pentateuch, the era of the Judean King Hezekiah, c. 715–687 BCE, a wholly new political/military era was reshaping the faith of the Israelites. Two hundred years had elapsed, a more settled urban and mixed agricultural economy had pushed aside the life of wandering cattlemen/husbandry and indeed the religious outlook of the earlier era. There had been much prophetical writing during this period, mostly critical of the Israelite union of Yahweh and Baal worship, a more syncretic integration of belief, highly influenced by the adjacent Phoenician cities. Also, because Israel was closer than Judah to the Mediterranean world of commerce, it was wealthier and the leadership inevitably corrupt. It was thus a lure for the powers that were to the north.

Most critically Israel as a state had now been overrun by Assyria. Judah was now under siege by this great and expansive power which eventually would push into Egypt itself, 674 BCE. Many thousands of Israelites had been deported to the vast and mysterious spaces of this empire. Indeed, ten tribes would disappear from the history of the Hebrews. Jerusalem itself became a city of refuge for many of these northern Yahwists. Hezekiah as related by the later Deuteronomic historians, at the probable behest of the priests of the 1st Jerusalem Temple, was urged to take down the various sacral "high places" an ancient tradition for worshipping and sacrificing, here going back to the Sumerian Ziggurats and also leading forward to the temples on the "high city" of Athens, (Acropolis).

But Hezekiah went further. The ancient bronze serpent of Moses, called Nehushtan, had been preserved in Jerusalem and the people had worshipped and made offerings to it as a source of miracles. This Hezekiah destroyed, clearly wanting to rid the Israelite religion and Jerusalem cult of symbols of magical worship, Moses-derived or not {2 Kings 18:4}. Possibly it resounded to the ancient symbolism of Yahweh as a war god, during a time to achieve pacification with the Assyrians.[11]

Another, not contradictory view of the surge for centralization and the attempt to rationalize the Judaic faith away from the magical and polytheistic urges of the masses towards Jerusalem, the Temple, the priesthood and the sacrificial wealth that would here accrue, was the national threat from Assyria. After three years of siege Samaria fell, and with a consequent vast deportation, c. 711 BCE. Hezekiah had to gird Judah for the next phase of Assyrian expansion. And when he attempted to co-opt the Assyrian advance they also came at him.

Rabshakeh, an emissary of the Assyrian king demanded surrender and spoke in Hebrew to the Judean delegation at the walls of Jerusalem, here with the population looking and listening {2 Kings:18}. The siege of Jerusalem however continued. Jerusalem held, possibly because the well at Siloam brought a continuous supply of Gihon spring water into this high city. And Hezekiah bought them off.

Contemporaneously the priestly class emended the books of the Pentateuch composed in entirety, Leviticus. Manasseh, the son of Hezekiah continued the sponsorship by Assyria of Judah, this for forty five years, 687–642 BCE. But in addition to the new subservient political conditions Manasseh appears to have become a hated figure of the Deuteronomistic historians {2 Kings:21}. He reinstated the popular worship of the idols of Baal and allowed for pluralistic worship and sacrifice to the gods at the high places.

Amon, son of Mannaseh became king at age 22, following the death of his father. He attempted to carry out the policies of his father, but a within-the-Palace/Temple conspiracy had him assassinated two years later, to be followed by a general uprising against the conspirators by the "people of the land—*am ha arez.*" Josiah, son of Amon, at age 8 became King of Judah from 640–609 BCE {2 Kings:21, 22}.

In a great reversal, Josiah is now seen as the restorer of Davidic fidelity to the traditions of Yahweh, the reforming prophets, and the spirit of Judaism as now determined by the diverse Levitical and priestly elements in newly threatened Judah. It was at this time that the Book of Deuteronomy was supposedly discovered within the Temple and then later placed within the Pentateuch. So too here were created the historical writings in Samuel and Kings. The books of Joshua and Judges were redacted and separated from J and E and the Torah, to be part of Deuteronomic history.

The book of Deuteronomy, even more than the priestly and prophetic speeches, writings, and centralization of worship attributed by the historians to King Hezekiah, becomes a central modernizing document in Jewish history. Here explicitly stated, worship and sacrifice in the diverse high places are condemned. Instead, sacrifice, burnt offerings, tithes, donations, and votive gifts are now to be given to "the place where the Lord your God will choose as a dwelling for his name" the Temple {Deuteronomy 12:1–19}. The Temple is no longer a mere physical home for Yahweh.[12]

The book of Deuteronomy as the culmination and summary of the five holy books can be described as follows: "Maintenance of the covenant relationship between Israel and its divine sovereign through the rule of faith and law within the community is the principal concern of Deuteronomy."[13] But it also firmly establishes the rule of the priesthood.

Perspective

The original Decalogue, the Ten Commandments are thought to have been written in very short imperative apodictive utterances, "you shall, shall not." In {Exodus 20–21} composed by the P author(s) in the time of Hezekiah, 700 BCE, and in {Deuteronomy 5:1–20}, Josiah's kingship, c. 630 BCE, the crucial injunctions against creating idols and worshipping other gods are phrased essentially the same. The greater difference is in the treatment of the Sabbath; Deuteronomy gives this law more of a social than a cosmological inference as in Exodus.[14]

In the time of King Ahab of Israel, c. 850 BCE, the prophet Elijah is repelled by the turn toward the worship of Baal and Asherah, the goddess of fertility, in the palace initiated after Ahab's marriage to Jezebel, a Sidonian. Elijah challenges Ahab to assemble the priests of these alien gods in a heavenly contestation {1 Kings 18:20–40}. Elijah and the God of Israel are victorious and the 450 priests of Baal are killed. Elijah then flees and, in imitation of the mission of Moses, is told by an angel of Yahweh to ascend Mt. Horeb in the wilderness where he has a miraculous, fire-and-brimstone meeting with the Lord {1 Kings:19}.

Clearly in Israel, as also in Judah, a popular syncretic form of worship and thinking saturates the popular mind. The monotheistic message of Moses to Israel is the provenance of only a small number of religious intellectuals, Levites/priests, scribes/prophets. The fall into Baal and Asherah worship in the north is easily understood. The economy and the relative wealth of Israel as compared to Judah more easily allows for this slippage into apostasy. A strict ethical monotheism is a difficult discipline to maintain, nationally, against the lure of material wealth and the beliefs of those that supply it.

Note that Manasseh, who became King of Judah in 687 BCE, and remained in power for over forty years under the vassalage of Assyria, no doubt maintained this power because he allowed the people of the land, the *am ha arez*, to maintain their polytheistic worship and the sacral groves on high. Example: ". . . and he [Manasseh] burnt his son [eldest] as an offering" {2 Kings 21:2–6}. It is clear that only in high intellectual circles, scribes, priests, Levites was the Decalogue injunction of Moses, not to take any idols, to worship, only one God to hold, observed.

The *am ha arez* needed to worship Asherah, the goddess of fertility, of the larger worlds of El and Baal, gods of the sky, the forces of nature, here to erect their wooden poles and other cultic structures, to sacrifice and engage in rites of joy.

The evidence is of a deep disconnect between this intellectual elite and the so-called people of the land. In the years after the death of Josiah, at the hands of the Egyptians, 609 BCE, the people were still worshipping the gods in Jerusalem itself, burning their children in the Valley of the Hinnom. As with the prophet Micah, Jeremiah who arrives in Jerusalem after the death of Josiah, observes the sacrificial corruptions of the Temple, the easy reversion of the populace to the traditional polytheistic practices of the various Levantine nations.

> Do you not see what they are doing in the towns of Judah and in the streets of Jerusalem? The children gather wood, the fathers kindle fire, and the women knead dough to make cakes for the queen of heaven [Ishtar]; and they pour out drink offerings to other gods, to provoke me to anger. Is it I whom they provoke? Says the LORD. Is it not themselves, to their own hurt. {Jeremiah 7:17–19}

> For the people of Judah have done evil in my sight, says the LORD: they have set their abominations in the house that is called by my name, defiling it. And they go on building the high places of Topheth [fireplace-shame], which is in the valley of the Hinnom, to burn their sons and daughters in the fire—which I did not command, nor did it come into my mind. Therefore the days are coming, says the LORD, when it will no more be called Topheth, or the valley of the son of Hinnom [Gehenna], but the valley of murder: for they will bury in Topheth until there is no more room. The corpses of this people will be food for the birds of the air, and for the animals of the earth; and no one will frighten them away. And I will bring to an end the sound of mirth and gladness, the voice of the bride and bridegroom in the cities of Judah and in the streets of Jerusalem; for the land shall become a waste. {Jeremiah 7:30–34}

Jeremiah had hoped that the Babylonian/Chaldean capture of Jerusalem in 597 BCE might inaugurate a new purification of the Temple and the city. But a revolt in 587 BCE caused the benign occupation to be ended and the Temple and walls of Jerusalem to be destroyed; more educated Israelites were sent off to exile. The people of land (am ha arez), the occupiers allowed to remain so that they could harvest the vineyards and the crops. While the Chaldeans/Babylonians looted the gold and silver of the Temple, the exiles took with them the many scrolls of their heritage.[15]

One must keep in mind that that time frame reveals a new world of intellect. Amid the devastating wars and the natural fears precipitated into these populations, there are writings, poetry, music, and throughout the world. The Homeric writings, c. 750 BCE and the poets of the Greek islands are now being disbursed far and wide. Even in Assyria, during the days of Hezekiah, c. 700 BCE, a great library was being formed in their capital, Nineveh. Hundreds of scribes and translators were transforming several thousands of years of literature, secular, mythological, and religious, harking back to the days of Sumerian greatness, 3000 BCE, to preserve and legitimize this heritage and the ruling powers that be. An Assyrian king even attempted to revive Sumerian, a non-Semitic language as the official tongue of his empire.

Just as Semitic Babylonia was being overrun by the Indo-European Medes and Persians, c. 550 BCE, the Chaldean King Nabonidas who was born in the Abrahamic city of Haran, and was probably of Indo-European heritage, sent his daughter to be a priestess in a temple at Ur, one of the great Sumerian cities. A devotee of the moon god Sin (Sinai?), he traveled to the Arabian city of Tima to study comparative religious practices for ten years.

The last Judean exiles left for Babylonia in 582, Jeremiah being forced to flee to Egypt. The Persian Cyrus conquering Chaldean Babylonia in 539 immediately sent back a group of Judean priests to Jerusalem to begin the reconstruction of city and Temple. They were to anchor his empire in regions of religious loyalty. The priesthood had been gone from Jerusalem for some 43 years. However, progress in Jerusalem was slow. Zerubbabel, one of the early leaders of the return from exile to Jerusalem, rejected offers of help from the Samarians and those other "people of the land, *am ha arez*" in rebuilding the Temple. These now-established outsiders in the provinces of Samaria and Yehud lobbied to inhibit the building of the Temple and the renewing of Jerusalem {Ezra 4:1–4}. By the time Ezra and Nehemiah arrived in Jerusalem, 450–400 BCE, one hundred years of Judean control of the Persian province of *Yehud* had been ongoing, and struggling. It is clear that a final separation and then, purification of the Jewish people from "outsiders" was necessary.[16]

The *Torah* now had been redacted, completed. It was to be the great document of sanctification, memorializing the history of a people and their "chosen ness" by the Lord. Devotion to the Book would sanctify this people. Under Ezra's guidance it was to be read with explanation even to the assembled returnee "elite," many with polygamous, polytheistic, concubine and slave families {Nehemiah 8: 1–8}. This Levitical elite, very loosely subscribed to the heritage of Mosaic Law. It was the task of the returnee prophetic and priestly elite now to draw together the evanescent strands of the Mosaic tradition. Without a political and military base, they would have to begin to reteach the covenant of this people with their God, to transform the chaos of political disintegration with the binding and now written words of Yahweh as dictated to Moses. They would now have to become a people of the Book.

> Blessed *is* the man that walketh not in the counsel of the ungodly, nor standeth in the way of the sinners, nor sitteth in the seat of the scornful.

> But his delight *is* in the law of the LORD; and in his law doth he meditate day and night.
> And he shall be like a tree planted by the rivers of water that bringeth forth his fruit in the season; his leaf also shall not wither; and whatsoever he doeth shall prosper. {Psalm 1:1–3, King James Version}

The Torah in Samaria

The power of the message of Babylonian exile and subsequent redemption in Jerusalem and the Yehud resonated deeply and widely. The Samarian leadership (of former Israel) also considered themselves as purveyors of the Yahwist faith here in the ancient northern homeland of Jacob and his sons; this in spite of the fact that many of them were converts from the Assyrian in-migration. They too had copies of the scrolls, the documents of the heritage {Jeremiah 41:4–5}. Before the middle of the fifth century, c. 450 BCE, hereditary Yahwist governors were also now in control of Samaria and Ammon (Trans-Jordan).

Those the Assyrians and Chaldean/Babylonians had left behind to tend the land, and who had incurred the wrath of the prophets for their syncretic and corrupt Yahwism, these also called the *ammei ha-aretz*, were suspect by the returnees. Increasingly intermarried and casual in their worship in both rituals and cult, especially the northerners of Samaria, all seemed different.

We must remember that the Yahwist faith was yet practiced by and large by those Israelites left behind after the Assyrian deportations, as well as the newcomers brought in by the Assyrians to repopulate the territory who had felt obligated to adopt the God of the region. Jeremiah recalls a poignant example of this steadfastness of belief:

> On the day after the murder of Gedaliah [the Judean regent chosen by the Chaldeans to administer Judea] before anyone knew of it, eighty men arrived from Shechem, and Shiloh, and Samaria, with their beards shaved and their clothes torn, and their bodies gashed, bringing grain offerings and incense to present at the [destroyed] temple of the LORD [Jerusalem]. {Jeremiah 41:4–5}

The same men who assassinated Gedaliah, caught them and slaughtered all but ten, who pleaded: "Do not kill us, for we have stores of wheat, barley, oil, and honey hidden in the fields" {Jeremiah 41:8}. Clearly many Yahwist peasants of Israel/Ephraim had remained true to the faith. They had recovered their economy and wealth in the 140 years (722–582 BCE) between the Assyrian and Babylonian/Chaldean occupations.

Samaria, the city, was a political latecomer of the Northern Kingdom. Originally Shechem (Jacob/Genesis and Joshua, then Jeroboam) and Shiloh/Saul

{1 Samuel 14:3} were richly important places of memory in the evolution of this people. The holy sites in the Northern Kingdom, after 930 BCE were at Beth-El and Dan {1 Kings 12:26–33}, and the capital of Jeroboam's secessionist northern tribesman was successively Shechem, Penuel {1 Kings 12:25}, east of the Jordan in Gilead, and then at Tirzah, c. 815 BCE {1 Kings 14:7}, north of Shechem. Forty years later under Omri, c. 875 BCE, a new capital, Samaria was constructed between Tirzah and Shechem {1 Kings 16:23–24}.

A delegation from Beth-el in the north, c. 520 BCE, which questioned the appropriateness of fasting on the anniversary of Cyrus' Edict of return, a happy day, causes a reconsideration by Zechariah {Zechariah 7:1–6}.[17] Both {2 Chronicles 30:5–11, 18; 34} and {Zechariah 7:1–7} convey a more conciliatory attitude toward Samarian Jews, implying that urban as well as rural Jews remained loyal inhabitants. {Nehemiah 13:23–29} {Josephus' Antiquities, 11:8.2} also argue for the continuity of Yahwism in this province.[18] Samaria between c. 375–335 BCE, the era of the Chroniclers in Jerusalem, reveals in its Aramaic legal documents that: "Most of the theophoric names are Yahwistic, indicating continued devotion to Yahweh and hence persistence of Judaism in the territory of the northern kingdom."[19]

Bickerman argues that the subsequent Samarian opposition to rebuilding the walls of Jerusalem, and the Temple on the return of the first exiles, 538 BCE, was a purely political one, thus too the rejection of their help by the returnees.[20] However, the Samarians maintained a strong Yahwist, if syncretic worship as the leadership were descendants of the original Assyrian colonists. The break with Jerusalem, came two hundred years later in 330 BCE, with a revolt against Alexander and the introduction of a Macedonian colony and military. The indigenous Samarians then moved their shrines to Shechem and became the Sidonians (Canaanites) of Shechem, no longer holy Mt. Zion (Jerusalem), but Mt. Gerizim (Shechem).

In these two hundred years they worshipped the Torah as did their Yehud counterparts. However, they had been under a different governing structure as a separate province under the Persians. It is only after the Hellenistic break did they gradually renounce the Judean emphasis in Scriptures of the greater religious significance of the prophets. In this the Samaritans concurred with the views of the Jerusalemite priesthood and then the Sadducees. The Samaritan version of the Torah is closer to Qumran documents as well as the Greek-language Septuagint version of the Torah that was worshipped in Alexandria, as compared to the much later rabbinical Masoretic text.

In order to understand the transformations of Judaism as it evolved beyond Ezra's Torah, the question of Samaria and the Samaritans must be raised. Why was their pure version of the Torah as the Law given to Moses by the Lord, not the ultimate form of the faith? Why did the Samaritans decline and practically disappear, now a quaint backwater sect of worldwide Judaism?

Indeed there were events. The blow inflicted by Alexander after the Samaritan revolt shortly after 330 BCE diluted Samaria with even more nonethnic Israelites, the Macedonian troops now stationed there with their families. Also, more cooperative Judea made peace with the Greeks until the Maccabean war against Antiochus which ended in victory for the Jews. Then John Hyrcanus, the Maccabean/Hasmonian King/High Priest of Jerusalem destroyed the Samaritan Temple on Mt. Gerizim in 128 BCE, even as he persecuted the Judean Pharisees. This was followed by an ultimate attack on both Samaria and Shechem in which Hyrcanus followed the Roman example with Carthage, obliterating the city.

Yet these cities again rose up to some level of prosperity. Herod committed to their rebuilding, c. 10 BCE, and re-named Samaria, Sabaste, after the new Emperor of Rome, Augustus. Josephus reports that in 6–9 CE Samaritans invaded the Temple in Jerusalem during Passover and profaned its sanctity by scattering human bones within.[21] And yet when the great revolt of Judea against Rome erupted, 67–70 CE, the Samaritans joined in with their Jerusalemite counterparts and suffered a final destruction of Shechem by the Romans.

But, were these blows, not too different than those suffered by Judea over the generations, enough to erase the Samaritan vision of the holy books, and the ancient tradition of "Ephraim" from historical memory?

A New Era

A majority of the Israelite population in Babylonia stayed on, prosperous and secure. Many moved to the cities of Persia, where they were useful to the monarchy; there existed there a relatively uncouth population of peasants and warriors. Hebrew communities could soon be found in the Indo-European cities in Asia Minor, such as Sardis, now also under Persian control.[22] The faith of their fathers was now portable. The holy writings could be copied and taken to new places where new communities of this ancient faith could be established.

By the days of Ezra and Nehemiah, c. 450 BCE, Israelites were widely dispersed in Babylonia, Persia, and the Ionian cities. The Israelites of Nippur became wealthy, 28 settlements being recorded in this area, with extensive involvement in banking, agriculture, trade, and in military settlements. Some of those who chose to return to Yehud and the growing settlement in Jerusalem were permitted to bring male and female slaves with them {Ezra: *passim*}. It is this polyglot intermarried population that both Ezra and later Nehemiah railed about. Their concerns involved political orthodoxy, religious practice and linguistic unity, not ethnic purity.[23]

The diminished land of Persian Yehud that the first returnees encountered, c. 538 BCE, was but a shadow of the former pride of nationhood. Perhaps 25,000 inhabitants lived in this small region centered around and including Jerusalem.[24] Edomites, later called Idumeans, had occupied southern areas of ancient Judah, with its capital, Hebron. Ammonites and Moabites had returned to the lands east of the Jordan, where the assassins of Gedaliah had fled. Phoenicians moved south along the coast and the fertile valleys, the ancient tribal home of Asher, Zebulon, and Issachar. The ever-resourceful former Philistine towns along the southern coast again had long expanded east into the Sheppelah hill country, where they had extensive olive plantations, often overseen by Judean management.[25]

Persia's cultural leniency allowed for the infusion of a wide variety of foreign inputs. For example, there were to be found in the Yehud during this period, Greek legal seals (*bullae*), coins with mixed Greek/Phoenician/Persian motifs, words and phrases in Greek, illustrations of the god Zeus, an Attic (Athenian) Owl, or the head of Athena. These were minted in various cities of Phoenicia, even Samaria, then under Persian control, and also during the time of the wars with Athens and Greece, fifth century BCE.[26]

There are descriptions and illustrations of a silver quarter shekel coin inscribed yhd—Yehud, in Aramaic lapidary script—early fourth century, c. 390 BCE. This coin shows a bearded helmeted Greek warrior on one side. On the other side, a winged wheel {Ezekiel 1:4-28}, Yahweh's glory, sits a bearded male divinity, carrying on his hand a falcon or eagle. Question: How and why, considering Persian relations with Greece at this time and the strict Jerusalem priesthood's view of "graven images" could a coin of this sort be minted in Yehud, and under Persian governance?[27]

In the Yehud, the rise of scribes and the end of the absolute political dominance of the high priest, (Persian hegemony), coincides with the introduction of the written Torah, the widespread availability of the writings of the Prophets, and of course the gradual urbanization of even backwater Palestine {Malachi 2:7; Haggai 2:12}. In Chronicles there is even an equating of Levites with scribes {2 Chronicles 34:13}.[28] Chronicles further relates that in the fourth century, the Torah came to be taught in all the cities of Judah {2 Chronicles 17:9}.

Scribes (*Soferim*) were everywhere. At the city gates, in the plazas, by the Temple, they assisted the ordinary folk with the requirements of a contract society. But they were also out in the countryside helping the faithful to understand the meaning of the holy laws of the Pentateuch and guide them in their day-to-day sanctities of family and ritual commitment. The seeming ethnic exclusivity hearkened to by Ezra and Nehemiah, as for example against intermarriage with the Samarians, the latter still devoted to the Temple and the Israelite traditions, was basically an issue of politics as well as religious orthodoxy. Yet there was, given a time of peace, an openness to proselytism that could be argued for from the holy writings, stemming not only from {Ezra, 6:21; also, Exodus 12:49; Leviticus 19:34;

Zechariah 8:23; Isaiah 56:7}. "Only a Jew was a true believer, but everybody could enter the congregation of the Chosen People" (Elias J. Bickerman).

How Many Torahs?

There are those today who cannot accept that the Torah is a work of human minds and human hands. No matter the problematic contents of good and evil, and as committed by Israelites, the Torah as existing today is viewed by the literalists as the word of God as transmitted by Moses the prophet. True, few of the most ultraorthodox Jews will see Moses as more than a prophet, a gifted human being touched by God, but yet so tainted by his labors below with the "stiff necked" escapees from Egypt, that Yahweh would not allow him to enter the Holy Land, Canaan, his mission in life.

It is probably true, if sad that many of these literalists follow the teachings of a leader who communicates the "truths" of the Torah to them to be obeyed under the tutelage of this teacher, a rabbi, but he could be a priest, minister, or mullah. True literalist believers need to submerge themselves under the guidance of someone, who though appearing and acting mortal, has taken on the role as vested communicator of truths from on high. They rarely actively live in the world where they must test factually their secular commitments and wagers.

Today, most Jews, and of course members of other religious denominations, must temper their religious beliefs and values in terms of the demands of the secular life, the responsibilities for decisions and actions in the economic and social domains. They live in a world of probabilities, actions taken with recourse to modification or alteration, given new facts, new events. There are few absolute truths in the secular world where humans must undergo constant traumatic challenges and realities. Here the study of the historical Torah can take on real significance.

Understanding that these five books are the product of centuries of human experience, heartbreaking human experience at times, and seeing the layers of philosophical, moral, and literary effort expended to illustrate the drama of human nature as it explodes over time in the life and death of a tribe, a nation, and a people, adds incomparable luster to this majestic undertaking. It may not be the literal work of a supernatural being, but it is the serious and reflective work of great minds and great artists.

Naturally the final redacted product as it found its way into the hands of wise Ezra, and as he lectured to his milling crowd at the gates of the holy city, was not the final product that found its way into the various editions of the five books as they have come down through history. The critical issue is not the number of variations, Qumran, Samaritan, Sadducean, Septuagint, Masoretic, but the fact that this work was a serious attempt to create a standard for a holy people, a moral people, a people chosen to be such. By revealing the warts along with the blessings of Israelite life over these centuries, the writers, editors, redactors reveal to us much of the mystery that lies in human behavior. It raises all the great questions of human life. Thus it should be studied seriously and respectfully in order to appreciate the wisdom that lies herein

The Torah, as we have it in our hands and before our eyes and minds today, may not be a creation of a supreme being. But it is as close as we humans will ever get to experiencing both the glories and tragedies of human existence. And still, we must concede that this human existence is indeed a product of a higher law, but a natural one that will probably remain forever beyond our ken, both as guide to action, and as metaphysical revelation as to what we humans are.

History Has Its Demands

The Torah was not the endpoint of historical Judaism. Almost as soon as it was collated as part of the priestly functions of the Second Temple, the awareness spread throughout the various Judaic communities that the interpretations and vicissitudes of life were producing literary responses. These arose out of the ever-increasing self-awareness of the intellectual leadership among the Jews. They were not merely prophetic and moral jeremiads, but also poetic and philosophic responses to life as it moved through time.

This accretion of thinking and writings, a cultural explosion of human nature in its most total envisionments spurred on this evolution in Judaism and its growing impact on the outside world. Just as the expansion of the Philistines, the Ammonites, and then the Assyrians and the Babylonian Chaldeans had exploded their own responses in the political and military dimensions of Israelite Judaic institutions, so too did these foreign incursions leave their literary and philosophical imprint.

This is the next story in Judaism, the evolutionary growth of Jewish intellectualism and its impact on the nature of Judaism, a new revolution to come. Here, the creation of Holy Scripture.

CHAPTER FOUR

Scriptures

Reprise

The first Judaic religious revolution took place with the breakup of the united monarchy, after Solomon's death in 925 BCE. As we have noted in the previous chapter there is reference in the Pentateuch of much historical and theoric writing before this event. But monarchical division did accelerate the Levites, scribes, priesthood of the Temple to quickly get on with a historic envisionment of the Mosaic tradition, but within the still existing traditions of the northern Elohistic (E) and the southern Yahwist (J) components of this new religion. Thus were Genesis, Exodus, and Numbers set down in Hebrew.

It took the crisis of the Assyrian invasions two hundred years later, c. 725 BCE, and the destruction of Israel as an independent nation to precipitate the unification of these two writings, and then the addition and editing into this material of the (P) priestly component of the Torah, now with the addition of Leviticus. Another hundred years, 630 BCE, and Judah is under foreign pressure and a hurried new folio of writings, both historical and sacral appear on the scene, perhaps precipitated by a new group of intellectuals, priests from Shiloh. The separation of Deuteronomy discovered by King Josiah of Judah's priests, supposed to have been the first book of the new history of the Israelites, but later added onto the four existing parts of the Torah creates the Pentateuch plus the early prophetic writings starting with Joshua and continuing on until 2 Kings and afterward.

In the meantime much prophesy critical of the people and the leadership had been put to the pen by these wandering visionaries, and there is a great literature in the making opposite but not necessarily critical of the Torah. Judah is destroyed and occupied by the Chaldean Babylonians from 592 BCE. Cyrus and the Persians allow the exiled Judeans to return to his new province of the Yehud and rebuild their Temple in Jerusalem, 538 BCE.

Political Quietism and Literacy

When the prophets, scribes, priests, in waves, returned to the Yehud, c. 538–516 BCE, to rebuild the Temple and the city on Mt. Zion, this new generation, was composed first of Isaiah III, Haggai, Zechariah, and Malachi. Almost one hundred years later, an interim period of apparent political disorganization in the Yehud, the successive arrival of the scribe and priest Ezra from Persian Babylon and then Nehemiah from Persia itself as regent of the Yehud, c. 475–425 BCE, constitutes a transformational moment in the history of the Jews and their religion. Ezra brings the leadership together at the gates of Jerusalem to hear a reading of the now entire and redacted Torah, a document of which they are now apparently ignorant. He needs to read and explain. The people had changed in outlook, the world had changed. Even Persia was now in contraction as the Hellenes were then advancing in power and influence.

Our knowledge of the period: the Babylonian captivity and beyond derives from more than the historical material gleaned from the archives of the nations involved. The contemporary prophetic books Exekiel; Habakkuk, 2 Isaiah (early exilic period), and later, Haggai; Zechariah, tell us much. The following were edited in the fourth to third centuries, Persian/Greek period: 3. Isaiah; Chronicles 1 and 2; Ezra, Nehemiah, 1 Esdras, (the Septuagint version of Chronicles).[1] The original documents of Malachi, Ezra and Nehemiah were in all likelihood written at the time of the events being discussed, 458–440 BCE. But the reader cannot be assured that the modern exemplars of the ancient editing conform closely to the original memoirs and writings.[2]

There is a pacifist outlook now among the Jews about Israel not needing armies, c. 399–350 BCE,[3] a political quietism under Persian rule. No longer is there a Messianic age to be anticipated. Our captivity, Israel, is due to our breaking of the King's covenant with the Babylonians {Ezekiel 17:11–21}. The creation under Ezra, scribe as well as priest, after, c. 450 BCE of a written Torah now engendered a more democratic religious environment in Judea. Charismatic and priestly control was to be buffered by public, written documents. "I see a flying scroll; its length is twenty cubits, and its width ten cubits" (c. 30 × 15 feet) {Zechariah 5:2}.[4]

The final prophetic books, (Nevim) especially Malachi, written in the time of Nehemiah, c. 445 BCE, marks a separation in the Hebrew Bible, and inaugurates a new genre of holy writing, Kituvim.[5] There is an outpouring of writings by Jews, some of ostensibly sacred intentionality, furthering the meaning of the faith, others on historic dimensions of the faith, philosophical speculations, as well as much moral questioning. There is no doubt but that the later Septuagint, in Greek, in Alexandria, c. 280–260 BCE, expanded this activity, since it could be joined to the larger corpus of Greek intellectuality and literature, now widely disseminated throughout the literate world, even the Persian provinces. This too was a historic literary tradition almost as ancient as the Hebrew.

In the Yehud, the rise of the scribes and the end of the absolute dominance of the high priest coincides with the introduction of the written Torah, the widespread availability of the writings of the Prophets, and of course the gradual urbanization of even backwater Palestine. {Malachi 2:7; Haggai 2:12} In Chronicles there is even an equating of Levites with scribes {2 Chronicles 34:13}.[6] Chronicles further relates that in the fourth century, the Torah came to be taught in all the cities of Judah {2 Chronicles 17:9}.[7]

In the 200 years of Persian peace, 538–334 BCE, and in spite of the Persian wars against the Greek states, c. 490–450, there was a cosmopolitan economic revival throughout the Persian provinces with much international trade, even in the largely Greek inhabited Phoenician cities, and in the protectorate Philistine towns. This resulted in a cosmopolitan atmosphere of thinking in the Yehud, the need for literacy or scribal assistance in carrying out family economic or other business or governmental relationships.[8]

The inherent religious, historical power of a restored Yehud, now with many outlier Judaic communities in Babylon, Persia, Egypt and wherever Persian expansion took them, were again looking at Jerusalem as their homeland, and sending money to upkeep the Temple. This expansion of a Jewish presence throughout the Diaspora gathered up the idea of a gentle proselytism {Zech 8: 23} {3. Isaiah 56:7}. "Only a Jew was a true believer, but everybody could enter the congregation of the Chosen People."[9]

The Chronicler writing in the period 399–350 BCE, emphasizes a new sense of personal, rather than corporate responsibility, the latter still was invoked by nations and kings and generals in war{Deut. 20:10–18; 1 Kings 15:29}. For Jews another passage in {Deuteronomy 24:16} is gentler "The father shall not be put to death for the child, neither shall the children be put to death for the father, every man shall be put to death for his own sin" also, {2 Chronicles 25:4}.[10]

The {Chronicler 2:15:2} also {Ezekiel 17:13} emphasize the subordination of political independence for the peace and security of "eternal" Persian rule, where the people of the book might maintain their faith, and "need not fight while the Lord is with them" {Chronicles, 2:15:2}.[11] *Qoheleth* (Ecclesiastes), written in Jerusalem in the early Hellenistic/Ptolemaic period, c. 320–200 BCE, and thus after the Alexandrian defeat of Persia, reemphasizes this political quietism, and the ever deepening analysis of the Judaic understanding of their monotheism. Ecclesiastes speaks of "one universal God of mankind." But also, it denotes a new acceptance of events that lie outside the scrutiny of God. "For everything there is a season, and a time for every matter under heaven: a time to be born and a time to die; . . . a time to weep and a time to laugh; . . . a time to mourn and a time to dance; . . . a time to love and a time to hate . . ." {Ecclesiastes 3:1–8}.

Hellenization of Judaism

The period in the history of the Jews that begins with the Persian occupation is deeply influenced by events in the rapidly changing politico-military-economic character of life. In a sense the Jews are now living in an international commercial world, far more culturally and intellectually influenced by outside forces.

Before, during the monarchies, the Mosaic teachings truly touched only the intellectual classes, Levites, priests, scribes, sages and then prophets. The gradually working through of the additions to the original Pentateuchal writings took place in the most secluded levels of society, within the Temple or the priestly retreats. Otherwise we would have never had to read the cries of moral anguish that rang out from the prophets. Not merely the elite in Judah and Israel, especially the official syncretism of the royal house of the latter monarchy, so close to the Phoenecian states, were called for their defilement of the Mosaic Law. So too were the *am-ha arez*, the people of the land.

As late as the time of Jeremiah, when Deuteronomy had been composed (discovered) and the historical writings were now recording the demise of Israel and the contemporary crises in Judah, the cultural development of the Judean and Jerusalemite masses remained primitive. The glorious rigor of the Mosaic teachings seemed moot. The people sacrificed to the Asherah, fabricated religious figures, baked offerings for the Baal, the ultimate sacrifice, the burning of their children.

The return of the exiles from Nippur on the Euphrates, the reforms of Ezra and Nehemiah building on a new generation of prophets, the internationalism of peaceful (in the Yehud and Samaria) Persian hegemony, and the active international trade in goods and ideas, decade by decade had their impact in the extensions of literacy, the readings of the Torah, the prophets, and now many writers.

It altered the vision of the average Israelite. With Alexander and the Greeks these changes were transformed from a strong wind into a typhoon.

From c. 330 BCE, the coming of Alexander, along with a new administrative regime, the Jewish scribe began to have an ever greater role in society. Business, administrative, and civil service required literate skills now written in Greek, Aramaic and Hebrew in the priestly domains. {Ecclesiastes 7:19}, c. 320–200 BCE, says that "ten rulers of the city are not worth one Sage." Sage and scribe are now intermixed as we enter a truly international intellectual world led by the Greek emancipation of individual secular thought from the overweening power of religion and myth. Since for the Jews, all law now came from the Torah, and so much contemporary decision making needed reconciliation with contemporary Hellenistic law, the scribe/sage needed to know the Torah and give modern legal interpretation of its ancient meaning.[12]

Thus the earliest impact of the Greeks on the Jews was the use of Greek in public affairs, government, and business. The Judean priest may sit with fellow "august" in religious, judicial/law judgments, in the *Sanhedrin* (Synedrion—Greek for Assembly—71 elders). However, scribes would advise the administrative elite, sit at the gate of the city assembly, and be consulted on political matters. They were our first Jewish "lawyers"! "Fight to the death for truth, and the Lord God will fight for you" {Sirach 4:28} c. 180 BCE.

The great Hellenistic moment came with the translation of the Torah/Pentateuch into Greek, c. 280–260 BCE, for the Jewish community of Alexandria, and for Greek-speaking Jews all over the world. It joined these Jewish writings, and soon the rest of the Scriptures including much of the Hagiographia into Greek, and became part of the international intellectual scene, unlike other religious writings from Egypt, Mesopotamia, Persia, which largely remained with the local priestly and indigenous populations. Manetho and Berossus, priests from Egypt were commissioned by Ptolemy 1, 280–250 BCE (as with the Septuagint) to translate their heritage for the Alexandrian library.

Manetho complied, with a short Greek-language summary. This included the story of Moses, here, not as a prophetic leader of the Israelis fleeing Egypt, rather a renegade priest of Heliopolis. For the Egyptian priesthood the most sacred psalms, hymns, and rites in the original cuneiform or hieroglyphics needed to stay with the priesthood: "The foreigner may not see it."—Manetho.[13]

Whereas the Law (Pentateuch) was translated into vernacular Greek, Koine, between c. 280-260 BCE, most of the prophetic and other books were subsequently, by 75 BCE, translated into Greek. Later many of these books were not accepted into the Hebrew canon, c. 90 CE, by the Pharisaic/Rabbis in Yavneh, Palestine, but were being accepted into the Christian canon, later assigned to the Apocrypha by the Protestants. "Many translators were involved, the Law (Torah) being more uniform and literal in its rendering than the other books which are often paraphrased." The word Yahweh was eliminated from the Septuagint in favor of "Lord" (kurios), "hand of God" becomes "power of God," "robe of God" becomes "glory of God." Extant codices are all Christian in origin. In general the Jewish rabbis renounced the LXX, after 90 CE, because Christians had begun using it as part of their proselytizing into the pagan, Greek-speaking communities. The New Testament uniformly uses the LXX for its quotations from the Old Testament scriptures.[14]

Septuagint: Except for changes in the name of YHWH to "the God" "the Almighty" the Greek rendering of the Torah was quite exact. "Torah" became "Nomos"=the Law to the wider Hebrew and Greek communities.[15] Thus the Torah, the prophets, and many writings of Jews, in Greek, Aramaic and Hebrew became available to the entire Hellenistic world, emanating from Jerusalem and Alexandria. And of course, Greek curiosity about the natural and human world, being proverbial, they were attentive to this seemingly new, if ancient faith.[16]

"For Hellenistic Jews in Alexandria, Torah was an institution that embodied the covenant between God and the nation reflecting a system of commandments and laws, customs and traditions connecting the history of the people with their judges, kings, and prophets = "nomos," similar to Paul and the Gospel of John."[17] We therefore can interpret this rich literature as being translated into a new language (Greek), for an important and educated community, one which does not limit itself to the religious exclusivity of the Pentateuch as the only Torah, as with the Sadducees and Samaritans. The hint is that the roots of pharisaic claims of the two-fold truth, the written as well as the oral Torah given to Moses by YHWH, goes back much further than the Hasmonean period after the Maccabean revolt, c. 165–37 BCE. It was only in the Maccabean period that the political struggle between Sadduceean and Pharisaic Judaism came into view. Its roots may have lain in Alexandria and the translators of the Septuagint

The Greeks found in Jewish history and now, ethnic exclusivity, a fascination. Aristotelian successors such as Theophrastus, c. 315 BCE, using information gathered by Hecataeus who accompanied Ptolemy 1 on his post-Alexandrian campaign into Syria, interpreted the Jews as a "philosophical race," with their "God of heaven," as signifying a natural theology.[18] Others called the Jews a nation of philosophers, (attributed to the writings of Megasthenes, Theophrastus of Lesbos, and Clearchus of Soli).[19] Hermippus, another follower of Aristotle said that the Jews believed in the immortality of the soul.[20]

Hecataeus' attitude toward the work of Moses heralded the beginnings of a dual fascination by two very different ethne of each other's values and way of life. Hecataeus on Moses: "He picked out men of the most refinement and with the greatest ability to head the entire nation, and appointed them priests; and he ordained that they should occupy themselves with the temple and the honors and sacrifices offered to their God. These same men he appointed to be judges in all major disputes, and entrusted them to the guardianship of the laws and customs. For this reason the Jews never have a king."[21]

Despite the Maccabean conflict with the Greek Seleucid regime in Judea, the Greek influence remained deep, culturally as well as intellectually. One rationale by the later Rabbis about this ongoing fascination by a large proportion of the Jews of the civilized literate world lay in the fact that they were now speaking Greek, often better than they spoke Aramaic or Hebrew, and thus reading the voluminous literature of the Greeks, and thus in part, becoming Greeks. The Rabbis invoked Noah: "May God make space for Japheth, and let him live in the tents of Shem; and let Canaan (Ham) be his slave." {Genesis 9: 27, J} = Rabbis = "Let them speak the language of Japheth in the tents of Shem." Japheth was the ancestor of the Aegean and western Indo-Europeans, Shem the ancestor of Elamites and Eber = Hebrews.[22]

The Disintegration of Temple Judaism

Prologue: It should be said that the Hasmonian period followed by the rule of the Herodians and then the Roman occupation to the time of the destruction of the Temple, consequent to the defeat of the Jewish revolutionists, 166 BCE–70 CE, is subject to much historical conjecture. In addition to {Maccabees I & II} and {Book of Daniel Ch. 11} the major defining of the different Jewish cults which vied for power during this period is to be found in the writings of Josephus, c. 35–95 CE, a Pharisee by education and a failed general of the Jewish forces opposing Rome. Josephus wrote in Aramaic and spotty Greek. He joined the entourage of the Roman Emperor Titus, and spent much of his later years in Rome, where he presumably died. Josephus exemplifies the complex Judaic/Hellenic relationship. A strong believer in the Jewish cause, yet a realistic appraiser of the cultural and military power of the Hellenistic world, including Rome.

The writings of the Christian fathers, Paul and the Gospels are also important in giving us a sense of the rivalries of these groups as well as the positioning of Christian belief. John the Baptist, Jesus, and Paul also communicated to the writers of the Gospels, after the destruction of the Second Temple. And these writings were closely contemporary to the circumstances they describe, as with Josephus. The Tannaitic writings, Mishnah, Tosefta, Baraitus, and other Midrashik collections, date from c. 200–250 CE, at least one hundred fifty years after the fall of Jerusalem and the dissolution of all the groups except the Pharisees. Finally, the often piquant stories of the great Pharisees/Rabbis, Hillel, Shamei, Zakkai, etc. must be thought of as a product of an oral tradition much later and finally written down under very different historical and religious circumstance, in the Galilee, and in Babylon.

The power of the Second Temple was great during the peace of the Persian era, 538–330 BCE. It served the Persians as a bastion of political/religious stability as they attempted to extend and then to solidify their empire. By the time of the coming of Hellenes, large Diaspora populations were regularly coming to Jerusalem with their gifts and tithing, this even from afar. Thus the failure of the attempt by the Seleucids to permanently extend their empire over the former rulers of Jerusalem, the Ptolemys, especially in Egypt, brought Antiochus IV, Epiphanes back into Jerusalem, c. 175–168 BCE to finance his military expeditions until Rome stopped him.

During this period the high priesthood of the Temple virtually became for sale. There were vast amounts of wealth now deposited there. The Hellenizing leadership sold out to Antiochus, soon leading to the revolt led by the Maccabeans, and then a semi-independent Jewish state. The victory led by this Hasmonian family eventually led in c. 140 BCE, to an extraordinary event, the virtual crowning of Simon, one of the surviving sons of Mattathias, as both king and High Priest of the Temple.

{1 Maccabees 14:25–49} speaks about the placing of a bronze tablet commemorating this event on Mt. Zion in which "... the great assembly of the priests and the people and the rulers of the nation and the elders of the country." Simon was so proclaimed. Ellis Rivkin calls this assembly a synagogue megale, an imitation of Greek democratic assembly prototypes, or of the Roman senate, the Boule. In one sense it is a violation of the Aaronic hereditary tradition of leadership exemplified in both the first and second Temple traditions. Yet it is still consonant with the Mosaic tradition of calling upon the (70) elders to help make critical decisions for the Israelite people {Exodus 18:13–24; 24:9}. First, these conclaves in the Hasmonen era were called the *Sanhedrin* (see above). After the destruction of the Temple, the Pharisees called these meetings of elite the Bet Din. In much later 3rd-century CE Tannaitic writings it was the Knesset ha Gedolah.[23]

Power drove the Hasmoneans to renege on their Maccabean orthodoxy. Early on they were eagerly continuing the Persian/Ptolemaic/Seleucid tradition of coinage, which combines both Judaic and Hellenic motifs.[24] The Hasmoneans adopted Hellenistic amenities, the baths, Greek schools, and Hellenistic domestic as well as official architecture. But now, there was a stricter obedience to the Second Commandment. These rigid Sadducean interpretations of the Second Commandment were meant to restrict more than merely "idolatrous worship." Yet the majority of given names of the Hasmoneans were Greek-Eupolemus, Jason, Josephus.[25] "... (S)ome highly educated and acculturated Jews (notice their names) had made a clear bifurcation between their Hellenistic education and their strong Jewish loyalties."[26]

The Hasmonean King/Priest, John Hyrcanus (134–104 BCE), son of Simon did introduce pagan mercenary troops, Greek fortress-and palace-building techniques and tax-collecting methods, Alexander's siege techniques against cities such as Samaria, Scythopolis, Gadara, Gaza, Dor. Alexander Jannaeus (Hasmonean King/Priest), John's Hyrcanus' son, (103–76 BCE) used troops from Cilicia, Pamphylia, Thracia, but no Syrians, for their hatred of the Jews. Earlier, his father Simon Maccabee had fought Hellenists and Syrian mercenaries in the Jerusalem Akra, in 141 BCE.

Alexander Jannaeus, son of John, (103–76 BCE) further used these mercenaries against the revolt of pious Jews. This so-called Royal Guard flourished under Aristobulus II, (66–63 BCE) son of Salome Alexandra, widow of Jannaeus, who called himself "Philhellene." During this period there was much conversion to Judaism amongst the Greek mercenaries. What could be considered both pseudo-"philo-hellenism" and "pseudo-Sadducean" orthodoxy is exemplified in the Jannaeus established tradition of coinage having a Greek legend but no improper images.

Thus was the coexistence of much Hellenistic institution building with proper Temple ritual. The pietists decried the vulgar Hellenism of the Hasmonean rulers. Some fled to the desert around the Dead Sea to pursue a more purified Judaism (Essenes/Qumran), others studied the Books of the Torah, Prophets, the new interpreters/writers, to search for a Judaic modernism that could save the ancient tradition, (Pharisees). The cult on the Temple Mount had been saved from the Antiochenes, but Jewish culture was now completed enfiladed by Hellenistic elements.

John Hyrcanus was especially notorious in having turned from his espousal of the beliefs of the Pharisees, to waging war against them when questioned about his wearing the mantle of both King and high priest. This had been a prerogative of the Zadokites/Sadducees, a tradition that stems from Moses' brother Aaron to the installation of the High Priest Zadok by Solomon. Civil war continued into the reign of Alexander Jannaeus over the nature of this radical reshaping of Judaism under the now revolutionary culture of the Greek occupiers. The splintering of the Jews into the various semipolitical sects continued: Sadducees, Pharisees, Essenes and Qumran separatists. Then in the time of the wars against Rome even more militaristic messianic visions of an Israel were restored.

The Hasmoneans, in general, at the prodding of the priests, did return to a policy of religious purification—(A) against idolatrous worship (B) for the forced conversion of neighboring peoples, internal pagans, and other religious groups, including the Samaritans (since the Alexandrian conquest and the building of their Temple on Mt. Gerizim, they were made into permanent deviants from Israel), the Idumeans/Edomites to the south, the Iturians of the north coast of southern Lebanon. For example, under the Hasmoneans, the populace of the city of Pella in Transjordan was given the choice of conversion or death.[27]

The evidence for the Sadducees, a political clique, as noted above, comes mostly from the writings of the Jewish/Roman historian Josephus, late in the first century CE {The Jewish Wars; *Antiquities*}, as well as often-hostile comments from much later Tannaitic and early Christian writers. For, these priests officiated at the bloody sacrificial rites of the cult and profited from what was even then, for many, a barbaric spectacle.

There are reasons for a more balanced evaluation. The Sadducees represented more than a mere aristocratic power- and wealth-hungry clique joined to the Hasmonean political and military subjugation of the area. The rigorous Sadducean priestly followers of Pentateuchal orthodoxy went further even than Moses, in banning all graven images and idolatrous figural representations. In the now- and ancient monarchy, the lions of Solomon's throne, cherubs over the holy ark, the serpent of Moses, the oxen supporting the basin in the Temple courtyard, calves at the sanctuaries in Bethel and Dan, were all implicit violations. The Sadduceean interpretation of the Second commandment was now far more fundamentalist than the mere prohibition of "idolatrous worship."[28]

The Sadducees, of course, in accepting the holiness of only the Five Books of Moses, denied the Oral Law now developing under Pharisaic interpretation, the latter seeking to harmonize the ancient texts with contemporary circumstance. The Sadducees believed in free will, but did not believe in resurrection or life after mortal death. They did not recognize as well, the holy status of the Prophets and the Writings as they were first preserved and edited. These had been compiled by the priestly/scribe elite in exile in Babylonia, spurred on by the earlier prophetic writings, the Deuteronomist historical and redactory editing. The Sadducees felt that all writings beyond the divine Law of Moses, the Pentateuch, were man made, subject to temporary utility, and not the material for Holy Writ.

The Saducean elite had been totally involved in Hellenistic material, cultural paraphernalia and institutions: gymnasia, games, baths, theatre, architectural styles and artistic tastes. The Sadducees' claimed that Pharisee logic would lead to more respect for 'the book of Homer' (by which they meant Greek literature) than the 'Holy Scriptures.'[29] The Sadducees, especially in Jerusalem, were devoted to the Torah and the cult, to protect the sanctity and independence of the Temple, to the extent capable under the suspicious supervision of Rome. Considering the wealth that still poured into the Temple during the days of sacrifice and other magnetic festal holidays for the Diaspora, they had a vested interest, and fought constantly for Hasmonean support against the Pharisees who contended for Temple control. There was blood in the streets here between the two dominant political/ideological groups.

But there were many groups of Jews disenchanted from the power struggles around the Temple. The Qumran dissidents in the desert and the Essenes represent the flowering of new visions of Judaic orthodoxy. The Qumran writings, as translated from their post-WW II-discovered scrolls, reveal an acquaintanceship with the Septuagint/LXX, c. 280–260 BCE, or a version of the Pentateuch from which it was translated into Greek. There are 27 fragments written in Greek, including parts of Leviticus, Numbers, and Deuteronomy. These separate Greek translations are different from the Septuagint, but closer to it than the much later rabbinic Masoretic text.[30]

Qumran beliefs were a rich mixture of contemporary eastern Hellenistic mystery religion beliefs in predestination, angels of good and evil, a solar calendar, and a Messianic view of prophetic fulfillment.[31] At the core is their concept of the community of belief (yahad). Their writings also hint at an acceptance of astrology, demonology, linkages of wisdom and spiritualism, initiation rites, a penal code, celibacy, and asceticism—all new to Judaism, and hearkening to later Christian belief and practice.[32]

The Essenes, as with the Qumran secessionists, reflect the influences of foreign elements on evolving Judaic beliefs and practices. By the time of the Essenes' flourishing, c. 150 BCE, (ending in 67 CE), the major writings of what would become the Old Testament had been collected and edited; the Qumran sect owned an accurate version of Isaiah.

The key to the anticipatory linkage with future and early Christianity is the Qumran groups' asceticism, belief in immortality, and salvation through the coming of a personal Messiah. What it signifies is the wide-ranging reinterpretations of Judaism (as was early Christianity) which the culture and civilization of Greece had inspired in this land of a now ancient and strongly rooted historical faith. Question: Was this wide range of interpretations of the now ancient faith a possible product of the many converts to Judaism? These new believers and those Jews of the Diaspora themselves influenced by the contemporary mystery religions could well have planted these seeds on Zion, in their pilgrimages to holy Jerusalem.

Importantly, we see in all these Judaic sects, including the surviving Pharisees and the late-coming Christians as well as those sects discussed above which would disappear with the destruction of the Second Temple, a sharp deviation from the religion of the independent Israelite/Judean monarchies, and then the priestly and Levitical returnees from Nippur to the Persian Yehud, who gave the Pentateuch its final redaction, c. 450 BCE. In the three hundred years between these achievements of Ezra, and the priestly crowning of Simon, the Hasmonean, (c. 140 BCE) by the *Sanhedrin/synagogue megala*, a vast alteration had come over the Jewish mind, and Judaism itself.

Pharisees

Josephus gave us the major overview of the groups in contention during the Hasmonean period, 166 BCE until the destruction of the 2nd Temple, 70–67 CE.

The Pharisees are identical with the scribes (*soferim*) and the sages (*hakhamin*), advocates of the twofold law, the written and the oral law.[33] Concerned with ritual purity, they separated themselves from the *ammei ha arets*—also they were allied with the *haverim*—associates. "Each individual who internalized this twofold law could look forward to eternal life for his soul and resurrection for his body."[34] The oral law was supposedly transmitted by Moses to Joshua, to the elders, to the prophets, to the Pharisees; each authoritative teacher could formulate oral laws that were binding on him and his disciples.[35] Relationship to God, "the holy one, blessed be he" signified a more personal relationship with God the father, by the individual, and the chosen people as a community—they wrote down none of their teachings, eschewed poetry and historical allusions, even for prayers and blessings; rather, they cultivated logical, deductive modes of reasoning and introduced proof texts. No priest or prophet or sage was necessary to approach God or a Temple. This allowed for complete Judaic observance away from the Temple and into the Diaspora. Rivkin believes that the Pharisees not only set the stage for Christianity but wanted to accommodate Judaism to the Greco-Roman civilization which emphasizes law, logic, reasoning, literacy.[36]

From the perspective of history and in consideration of the Saducean response, the most important historical contribution of the Pharisees was their belief that YHWH had given to Moses at Mt. Sinai the truths of the Oral Law, as well as the written Torah. The Oral Law was the means by which the Written Law could be interpreted for use in modern times. But its authority was hinted at by the existence of the prophetic and wisdom writings, the Nevi'im (Prophets) and Kituvim (Writings), to be acknowledged at a later point in time. These surely were an adjunct to the Torah, the Written Law, and its ultimate authority. This reality allowed for the search for living meanings in the Torah, relevant to all future generations of Jews.

In Jerusalem both the Sadducees and the Pharisees, the two dominant political and religious perspectives, attempted a harmonization with the modern. The Hasmonian king/priests had quickly succumbed to Greek civilization as Jews, even as the *hellenophile* chief priests were either killed or exiled as tools for Seleucid tyranny. The Saducean outlook had a unique version of a twofold truth. On the one hand they were highly traditionalist in their view of what consisted of the holy books of Judaism, here the Torah only. The rest of the writings, prophetic and wisdom, were mere embellishments. But also they had the Temple as the repository for their "being." In spite of the barbarity of the animal sacrifices, the corruptions of tithing and the wealth that they received from Diaspora Jews, the Temple as does later, the synagogue, harkened back to an ancient tradition, here it was the Davidic heritage and the creation of an Israelite nation.

The idea of an Oral Torah seemed specious, an artificial means of persuading the ignorant flock of the necessity to alter and reinterpret the ancient truths for modern times. The only way to do this was to argue, to create a "noble lie" of Plato, for persuasion and commitment. It also required much scholastic hairsplitting to rationalize the new moral and sacral basis so as to allow for its adjustment to the needs of this new civilizational reality. Thus the Saducean comments that the Pharisaic logic splitting ("Talmudic") would lead Judaism to Homeric thinking, as with the Greeks.

On the other hand Josephus, as a Pharisee, commented that in the Saducean espousal of a personal Hellenism, they really held beliefs and practices that were basically consonant with Hellenic radicals. The Sadducees may have been purists in their interpretation of the Israelite writings and traditions, but in their actual lives they were infatuated by the games, the dramas, the attire, the material artifacts of Hellenic high culture. Josephus associated the Sadducees with the *apiqoros*, atheistic Epicureans {Josephus *The Jewish Wars* II viii, 14; *Antiquities* XIII, v., 9}.[37]

> The Pharisees are extremely influential among the townsfolk; and all prayers and sacred rites of divine worship are preformed according to their exposition. This is the great tribute that the inhabitants of the cities have paid to the excellence of the Pharisees. {Josephus, *Antiquities* XVIII:1:3–5}

In this new era, even from Persian times, there were difficulties in interpreting the Sabbath ritual as expressed in all the books of the Pentateuch from Exodus and Deuteronomy. What kind of activities are allowed in terms of the rights of married women? This the Jews of Persian Elephantine, in Egypt, c. 425 BCE, were asking then of both Jerusalem and Samaria. The existing and ancient Egyptian law gave women far more rights, such as divorce and inheritance, than the Israelites or Babylonians did.

Talmudic tradition says that under the Pharisees, Rabbi (Aramaic for "my teacher") Hillel the elder, in Jerusalem during the reign of Herod, (37–4 BCE), had to deal with a crisis created by the prozbol {Deuteronomy 15}, who would loan monies to the poor close to the sabbatical year when all debts were cancelled. Many Jewish peasants and workers were forced into the hands of non-Jewish "loan sharks." Even more challenging was that such an ancient practice would close off loans in business affairs by Jews. His solution was to assign the loans to Jewish councils or others who were not under a personal obligation to forgive a debt.[38]

Later, after the destruction of the Second Temple in 70 CE, Rabbi Yohanan ben Zakkai in Yavneh, is said to have suspended the law of the suspected adulteress—{Numbers 5:(11–31)} and the purgation of blood-guilt by the sacrifice of an unworked heifer {Deuteronomy 21:(1–9)}. Both pharisaic decisions were examples of the need to reinterpret the primitive tribal ethic that was retained even in the later additions to the Pentateuch by the "priestly" writers and the Deuteronomic historians, from c. 700 BCE to c. 500 BCE.

Further, Rabbi Gamaliel II, teacher of Rabbi Akiba, c. 110 CE, had to decide that the requirement for two witnesses to attest to a woman's widowhood {Deuteronomy 19:15} was an unwarranted burden, one witness could attest, so that she could remarry. Akiba himself, c. 130 CE, altered the law {Leviticus 15:33} of separating women and men in terms of their bodily discharges, thus stigmatizing women as being defiled.

Two issues that occurred repeatedly in each generation, was the relationship of father to son and *lex talionis*, "an eye for an eye." The first {Deuteronomy 21:18} seemed to give the father life or death control over "the rebellious son" {Talmud: Sanhedrin 8}. The second seemed too brutal considering all the mitigating circumstances under which physical loss could take place.[39]

Such questions and doubts about a literal Torah interpretation were being asked by an increasingly sophisticated and worldly people. The breezes of Greek rationalism now required that even the Torah, when it commanded our behavior, needed to be reinterpreted in a new historical context. Less affiliated with the powers and wealth of the Temple and devoted to their prayer houses and study halls, the Pharisees were closer to the ordinary working classes. The emphasis on the holiness of the family and the sanctity of the home led to great concerns with purity, both in the dietary laws, and in personal cleanliness. They often fasted, and now believed in the physical resurrection of the dead {Mark 2:18}.

Rabbi Shammai, (c. 25 BCE–25 CE in Jerusalem) in response to a prospective convert's question as to how many *torot* existed: "Two, the Written Torah and the Oral Torah" {B.T. *Shah*, 31a}. Gamaliel II, over two generations later and after the destruction of the Second Temple and at the ancient Philistine city of Yavneh, which now became the center of a school which would evolve into *mishnaic* study, replied similarly to the question of a Roman consul {*Sifrei* Dt. 351, p. 408}.

An estimate of the work of Rabbi Hillel (c. 25 BCE–25 CE): "Scripture alone was not the whole of Judaism; that law and custom supplementary to the text of Scripture were as genuine expressions of Jewish history as were the norms and practices recorded in the holy classic. Hillel did not reject what had come from earlier ages; but insisted that in each generation scholars were entitled to search the Torah thoroughly, and with the assistance of reason and logic, able to derive new meanings and new legal prescriptions."[40] Hillel tried to search through the larger intent of the Scripture rather than its literal implications.

The Synagogue, "bring together," a Greek term, and a Hellenistic institution, was utilized by Diaspora and Holy Land Jews alike in the era before the end of the Second Temple. Norman Gottwald sees its origination as a Diaspora institution, no earlier than 250 BCE, shortly after the translation of the Torah into Greek, in Alexandria.[41] The synagogue was referred to as a *bet 'am* ("house of a people"), and it functioned in this capacity.[42]

The need to search for "larger intent" stimulated the building of the *proseuche* and *synagogue*. The former were places of prayer, (*proseuche*) {Acts 16: 13,16} here mentioned by Paul about Philippi a Roman colony in Macedonia.[43] Jesus, part of this new *pharisaic* tradition had supposedly studied with the great sage, Hillel, while Paul had studied with the elder Gamaliel, a *pharisaic* descendant of Hillel in Jerusalem. Paul, a member of the Diaspora, would have been aware of distinctions between these Jewish institutions.

Gatherings before the gates to hear discussions by various prophets were an ancient tradition in Judah and Israel. The housing of these meeting places, especially in the Diaspora, to read the Torah, or to translate passages into the various vernaculars, Aramaic or Greek for further study and prayer, without diminishing the role of the Temple, would constitute ordinary human behavior. {Acts, 6:9} mentions synagogues of freed slaves, probably from the harsh conquests of Roman, Pompey, c. 63 BCE. Diaspora Jews then living in Jerusalem included Africans (Cyrenians, Alexandrians) and others from Asia Minor (Cilicians, and Asians). The synagogues offered these displaced Jews support, study, and prayer. It was in one of these that they later contested the growing Christian *heresy* of St. Stephen.[44]

Holy Scriptures

The day of wrath was fast approaching, so said many of the preachers who roamed the land. The Essenes, including the Qumran community, too, had a vision of the approach of judgment day, but they awaited this moment in ascetic devotion. The Essenes maintained their pacific position until the final conflagration, 66–70 CE. But many threw in their lot with the Sadducees, Zealots, and Sicarii, *e.g.*, John the Essene: "In their monastic communities they paid little attention to the strife of the times, but waited patiently for the Lord's Anointed One, the Messiah. Meanwhile they lived by strict rules, in celibate communities, holding their possessions in common, keeping the Sabbath day, laboring in the fields during the other days of the week, and devoting themselves to fasting, prayer, and frequent ceremonial ablutions."[45]

So too John the Baptist, like many Jews, sought surcease from this heavy Roman universalism and militarism. He awaited the coming of the Messiah in acts of repentance, purity, self-discipline and in preparation for the great day of baptism in the waters of the Jordan. John was executed in c. 28 CE. With the subsequent crucifixion of Jesus, in c. 30 CE, his followers awaited his second coming, his resurrection as the *Messiah*. On that Day of Judgment, the Christ would redeem his people. Instead, there came a war of the unequal and Roman victory, 70 CE, along with the destruction of the Temple. Thence, began a new pathway of teaching and proselytizing for Paul and the writers of the Gospels.

"The Pharisees, on their part, held themselves from violence largely out of considerations of prudence . . . Caught, all of them, in a world of rapid and unpredictable change, the Pharisees made it their principle to live as nearly as conditions permitted according to their traditions. They felt that the only way to hasten the coming of the Messiah, and in the meantime to save Judaism . . . was to be scrupulous in religious practices that linked tradition with every detail of daily living . . . to fulfill to the letter the regulations for keeping the Jewish festivals, to tithe, to repeat the Shema constantly, to have a mezuzah inside the door and a phylactery on the brow; to be very particular about ceremonial purity . . . and dietary rules . . . and have judicial recourse only with the *Sanhedrin*"[46] And, of course they rejected Christ as the Messiah. A century later, one of the great Pharisaic scholars, Akiba, would pronounce Simon bar Kohkba, "son of a star," as the Messiah, c. 132–135 CE. Emperor Hadrian had them both killed.

It was in Yavneh (also called Jamnia), c. 90–100 CE, that Pharisee Johanan ben Zakkai and his successor, Gamaliel II, completed work on an authorized compilation of the Hebrew Biblical text: 1—Torah, (Law, Pentateuch), 2. Nevi'im (Prophets). 3. Kituvim (Writings) to create = TaNaK.[47] Pharisaic Rabbi Johanan ben Zakkai was protected by the Roman Emperor in fleeing to Yavneh during the war: "What does the Emperor demand of you but that you send him a bow and arrow." Meaning, peace and surrender.[48]

"While the scribes of the Second Commonwealth were collecting and ordering the sacred books, many Jews both in Palestine and in the Diaspora were circulating the didactic, historical and apocalyptic writings, some of them under the names of the patriarchs or prophets, in order to obtain greater authority for these writings. These books, even those written in Hebrew or Aramaic, were not admitted into the canon of Sacred Scripture by the rabbinic scholars of the early Talmudic period for one of two reasons: either the rabbis thought that they had been written after the close of the Persian period, when prophetic inspiration was supposed to have ceased, or else they regarded them as unorthodox in content . . ."[49]

Admitted were Book of *Daniel*, despite its Babylonian context, and Book of *Ecclesiastes*, ascribed to Solomon. Non-canonical Hebrew and Aramaic writings, such as *Sirach*, (Ecclesiasticus) translated into Greek by the writer Ben Sira's grandson, were highly regarded and circulated widely among the Jews of the Diaspora, and included in the Greek version of the Bible, the Septuagint, and then, either as a sacred or edifying book added to the New Testament in Latin, Armenian, Syriac. But *Sirach* was not included in the Pharisaic/Rabbinical rendering of the Wisdom Writings {*Kituvim*}.[50]

The scholars in Yavneh seemed deeply involved in their efforts for the restoration of the ancient creed. One would think that the Hebraic traditions, of the written Torah, as well as the Oral Torah with which the Pharisees and their rabbinic successors seemed deeply and centripetally involved, would now brook little room for an alien culture, Greek or Roman. Certainly we no longer hear of involvements with the Greco/Judaic thinking of the Alexandrians. After Philo, pagan philosophy and culture seem to disappear from Judaic records both in Egypt and in Judea. There is little evidence of religious or social intercourse between the two communities, though both lived under the same military thumb. Only Josephus writes to both worlds at the end of the first century CE.

Yet, it is recorded that Gamaliel II, Patriarch of the Yavneh Academy (Yeshivah), c. 90 CE, deeply involved with completing the defining text of the Hebrew Bible, Gamaliel II, was also running an academy for the cultivation and teaching of "Greek Wisdom."[51]

Continuity was eagerly sought. The convening at Yavneh, possibly under the same controversial Gamaliel II, at the end of the first century CE, was the *Bet Din*, the scholarly judicial court, successor to the Jerusalem Sanhedrin, the latter had included both priests and Pharisees, and which had functioned until the destruction of the Temple. Now there was an assemblage of rabbinical sages *Bet Din*, to decide issues of religious theory and practice within the community and the family, to the extent that the governing Gentiles would permit.

A Puzzle

The Pharisees had been actively arguing the Oral Torah to the Jews of Judea since the days of the Maccabean revolution. Many wise scholars/scribes were involved in these teachings from before Hillel, c. 25 BCE–25 CE, (the Pharisees Joshua be Perahiah; Jose ben Joezer, c. 165 BCE) to the martyrdom of Akiba in 135 CE. The subsequent Talmudic writings record this rich history and the Pharisaic attempts to modernize Jewish practices exemplified in the Law of the Oral Torah. Yet, all that remains contemporary to this long-existing Pharisaic heritage is the historic summary of the law and beliefs of the Israelite/Jewish people, the Holy Scriptures, as they were being written down by these same Pharisaic/Rabbinical scholars at Yavneh, c. 90–100 CE.

Why not at the same time, during this quiet interregnum, 70–100 CE, record the Oral teachings of these wise intellectuals? Why summarize the past, (Scriptures) without engaging the present, c. 165 BCE–100 CE? Why was there such an intellectual gap until the Mishnah was written down, 200–250 CE, this document with little reference to the historical past? Only then, centuries later, did the Oral Law for the Jews find its way into the written record, the Jerusalem and Babylonian Talmud. Yet we know that literary efforts with regard to the Jewish religious and moral experience were streaming into tangible written reality (note the so-called Apocryphal/Deuterocanonical Books) throughout the entire Pharisaic period!

CHAPTER FIVE

Talmudic Republic

The Challenge of Internationalism

Both the destruction of the Jerusalem Temple in 70 CE and the rise of Christian proselytism—Paul, were goads for the completion of the Holy Bible in Yavneh, c. 90 CE.

The Galilean intellectual, Josephus, was in Rome c. 65 CE on a diplomatic mission for the Judeans. He became acquainted with Poppaea, Nero's wife who was well-disposed toward the Jews, and who possibly directed the scapegoating for the great fire of 64 CE toward the Christian schismatics from Judaism. Paul was executed during this period, c. 62-65 CE.

In Chapter 4, we noted that the Pharisee/Rabbi Gamaliel II of Yavneh, himself deeply involved in assembling the final orthodox Judean version of the Holy Scriptures, was at the same time apparently directing a school for Hellenic studies, usually literature and philosophy. This fact seems to characterize the bifurcated state of the Jewish mind during these chaotic late first-century times. Josephus, a Judean with a middling knowledge of Greek, wrote the first of his books on Jewish history in Aramaic, and in Rome, the later works in assisted Greek. In Alexandria, Egypt, a very considerable Diaspora Jewish population was assembling its own version of the Holy Scriptures, this written in Greek. Increasingly during the latter half of the 1st century CE, Christian converts were utilizing this Greek version of the Old Testament.

Probably the greatest exemplar of the deep interpenetration of Judaism and Greek civilizational thinking was exemplified in the writings of Philo (c. 15 BCE– c. 54 CE). Born of a leading family of Alexandrian Jews, his father was a "tax farmer" among the native Egyptians along the Nile. Philo received a deeply orthodox education within this community. At the same time he was exposed to the writings of the major Greek schools of philosophy. These made a deep impression on his thinking about Judaism. The significant writings for him came from Plato, the Pythagorean and Stoic schools, the latter well represented in Rome in his own lifetime. And while he wrote in Greek, Philo had some acquaintance with Hebrew. He also was well aware of the different schools in Judea competing for dominance, as well as survival under Roman and Herodian governance. So deeply was Philo immersed in the life of the Jewish community of Alexandria, that he recommended the death penalty for any Jew who participated in a Pagan cult practice {Philo Spec. 1:315–316}.[1]

Philo, in his philosophical writings held that all truth was contained in the holy laws of Moses, the Pentateuch. All the knowledge and truth of Greek philosophy was already expressed in the Mosaic laws (a view held by the Jewish historian Aristobulus). The scriptures, he interpreted allegorically, and in great detail. This was already an ongoing tradition among the Pharisees. Monotheism, raising up a God of absolute majesty and sovereignty, a God who must not be described in images or idols, thus renders Judaism as the highest religion. He did fight against the extreme allegorists who would have the most important Jewish rituals and traditions such as circumcision declared to be allegorical statements of the biblical tradition and not mandatory, this view soon to be the orthodoxy of schismatic Christianity.[2]

The Jews were chosen by God because of their current virtuous devotion as well as a long historic tradition of being subject to his laws. Philo grants that these laws are now available to the world. Moses' laws are humane, righteous, and rational. Thus is explained their appearance at a later stage in human knowledge as in the philosophy of the Greeks.

"Philo's literary labours have a twofold object, being directed to expound the true sense of the Mosaic law . . . or to convince heathen readers of the excellence, the supreme truth, of the Jewish religion, whose holy records contain the deepest and most perfect philosophy, the best and most humane legislation."[3] Yet, at times he viewed the Jews, especially of the Yehud, as *barbaroi*, outside the Greek, and possibly Mosaic worlds {*De Vita Mosis* 2:27}.

By contrast, Josephus (c. 37–95 CE) coming into the world a half century after Philo, represents a final and explicit defense of Judaism to the Greco/Roman world. Born to a Judean family having high priest ancestors, Josephus was educated in Essene and Pharisaic doctrine, became a committed Pharisee. In Rome he wrote "The Jewish War," c. 75–80 CE in Aramaic, perhaps as an apologia to the Jews of Judea and Babylon for his turncoat behavior, then translating it, with assistance, into Greek. In subsequent books, *Antiquities*, c. 93 CE and in *Contra Apionem*, c. 95 CE, mostly using available Greek language and biblical sources, he was at pains to underscore the differences between Greeks and Jews, the durability of the now ancient faith against the inadequacies of Hellenic religious practices.

Josephus claimed that in reality Jews were divided from Greeks more by geography than from their study of the original teachings of Moses, as set forth in the Torah {*Contra Apionem* 2:123; 2:168}. In Plato's *Republic*, the requirement for citizens to study their laws, restrict contact with foreigners, comes directly from the Mosaic laws {*Contra Apionem* 2:257}. The creation of new gods, bizarre worship by poets and artists, is why Plato banned them from his Utopia. The Jews, in contrast to the Hellenes, had always held strongly to their philosophy by already ancient practices. Philosophers such as Pythagoras, Anaxagoras, Plato, and the Stoics, had gained much law and tradition from the Jews in spite of the powerful and the envious.

"Greek philosophers were only the first of those drawn to the laws of the Torah, adopting similar views about God, teaching abstinence from extravagance and harmony with one another. The masses followed suit. Their zeal for religious piety has now spread around the world so that there is hardly a single polis or ethnos, whether Greek or barbarian, unaffected by observance of the Sabbath, various Jewish practices, and even dietary restrictions. Indeed, they labor to emulate the concord, philanthropy, industry, and undeviating steadfastness characteristic of Jews" {*Contra Apionem* 2.280–284}.[4]

There is no significant Graeco-Jewish literature after the first century CE. Neither Christians nor rabbinic Jews who wrote in Hebrew and Aramaic had any interest in writing down what Greek Jews wrote. This is in part due to great conflicts between Jews, Greeks, and Egyptians in Greco-Roman Egypt in the 1st century CE and then the great revolt of the Jews that spread across the Roman world in Cyrene (Lybia), Egypt, Cyprus, and Ctesiphon (Mesopotamia) between 115–119 CE.

Disintegration

In c. 70 CE, the estimates for Jewish populations, are as follows: one million in Palestine, Eretz Israel, approximately three million in Egypt, North Africa Cyrenaica, Mesopotamia, Persia, Asia Minor.[5] Jean Juster estimates that there were seven to eight million Jews in the first century CE, a figure that Baron endorses.[6] There is no question but that a very large proportion of these Jews were "god-fearing" converts to the "God of Heaven," fascinated not merely by Jewish monotheism and rigorous moral beliefs, but also by the ancient heritage symbolized in the Pentateuchal Laws of Moses.

Jerusalem, c. 70 CE, now had about 70,000 people; many of them forced converts to Judaism under the Hasmoneans, or converted Greek mercenaries and their families. Alexandria, which was now the great city of the empire beyond Rome, is estimated in the first century BCE, the era of Philo, to have had a population of 300,000 free citizens and an almost equal number of other residents, slaves as well as aliens. The Jewish community of Alexandria numbered about 180,000, in that period.[7]

It is difficult to fathom the extent of the impact on the very life of the Jewish community in Palestine, in the post-war period after 70 CE. Many parts of its geo-political structure, Idumea (southern Judah) and Ammon (east of the Jordan), were severed from Judea, and these Jewish populations set out on their own. Yet, from one million people in greater Judea, c. 70 CE, the population was still in the 750,000–800,000 range almost one hundred years later after the Bar Kokhba revolt, c. 150 CE.[8]

The massive turn of the "god fearers" to the religion of the people of the book was deeply jarred by the revolt of 67–70 CE. Here are included segments of all the Judaic sects, now including "zealots" and "Sicarri" extremist guerilla warriors who rose up against Rome and were defeated. The Pharisees themselves sought final protection under Rome, Josephus himself aligning his future with the winners. A nephew of Philo became an apostate governor in Judea under the Romans. The two following wars 115–118 CE and then the Bar Kokhba revolt of 132–135 CE were the final nail in the coffin of international Judaism, humbling events in the aspirations for Jewish political independence. The preeminent Rabbi Akiba of the Yavneh school is said to have regarded Bar Kokhba as the "son of a star," the *Messiah*. Both were killed by the Romans.

Christianity, by the 2nd century CE, was rapidly spreading as an underground "mystery religion," now clearly separated from the mother faith, Judaism. Thus the Jews became not merely a "nation of philosophers," a "people of the book," but now an *ethne*, a people alone, without a national home or temple, cultivating an ancient intellectual and literary heritage, symbolized by the later systematization of the Oral Law in the Mishnah, c. 200–250 CE. Even more, Judaism turned away from the alien and hostile majority and intellectually and socially began to mine the meanings now contained in the ancient writings

We noted at the close of Chapter Four, "a puzzle," there is no contemporary written record of the teachings of the Pharisees. Perhaps it was that the Oral Law needed not to be written down for the Jews to follow the pharisaic teachings, then, bitterly contested by the Sadducees:

"The overwhelming majority of sayings attributed to the Pharisees in Rabbinic literature comes from the later sages, Hillel and Shammai and their academies (Beth Hillel and Beth Shammai). We thus have no idea how many of the anonymous references to the Pharisees actually apply to the Hasmonean period. With but rare exception, it is impossible to date such material confidently. It is no less difficult to understand why so few traditions of these early sages were preserved by the later rabbis. The relatively large time gap between the Hasmonean period and the first redaction of rabbinic sources in about 200 CE may in part account for this phenomenon."[9]

Mishnah, The Repetition

The memory of this now hoary historical pharisaic/mishnaic tradition now takes its form in the third century, CE. One of the earliest mishnaic discussions of Halakhah, law of the Torah, written and oral, is said to involve Jose ben Joezer, c. 165 BCE, a writer who also expressed concern about the growing Diaspora community apart from the precincts of the Temple. He recognized their need to be in full contact with halakhic interpretations that would maintain the bonds of Israel: "Scriptural grounds on which to justify long established usage not expressly ordained or permitted by Scripture."[10] It was this commitment by the later schools of Hillel and Shammai in Jerusalem in the Herodian period, that would preserve for the Israelites a life under the law, including Temple law, this in spite of their opposition to the controlling Sadducees. The writings of the Mishnah thus pursued all issues arising out of the written law, small and large. "Therefore the oral law preserves with equal piety, customs, and discussions arising out of the lightest as out of the weightiest precepts of the Law revealed to Israel at Sinai."[11]

The escape from Jerusalem to Yavneh after 70 CE turned the various almost-independent Mishnaic efforts of pharisaic scholars into a crash course of systematization. In perspective, Yohanan ben Zakkai directed his colleagues, beyond their work on the final compilation of the Holy Scriptures, to three areas of study: (1) The development of the technique of Midrash, as a way to deeply analyze and subject Scripture to careful exegesis; (2) Following that, a study of Halakhah, the legal tradition and rulings by sages given over the generations; and (3) Haggadah: philosophy, theology, lore, ethical guidance, and even fables that add dimension to the understanding of Scripture.

An halakhic example in the Mishnah is the decision that civil cases are to be tried by three judges, because in Scripture the case of a thief was followed three times by the word *Elohim*, when discussing the juridical procedures to be followed.[12]

Perhaps symbolic of the era to come was the cited dispute between Rabbi's Tarfon and Akiba, the latter a student of Gamaliel II, c. 120 CE, as to which was more important, learning or deeds. Later rabbis would nod in agreement with the ironic position of Akiba against Tarfon, ". . . learning is greater, for learning leads to deeds" {B.T. *Qid.* 40b}.[13] By unanimous consensus, his contemporaries and followers regarded Akiba as the most brilliant of all the Yavneh scholars in developing mishnaic thinking. As he analyzed the legal ideas of the Scriptures even single letters in the pentateuchal verses were forced to reveal their deeper oral meaning in crucial passages, these given revealing import in Akiba's midrashic homilies

Surprising too, was the convening at Yavneh, possibly under the same controversial Gamaliel II, at the end of the first century CE, of the *Bet Din*, the scholarly judicial court, successor to the Jerusalem Sanhedrin, the latter including both priests and Pharisees, and which had functioned until the destruction of the Temple. This was an initiating assemblage of rabbinical sages, *Bet Din*, to decide issues of religious theory and practice, but also leadership issues in the now defensive Jewish community. They functioned to the extent that the governing Gentiles would permit. And it was this same *Bet Din* assemblage which finally ousted Gamaliel II from his leadership role.

In the Talmud, the *teaching* begins with these Tannaim, *teachers*. The Mishnah, *repetition*, c. 200–250 CE, was an attempt to reconcile the now many compilations about the oral law with the written law. How did it apply to the contemporary circumstances of the day? The pentateuchal legislation of the last four books arose out of a very different cultural and political setting of the Hebrews. To live again, after a thousand years of evolution it needed commentary, Midrash

Rabbi Judah Ha Nasi, in Tiberias, d. c. 217 CE, during a period of relative Roman toleration brought together the Mishnah, this, the first part of the Talmud. Judah Ha-Nasi, a man of powerful personality and intellect, as well as inheriting great wealth in this poor land, represents a unique point of departure in the development of Talmudic Judaism. "Judah 1, son of Simon, with his vast landed possessions, his luxurious court, his large retinue of slaves and a foreign bodyguard, resembled a hereditary vassal prince of Rome much more than the head of an academy of learning. The Jews, although paying heavily for the privilege, rejoiced in finding 'learning and worldly greatness united' here in one person."[14] He was noted for his entourage of devoted scholars, many of whom he personally supported. His theme: "It is the unlearned who bring trouble into this world."[15]

"The Mishnah is thus the repository exclusively of the teachings of a scholar class. And since these teachings are set forth as authoritative and binding, and since they are teachings which, for the most part, are not written down in the Pentateuch, they testify to a system of authority that is self-assumed, self-asserted, and self-validated. . . . The Mishnah thus bears living witness to a revolutionary transformation by virtue of the chasm which separates its system of Law from the Pentateuchal system of law, and its scholar class from the Prophets and Priests of

Scriptures. . . . Nor was there any inner logic that the Written Law, explicitly proclaimed by God himself as immutable, should be supplanted by whole categories of law not even mentioned in the Pentateuch."[16]

In the period after Akiba, c. 135 CE, supposedly, a number of Mishnahs had been created along the way, organizing Halakhah along certain logical lines—collections and digests of the oral law as it relates to Torah. Judah Ha-Nasi's achievement, d. 217 CE, in Sepphoris, (Galilee) comprises the most completely organized and accepted Mishnah. The Tosefta (supplement), Baraitas (excluded traditions), plus other groups of independent midrashic collections by various sages commenting on the last four books of the Pentateuch, were also transmitted to the academies (Yeshivahs) at this time, c. 200 CE and beyond.[17]

It is important to note that the haggadic elements, (non-halakhic commentary as in the historical elements of *Genesis*) in the later Talmud, date from the fifth century CE and beyond, literary commentaries which go beyond the new Mishnaic laws, Halakhah.[18]

These independent halakhoth, where the oral decisions had been interpreted on the basis of the Old Testament, were thus gradually collected, and then in Usha in the Galilee, arranged alongside the Mishnah and Tosefta.[19] The significant achievement of Judah Ha Nasi, (the Prince), lay in bringing together in organized form the work of his predecessors as the beginning of a legal system based on scriptures. His Mishnah (Repetition) was written in Hebrew. It had six orders: agriculture; festivals; women; civil law; holy things—sacrifices of animals; purifications—dealing with the ritually unclean.[20]

A famous example of Judah Ha-Nasi's legal thinking:

> The saving of a man's life takes priority over a women's . . . The covering of a women's nakedness takes priority over a man's. A woman's ransom has priority over a man's. A man in danger of being forcibly sodomized has priority over a woman in danger of rape. A priest takes precedent over a Levite, a Levite over an Israelite, an Israelite over a mamzer, a mamzer over a natin (from nathin, a Gibeonite descendant) a natin over a proselyte, a proselyte over a freed slave.
> Under what circumstances?
> When all of them are equivalent (in other regards)
> But if the mamzer was the disciple of a sage, and here compare with a high priest. If a king dies any Israelite is suitable to mount the throne. If the priest was an ignoramus, the mamzer who is a disciple of a sage takes precedence over a high priest who is an ignoramus. {*Mishna*: *Horayot*, 3, 5}

The Tosefta adds:

> A sage takes precedence over a king
> For, if a sage dies, we have none who is like him. Tosefta *Horayot*, 2,8}[21]

Judah Ha-Nasi:

> "He who translates a verse with exact literalness is a falsifier, and he who makes additions is a blasphemer."[22]

Gemara (Aramaic for Completion, Decision)

> When a man is brought in for judgment in the world to come, he is asked, "Did you deal in good faith? Did you set aside time for the study of Torah? Did you engage in procreation? Did you look forward to salvation? Did you engage in the dialectics of wisdom? Did you look deeply into matters?" {B. T., Shab. 31a; from Rabbah, a fourth century rabbi}[23]
>
> ... if all Israel only twice will properly keep the Sabbath (as the rabbis instruct), the Messiah will come. {Talmudic teaching.}[24]

The fact that the Mishnah was largely an historical Halakhah, without source commentary, seemed to necessitate amplification. It needed explaining, from both the biblical writings and the post-biblical teachings. The Gemara, both Palestinian and Babylonian, now written in Aramaic, provided principles, human and scriptural sources, and relationships, that the Mishnah had merely implied, "according to everyone." Still, it was the accepted summa of over three hundred years (165 BCE–200 CE) of oral commentary on the meaning for "today" of the written and unwritten Torah.[25]

The death of Judah Ha-Nasi, c. 217 CE, coincides with historical trends in the world far from the hidden enclaves of the Tannaim in Galilee, Sepphoris, Usha, Tiberias, and Bet Shearim, the latter, the place where a historically important Homeric-styled Greek written epitaph (c. 225 CE) of a young Jewish man was discovered. The Christian Alexandrians, Clement and Origen were simultaneously deeply involved with their biblical (Septuagint) and Hellenic studies for the philosophic deepening of Christian thought.

Christianity, now a flourishing underground religion throughout the empire was producing a number of potentially schismatic tendrils, Marcion and Montanus both from Asia Minor, added to the challenge of Gnosticism's mystic dualism, with a direct attack on Christianity's Judaic roots. Emperors such as Nerva, c. 98 CE, Antoninus Pius, c. 140 CE, and especially Alexander Severus, c. 225 CE, the latter of Syrian heritage, were at the least, tolerant of the new sense of exclusivity of the Jews, in contrast with the harsh inflictions of emperors Caligula, Claudius, Vespasian, Titus, Domitian, Trajan, and Hadrian.

"Without ever saying it in so many words, emperor after emperor allowed Jews individually to abstain from all public ceremonies which they viewed as idolatrous, and collectively to exclude from their synagogues any form of worship objectionable to them. The emperors were satisfied with the Jews' regular prayers and sacrifices for their welfare and occasional dedications of particular synagogues. Flaccus' attempt in Egypt (Roman governor), followed by Caligula's general intention of abrogating this privilege of abstention, met with such stout resistance of the Jewish masses that no later emperors ever reverted to this attempt. Some emperors, individually friendly to Jews, aided them positively in the erection of synagogues and donated equipment. For such actions, Alexander Severus received the derisive nickname archisynagogus."[26] Alexandeer Severus, a very young Emperor ruled from 222–235 CE.

The *amoraim*, those scholars responsible for the commentaries of the Gemara which attempted to reconcile Mishnaic Law with Scriptural Law, (these the three domains of the Hebrew Bible—Torah, Prophets, Writings—*Tanakh*), continued their work of modernization both in Palestine and in the Babylonian Diaspora. This essentially scholastic endeavor was quite different from the later scholastic intellectual traditions in Christian Europe.

Christian scholasticism of the period 1100–1500, attempted to reconcile the writings of the Christian fathers, c. 70–450 CE with the infusion of classical Greek and Roman writings into northern Europe through the aegis of Islamic and Jewish scholars such as Averroes and Maimonides. It was centered in the newly evolving universities of Europe and developed by a now (after c. 1000–1100 CE) elite and celibate class of monks and priests.

By contrast the Talmudic rabbis had no longer, c. 250–600 CE, any interest in the world of the Greeks. Their great concern was to concentrate the attention of the Jews on their own "twofold truths" the Written and Oral Law, as now laid down in the Hebrew Bible, the Masoretic text, and the Talmud plus other accepted writings. And this teaching was to go out to the entire Jewish population, universal literacy for the males. The Rabbis were family men who arose to Talmudic intellectual preeminence from their own constituency. Their positions of eminence were largely nonhereditary, and without significant material recompense, except for the claims of the Exilarch and sometimes the Gaons of the Yeshivahs, in both Babylon and the Galilee, who claimed descent from the Davidic line.

Thus, the Amoraim, from 250 CE, the interpreters, inherited the task: the dialectical shaping of proof and analysis to result in bringing about true understanding of things. This also allowed for the possible rejection of past interpretations.[27] In the Gemara, the decisions of the Mishnah are not only discussed, explained, or developed, but all kinds of additional matter are suggested to the writers—haggadic interpolations: narratives/recitations, accounts tangentially based on scripture, and philosophical interpolations.[28]

"Prose mingles with poetry, wit with wisdom, the good with the bad, . . . it makes the Talmud a somewhat rambling compilation . . . it is almost an encyclopaedia in its scope, a storehouse reproducing the knowledge and thought, both unconscious and speculative of the first few centuries of the Christian era."[29] Law and religion are here, one. "Talmudic discussions were often merely specialist and technical—they were academical and ecclesiastical debates which did not always touch every day life; sometimes they were for the purpose of reconciling earlier views, or they seem to be mere exhibitions of dialectical skill . . . that spirit . . . impelled Jewish scholars of the middle ages to study or translate the learning of the Greeks."[30]

The Amoraim: Five generations in Judea, Galilee, leading to the fifth century, and the completion in Palestine of their version of the Talmud. Eight generations in Babylonia, to the beginning of the sixth century, for the completion of their version.[31] Messianic hope for salvation, the religion of Torah, and rabbinic authority were now linked. "Talmudic Midrash"—interpretation, commentary, exegesis, amplification—applied to all scripture. It had been informally carried on since the days of Ezra. It was especially and supposedly developed and taught in Tannaitic times, first to second centuries CE (in Yavneh), and applied to four books of the Pentateuch, Exodus through Deuteronomy (excluding Genesis), because these contained the bulk of *Halakhah*—the law. The Law is given to Moses by YHWH. Moses is not the originator of biblical law, God's law, written and oral, was transmitted through Moses. . . . no written code can be transmitted without supplementary instruction. Supplementary instruction was what *midrash* provided.[32] Not only were literal meanings of the Bible investigated, but also new exegesis supplied the old folkways with scriptural sanction, or released new law (*Halakhah*). They now found law, mystic doctrine, prophesy and history, parable, warning, consolation, commandment and ideals, to be met in each verse."[33]

It is fair to argue that life under Rome, especially during the later persecutions of Constantine, Constantius, Theodosius II, throughout the fourth century when Christianity became the only official religion of the empire, weighed heavily on the life and work of the Galilean Rabbis. Emperor Zenon in Byzantium after Christians burned the ancient synagogue in Antioch, including the burial vaults: "Why did they not burn the living Jews with the dead?" It is estimated that in Palestine there were 150,000 to 200,000 Jews in the sixth century as compared as noted earlier with 750,000–800,000 after the Bar Kokhba revolt, c. 135 CE. By the end of the fourth century, to the beginning of the fifth century c. 425 CE, the Palestinian Talmud had come into being. The Patriarchate of the Jews was abolished in 425 CE by Theodosius II, giving Jews no official internal legal force.[34] Thus work on the Jerusalem Talmud was probably truncated by "events."

Rabbinic/Babylonian Judaism

The heirs of the Mishnah harnessed its power to a system known as Rabbinic Judaism, a holy way of life taught by a master of Torah. Such a person, Rabbi Abba' bar Ayyvu, a student of Judah Ha Nasi, who had come down from Babylon, was the first non-Judean to be ordained by the Galilean Yeshivah to return to serve his Diaspora community in the interpretation of the Torah, c. 250 CE.[35] Rabbi Abba was now the ordained student of Judah Ha-Nasi, who, after his teacher's death, returned to Babylon. Under Sassanian (Persian) rule (227 CE), policies continued that in the beginning were far more tolerant of Jews than would have been those of the subsequent Roman and Christians rulers to the south. Rabbi Abba was the first of the deeply intellectual Babylonian Jewish leadership in that 70-mile enclave along the Euphrates, Pumbeditha and Nehardea in the north and Sura in the south, an area which became almost a nation of Jews, in itself, and by the local Jews, called "Israel."

Rabbi Abba's famous epigram to his Babylonian flock: "Do not marry two women; if you do marry two, then take a third." Thus we sense the ongoing orientalism of Judaism.

An important dimension of the growth of Talmudic thought was the institution of the Kallah, twice-a-year assemblages, from the mid-third century CE, under Rab Samuel and Abba, in the Babylonian Academies, (Yeshivoth), starting with Nehardea, then Sura and Pumbeditha, finally, the survivor in Baghdad under the Muslims. Here were gathered vast numbers of students of all ages and attainments, to discuss questions and decisions on issues of Torah or Mishnaic/Talmudic interpretation. "Thus the Babylonian academies combined the function of specialist-law schools, universities, and popular parliaments. They were a unique product of rabbinism; and the authors of the system were also the compilers of its literary expression, the Talmud.[36] Early spring and fall, lectures and discussion sessions were scheduled before the traditional festivals. Sura was not large enough to provide all the lodgings necessary to accommodate the crowds.[37]

By the beginning of the 11th century the Babylonian academies were in decline. Only Pumbeditha now based in Baghdad was functioning. A German Jewish traveler was able to visit the city and to report that at this particular Kallah 2000 Talmudic scholars were in attendance under the direction of Sherira or Hai Gaon and their *meturgemans*.

The greatest of the Gaons arrived almost a century earlier from his birthplace in Egypt. This was the appointment in 928 CE of Saadia (882–942 CE) to the Gaonate of the Sura Yeshivah, then also located in Baghdad. By this time the Caliphate was in serious decline. Turkish mercenaries were in control; the Caliphate would soon be replaced by Seljuk Turk invaders. The power of Baghdad had previously been weakened by the revolt and a generational existence of a kingdom of African slaves in the south at Basrah.

Saadia had by then polemicized against the separatist Jewish Karaites, wrote a Hebrew rhyming lexicon, and translated the Hebrew Bible into Arabic, "Were it not for Saadia the Torah would almost have disappeared from the midst of Israel; for it was he who made manifest what was obscure therein, made strong what had been weakened."[38]

The intellectual influences which moved his mind came from the Babylonian Islamic philosophers of Baghdad and Basrah, the *Mu'tazilah*, a doctrine involving *Kalam*, 'speech about theological matters,' especially the boundaries and powers of reason to deal with religious knowledge. Here, Saadia, in his *Book of Beliefs and Convictions*, (*Creed and Faith*), endeavored to argue that reason and revelation lead to the same religious truths, here he echoed Philo, almost a thousand years earlier, and thus himself anticipated the culminating medieval philosophical summa of Jewish philosophy, the Spaniard, Maimonides, d. 1204 in Cairo.

What Saadia was motivated to think and write about were issues that were long ignored in Talmudic study, thinking rationally about affairs outside the Jewish world of family, ritual, lawful behavior, and keeping the faith. The new and unencumbered winds of thought were already emanating from Spain, which simultaneously was undergoing a renaissance under liberal Muslim auspices.

In the West

The Jewish community of Spain was organized about two centuries after the Arab conquest of 715 CE. In c. 950 CE, Hasdai ibn Shaprut (roughly contemporary with Saadia in Baghdad), its leader, established Talmudic law, probably Babylonian in origin, within a Jewish population now estimated to have grown to c. 250,000. This was a long-established pre-Christian population added to by in-migration from various parts of a more intolerant world, this especially after the Arabs ousted the hostile post-Visigothic rulers.[39] Singer sees Shaprut as initiating the intellectual leadership of Spain, over a declining Babylonia.[40]

Solomon Ibn Gabirol was the first universally acclaimed Jewish philosopher in Spain, c. 1020–1070 CE ("Avecibron" in the Christian world). Gabirol wrote in Hebrew, and in these generations was as well known and influential throughout the Mediterranean as was Saadia.[41] Other intellectuals, poets, stylists, jurists, were Samuel ibn Nagdela of Granada, (993–1063 CE) Jekutiel ibn Hassan (d.1039) of Saragossa, and Isaac ibn Albalia (1035–1094) at Seville. Spain was branded deeply into the Jewish consciousness. As with the earlier Babylonian renaissance, it was a new Canaan, and they set down deep roots.

The Spanish Muslims, mostly converts from the indigenous population of Visigothic Christianity, had enthusiastically taken to the international culture that both Arabs and Jews had communicated from the eastern Mediterranean. This beautiful land seemed to stimulate poetry, philosophy, even science, amid a surge of economic development. The Jews moved into positions of power throughout the south, centering in Cordoba and Lucena. The latter, with an important Jewish academy, was thought to have a population whose majority was Jewish.

The important Spanish Islamic Aristotelian judge, physician, and philosopher Averroes, 1120–1198, of Cordoba, attempted to carve out a place for secular reason and philosophy within the Koranic domain. "The opponents of Averroes regarded him as a Judaizer."[42] A younger contemporary of Averroes, also from Cordoba, at that time with a very large and prosperous Jewish community, Moses ben Maimon, (Maimonides) 1135–1204, fled that city with his family, c. 1148, when the fundamentalist Almohades sect from North Africa overran southern Spain and inaugurated a horrendous assault on the Jews. Many other Jews fled north into the receptive Christian provinces, the feudal Christian princes eager to obtain the skills the Jews would provide for them, and thus the means to recapture Spain for Christendom. Maimonides settled in Egypt, after much wandering, writing philosophy that attempted to reconcile the corpus of sacred Jewish texts with the new secular philosophical revival of Greek learning that was then swirling through the civilized world. Eventually he became court physician to Saladin, the Kurdish ruler of these domains. Maimonides was to become the greatest of the medieval Jewish scholars, and one of the great achieving minds of history.

Even as he wrote his influential "Guide for the Perplexed," in Arabic, but with Hebrew script, he would write to the rabbis of Lunel in southern France, now led by his old friends from Cordoba, the Bene Tibbon family (Samuel and Judah), c. 1200 CE, that he was looking forward to European leadership in the evolution of Jewish learning.[43] "Man must keep his eye constantly fixed upon one goal, namely the attainment of the knowledge of God, may He be blessed, as far as it is possible. . . . [M]an's only purpose in eating drinking, cohabiting, sleeping, waking, moving about and resting should be the preservation of bodily health, while in turn, the reason for the latter is that the soul and its agencies may be in sound and perfect condition so that he may readily acquire wisdom, and gain moral and intellectual virtues." {Maimonides *Introduction to Commentary on Tractate Aboth, Mishnah*, Chapter 5.}[44]

George Sarton, historian of science, estimates that in the heyday of Spanish science, 1150–1300, there was a total of 85 scientists worthy of international historical recognition for their achievements: 35 Jews; 30 Muslims; 20 Christians. Thus the Jews contributed 41 percent of this scholarly tradition. Salo Baron estimates that in 1300 CE, the Spanish population, including, Muslim Granada, was 5.5 million; Jews—150,000, or 2.5 percent of the population. (It is probable that there were more Jews in Spain at that time than Baron estimates, when late converts to Islam and Christianity are included {author's note}.)[45]

Maimonides, under the press of Muslim fundamentalism probably converted to Islam along with his family when he fled Spain for North Africa. Finally arriving in Palestine, then under Christian control, he reclaimed his Jewish identity, and eventually settled in tolerant Muslim Egypt. Other Jews fled north to the advancing Christian armies beginning in the mid-12th century. At first they were welcomed for their skills, both economic and intellectual. A century and a half of freedom and prosperity was had, mostly in Aragon and Catalonia. But as the indigenous Christianized communities began to mature they increasingly resented the Jewish presence and domination. A most famous event was the public religious debate staged by the King in Barcelona, 1263 CE, which pitted the then-most learned Jewish intellectual Nahmanides ("Ramban"), d. 1270 CE against an apostate Jew.

In the end, c. 150,000 Jews picked themselves up first from Spain, then from Portugal, c. 1492–1497, simultaneous with the Italian Jew, Columbus, sailing west under the Spanish flag to discover the New World. The expulsion from Spain left many a *converso* within the bosom of Spanish and Portuguese life. These nations were the better for their inhumane acts.[46]

Ashkenazim

To the north the awareness of the new intellectual currents was slower in coming. Talmudic learning as it was derived from Babylon and Palestine seemed critical in maintaining the glue of survival. Charlemagne, founder of the Holy Roman Empire, and his son, Louis the Pius, gave private charters to Jewish merchants, c. 800–825 CE. They both invited the Jews to settle in the empire, to promote trade and crafts. In Mainz, a large community of Jewish families had settled from Italy and France. Gershom ben Yehudah, c. 1000, d. 1028, the most important rabbinic leader of this community, was interpreting the Talmud and Bible on his own, with no gaonic correspondence from Babylon or Jerusalem. In an "Enactment" to Ashkenazic Jewry, "It is a commandment to listen to the words of the sages" {B.T., *Yev.* 20a}, and seeing the need to live within a majority Christian moral environment, he ruled against polygyny and the forced divorce of a woman, the former permitted by the Hebrew Bible and the Talmud.[47]

To the west, Shelomo ben Yitzhak—Rashi, 1040–1105 CE—the greatest European expositor and commentator of the Babylonian Talmud, in Troyes, France, was a self-taught scholar. He earned his living as a seller of wines. But he founded an academy in that city to teach others. At roughly the same time as

Rashi was writing his Talmudic commentaries, as was then beginning to happen in Spain, religious attacks occurred in the Rhine River valley, 1095 CE, with widespread Crusader mobs butchering the Jewish communities in Worms, Speyer, Cologne, and Mainz. The Talmud and the Jews of Europe would now undergo centuries of continuing pogroms, sieges and persecution.

And yet they survived, wandered to and fro, wherever they might find refuge and usefulness from the powers that be. Their only solace was this literature that they carried within their communities, the Talmud and the Holy Scriptures. It formed an invisible defense line against the surrender of their personal and social beings, an education within itself, a community that survived mostly in poverty with practically one hundred percent literacy, a community unique in the history of civilization.

Judah Goldin on the Talmud: "To speak of it as encyclopedic is perhaps useful to suggest its catholicity of interests; but the character of its discussions is as unlike an encyclopedia as is a round-table discussion unlike a polished essay. . . . To them (Sages) it was a sea, full of life and action, with deeps and shallows; skill was indispensable to navigate it; but the expanse was wide and the horizon rich and the voyage rewarding. And because the waters never stood still, they never grew stagnant."[48]

Their Torah, Scriptures, and Talmud were one dimension of their lives with which the Gentile world could not interfere. Other communities of Jews, now spread among the nations and the continents, would mentally or physically, share their burdens. The Jews became, in the words of the *Codex Theodosius*, 438 CE, "*the nefarious sect.*" The disciplines evoked by Torah and Talmudic learning had to permeate their lives. It was the only hope for the survival of the Jewish community until the coming of the Messiah and eternal redemption.

In fulfilling this intellectual and moral devotion, each male would thereby be transformed into a rabbi, hence into a saint. When all Jews had become rabbis, they then would no longer lie within the power of history. The Messiah would come.[49] Talmud study, the oral Torah given by God to Moses, this study became universal for Jewish boys and men. No Jew, as earlier noted, was considered incapable of adding new and original ideas to this learning.[50]

The rabbinic sages sought the company of their communicants, other Jews. They lived in villages, not in monasteries, owned property, and became part of village communal life in administration or business. Entrance to rabbinic schools was open to all depending on ability and inclination. They actively proselytized for new candidates for their schools. The rituals of the table, saying blessings, and prayers could be learned from the rabbi, no secrets from the ordinary Jew. The ideal was for all male Jews to become rabbis. The rabbis wanted to transform the entire Jewish community into an academy (*yeshivah*) where the entire Torah was studied and kept.[51]

Thus the Jewish community took on the character of an evolutionary outlander, in defense, nurturing the ancient mammalian attribute of high intelligence, obscurity, alertness, adaptability. Literacy was its great reservoir of perseverance in the cultivation of the moral and social discipline necessary to surviving, existing on the edge of the larger political, military, even religious powers that now dominated. No longer could Judaism easily proselytize for new recruits, as in the first post-Babylonian exile and then the Hellenistic era. The inclination was now negative. A deeply centrifugal ethnicity arose whose social profile was increasingly anathema to the Gentile world. No longer would they struggle with sectarianism. With few worries over schismatic Jews (Samaritans, Karaites), the great concern was with the powerful "pagan" outsider.

Universal Literacy

Lod (Lydda), c. 300 CE: Rabbi Hanina bar Hama to Rab. Hoshaya, while touring the synagogues of Lod: "How much {money} have my ancestors invested here {in these buildings}" R. Hoshaya: "How many souls have you lost here? There is no one studying Torah" (wrong prioritization of values).[52] "(Regarding) a small town in Israel (Galilee), they (the townspeople) built for themselves a synagogue and academy and hired a sage and instructors for their children. When a nearby town saw (this), it (also) built a synagogue and academy, and likewise hired teachers for their children" {Seder Eliyahu Rabbah 11}.[53]

In the post-Temple period, delegations of rabbis were sent throughout Palestine to establish for the towns teachers of Scriptures and the Oral Law. In one place they found neither. They summoned the elders of the town: "Bring us the guardians of the city." The sentries were brought. "These are not the guardians of the city, these are its destroyers. . . ." "And who are its guardians, the people asked?" The sages replied: "The teachers of Scriptures and the teachers of the Oral Law.[54]

Why the Talmud? Atonement or reconciliation for the commitment of sins by Israel, became the rationale for the study of the Torah, the keeping of the commandments, and doing good deeds. The study of Torah was now primarily an intellectual process whose supernatural effects were secondary. The resources of the schools lay in the knowledge of the laws and traditions of the Torah of Moses. The rabbis were expected to have knowledge of the holy books as did other holy men in other religions. But they themselves respected legal learning and the capacity to reason about real cases. The whole process of learning, not merely its creative and innovative aspects, was regarded as sacred, for the words themselves were holy.[55]

Again, the value of the analysis of God's law was as important in Talmudic religion as the content of that study, the hairsplitting dialectics of medieval rabbis reflects their interest in internally consistent knowledge, making distinctions between areas of knowledge, the integration of teachings from widely disparate fields into a single web of unifying principles. "It gave Rabbinic studiousness a scholastic tinge that continued to sharpen as later centuries wore on. Text commentaries over the centuries were jammed into each page of the Talmud. Rabbinic intellectualism turned into disciplined argument; the interplay between proof and refutation, and then, into a holy activity."[56]

To the bridegroom, from the Rabbis: "One should always sell everything one possesses in order to marry the daughter of a scholar; if he does not find a scholar's daughter, he should marry the daughter of the great men of the generation (the communal leaders); if he does not find a daughter of great men, he should marry the daughter of archisynogogi (lay head of the synagogue); if he does not find a daughter of archisynagogi, he should marry the daughter of charity supervisors; he should marry the daughter of elementary teachers, but he should never marry the daughter of the people of the land (*am ha-aretz*/illiterates)."[57]

In the *shul*, the teachers were often uncouth and brutal at all grade levels in the cycle of learning, allowing little freedom. The consequent appearance of a more Dionysian form of Ashkenazi Judaism, represented by the Hassidic movement of the mid-18th century in Eastern Europe, a reminiscence of the kabbalistic mysticism of late medieval Spanish Jewry, represented an emotional release from the Talmudic rigor and inflexibility that had held the Jewish community together for so many centuries. Hassidism also came to influence at the time of the Enlightenment, an opening door for the Jews to reenter the world community. It helped to ring the bell for Ashkenazic Talmudism.[58]

"During the Middle Ages the Jewish communities no longer contemplated battle. The medieval Hebrew poets did not celebrate the martial arts. The Jews of Europe were placing themselves under the protection of constituted authority. The reliance was legal, physical, and psychological."[59] The implication is one of surrender and apathetic reception of the good or evil that was imposed upon this people by the powers-that-be. The further implication is that the Jews struggled mightily to survive economically, finding every empty niche—banking, loan-sharking, peddling—that remained open to them, if only to nourish their families. The Talmudic education here in its continued evolution at the hands of Ashkenazi scholars such as Rashi, c. 1100 CE, furthered this development of Jewish Law, *Halakha*. It became the rod of survival by emphasizing the endogamatic preservation of Jewish ritual, ceremony, family life.

The development of the European Talmudic academies, the *Yeshivoth*, served the function of creating the wisest teachers, rabbis, who might both internally adjudicate and lead the Jewish communities scattered over the face of Christian Europe in their attempts to survive as practicing Jews. Here a different form of knowledge accumulation occurred than was traditional in the classical Hellenic and Hellenistic worlds, perhaps even different in its emphases from that of the great Spanish Jewish scholar, Maimonides. When living in Egypt under Muslim rule, Maimonides attempted to extend the vision of the ancient Asiatic Talmudists into an accommodation with the growing awareness of the larger world of Greek knowledge as it was being rediscovered in this late-medieval era, the Mediterranean world of c. 1200 CE, but not in northern Europe.

The later reaction against Ashkenazic Talmudism was that it had become casuistic, scholastic, and preoccupied with the splitting of hairs about the meaning of the holy writings as applied to life within the Jewish community. Talmudic disputation became a type of chess game where one could argue about the most subtle and ingenious meanings from the ancient texts and the earlier Talmudic sages that none before might have intuited. This was a game of finding subtle meanings within the textual traditions of the past, rarely relevant to the world external to Jewish existence. Thus, the later Jewish disdain for this self-absorbed world, even in raw survival. The Ahkenazim were maintaining this experiential autonomy of knowledge making, even while the Renaissance was opening up to the outside Gentile world, a revolutionary vision of life and experience.

> The Polish Jewish schoolmasters . . . with rod and angry gesture, instructed Jewish boys in tender youth to discover the most absurd perversities in the Holy Book, translated into their hateful jargon, and so confusing the text with their own translation that it seemed as if Moses had spoken in the barbarous dialect of Polish Jews. . . . the neglect of all secular knowledge, which increased with every century, had reached such a pitch that every measured oddity, even blasphemy, was subtly read into the verses of Scripture.[60]

From a perspective of an additional century, however, one can better appreciate the role of Talmudic study, a universal preoccupation and discipline for all Jews in the period before the *Haskala*, the Enlightenment emancipation. It created, in the first place, an elite that was independent from, perhaps even higher in status than the role of those few ambitious and chance-taking Jews, who took on the Christian world in the open economic areas of life. The highest levels of Jewish attainment involved the subtle hairsplitting, chess-game dialectics of the Yeshiva scholar. And to him the brightest young wives from the wealthier families were offered. And there were many children who were born to these "house" intellectuals, they, completely irrelevant to the outside world.

But more: this world lived through these talmudic "games," the stuff of their moral and social existence. These created meanings allowed for a dynamic that was internally rich in social movement and advancement, even without the tangible wealth to show for it.

In short, materialistically deprived, it was a culture steeped in symbolic and fluid attainments, even if the knowledge, the grist of these attainments, had nothing to do with the dynamics of material events in the external world of feudal, national, religious wars, the power plays of secular and Christian life. As long as the knowledge structure of Christian thought was not in advance of the Talmudists, as their several famous debates in Spain, Paris, and Rome seemed to have shown, this Talmudic world remained happily inured to the events of the outside.

One could compare the Talmudic sociocultural world with that of the Catholic Church. Here monks, priests, bishops, cardinals, and the Pope played a hierarchical game of positional status, hardly related to the material dynamics of economy, trade, craft, even agriculture. Yet the power shifts, the political, military, and social impact of the dynamics of Church hierarchy and power were enormous. Today the same status games, mostly impotent, are played within the secular academy.

Within the bounds of Talmudic Judaism, the power, leadership, hierarchical positioning of religious knowledge, became the fuel of this society, marching in place, going nowhere materially or politically, no less militarily. Rather, it just impacted on the internal redactions issuing out of the ever-growing commentaries, disputations, and analyses that made up an infinitely expanding literary and intellectual heritage, the Talmud.

A critic, Graetz, on Talmudic study: "The perverse course of study . . . had blunted their minds to simplicity. They had grown so accustomed to all that was artificial, distorted, super cunningly wrought, and to subtleties, that the simple, unadorned truth became worthless, if not childish and ridiculous, in their eyes. Their train of thought was mostly perverted, uncultivated, and defiant of logical discipline."[61]

However, Graetz, on their entrance into modernity: "As if touched by a magic wand, the Talmud students, fossils of the musty schoolhouses, were transfigured, and upon the wings of the intellect they soared above the gloomy present, and took their flight heavenwards."

Graetz again, on Talmudic study: " . . . the acumen, quick comprehension, and profound penetrativeness which these youths acquired in their close study of the Talmud rendered it easy for them to take their position in the newly discovered world. Thousands of Talmud students . . . became little Mendelssohns; (Moses Mendelssohn, 1729–1786) many of them eloquent, profound thinkers. With them Judaism renewed its youth . . . In a very short time a numerous band of Jewish authors arose who wrote in clear Hebrew or German style upon matters which shortly before they had no knowledge . . . They found their level in European civilization more quickly than the {Christian} Germans, and—what should not be overlooked—Talmudic schooling had shaped their intelligence."[62]

And thus began the great transition, a revolution in the life and thinking of the Jews that overturned fifteen hundred years of imposed encapsulation. This isolation had created a unique culture and mentality for Judaism. Little did the Jews understand that the oncoming dissolution of the barriers of entrance to the outside world, itself undergoing revolution, would carry with it enormous revealed promise for the Jewish mind, but also terrible consequences.

CHAPTER SIX

Haskalah: Crisis

Renaissance Revolution

It is not coincidental that the opportunistic ruling cliques of Spain sent the *converso* Columbus, on his way west in 1492 CE, at the same time that stubborn Jews were being expelled, sent on their way north, east, and south. The world even then was bubbling with the new technological and intellectual innovations of the Renaissance. Economies were percolating, trade expanding, a world opening up even as the Portuguese explorers, many armed with the maps created by Jewish scholars, *e.g.*, Abraham Zacuto and Joseph Vecinho, were guiding them around Africa to the spices, textiles, and the richness of the unexplored East. It is no coincidence that the Hanseatic German, Nicholas Copernicus, 1473–1543, and the heretical German theologian, Martin Luther, 1483–1546, were contemporaries, movers in the astronomical/scientific and religio/political sense. The world was hurtling toward a new cultural and historical ethos.

Perhaps the most influential Jewish/Italian writer of this period was Simeone Luzzatto c. 1583–1663, co-rabbi with Leon of Modena of the Venice ghetto. His *Discourse on the Status of the Jews*, in Italian, was an apologetic for the usefulness of the Jews to modern states. Later, these arguments would be used by John Tolland, 1714, in England, arguing for the naturalization of the Jews. Luzzatto distinguished between different groups of Jews, the Talmudic scholars, followers of the Kabbala, Karaites, also different nationalities of the Jews from Venice, Constantinople, Poland, Damascus, Germany, etc., yet a common character.

Luzzatto: the Jews were, ". . . a nation of timid and unmanly disposition, at present incapable of political government, occupied only with separate interests, and caring little about public welfare. The economy of the Jews borders on avarice, they are admirers of antiquity, and have no eye for the present course of things. Many are uneducated, have no taste for learning or the knowledge of languages, and in following the laws of their religion, they exaggerate to the most painful degree. But they have also noteworthy peculiarities—firmness and endurance in their religion, uniformity of doctrinal teaching in the long course of more than fifteen centuries since their dispersion; wonderful steadfastness which leads them, if not to go into dangers, yet to endure the most severest suffering. They possess knowledge of the Holy Scripture and its exposition, gentleness and hospitality to the members of their race—the Persian Jew in some degree suffers the wrong of the Italian—strict abstinence from carnal offenses, extraordinary carefulness to keep the family unspotted, and skill in managing difficult matters. They are submissive and yielding to every one, only not to their brethren in religion. The failings of the Jew have rather the character of cowardice and meanness than of cruelty and atrocity."[1]

The great stain on the Jewish community of Holland during this period was, of course, Baruch Spinoza, 1632–1677. He was excommunicated from the Jewish community and its synagogue. So too was the tragedy of the Jewish dissenter Uriel da Costa who killed himself in 1640, when he was twenty-three, before any of his writings had been published. The immigrant Jews feared heretical thinking, not wanting to endanger their position with Dutch religious leaders. Spinoza was able to read the rich revolutionary literature available in Holland at this time, which the Dutch churches did nothing to censor. Spinoza was therefore influenced by René Descartes, Giordano Bruno, Thomas Hobbes, also Sephardic Jewish philosophers Maimonides, Gersonides, Hasdai Crescas. Little did the Jewish/Sephardic leadership realize how quickly the breezes of intellectual liberty would make themselves felt in this newly dynamic world of Europe, north.[2]

There is a possibility that the learned and cosmopolitan Rabbi Mennasseh ben Israel (Rembrandt made an etching of him), who was in negotiations with Cromwell and then went over to England to obtain entrance into that nation for the Jews, would have intervened to stop the excommunication of the young Spinoza from the Jewish community. Jewish communities that had been part of the Jewish Sephardic Renaissance, such as the Portuguese/Spanish refugees who in the 16th century made Holland their home as well as others in Ottoman, Turkey or in Renaissance Italy itself were already deeply involved in the intellectual and commercial explosion in perspective and wealth of this era.

When Gutenberg invented the movable type printing press, c. 1450, the Jews of the continent were quick to use this technology for their own purposes, both commercial and communitarian. Patai reports that ". . . in Cremona, (Italy), the Inquisition destroyed at one time 12,000 books which were in possession of the eighty Jewish families in the city. This astounding figure indicates the extent of Renaissance Jewish bibliophilism, for some Jews it became a veritable passion."[3] Hundreds of Jewish scribes made their living in Italy. At the end of fifteenth century many Jewish printing presses were in operation, even translating into Yiddish.

Thus we have in the sixteenth-century Reformation awakening in the German north, a Luther expatiating on the Jews, perhaps expressing subliminally his own precarious political position: ". . . they hold us Christians captive in our country. They let us work in the sweat of our noses, to earn money and property for them, while they sit behind the oven, lazy, let off gas, bake pears, eat, drink, live softly and well from our wealth. They have captured us and our goods through their accursed usury; mock us and spit on us, because we work and permit them to be lazy squires who own us and our realm; they are therefore our lords, we their servants with our wealth, sweat, and work: . . . Moses could improve Pharaoh neither with plagues nor with miracles, neither with threats nor with prayers; he had to let him drown in the sea."[4]

Well before the final expulsion of Jews from Spain and Portugal at the end of the 15th and beginning of the 16th centuries, Muslims also, the Jews throughout fragmented Europe had been driven hither and yon by a steady sequence of pogroms, economic restrictions, taxes, and especially expulsions. This was true into the 16th century when many of the most opportunistic became *"Schutzjuden,"* seemingly indispensable for their linguistic, financial, and craft skills. As they moved into the east, especially Poland where the feudal aristocracy desperately needed these skills, they attained a measure of autonomy, by 1474, in their own Kahals. The coincidental anti-Semitism of the population, and a Cossack pogrom in 1648, finally drove many westward back into the Germanic states, themselves attempting to cope with this upsurge in Jewish entrepreneurship. This was especially true by the beginning of the 18th century.

The Germans proper, ever ambivalent about these Jewish populations within their midst evicted, then invited, then evicted once more, this wandering, alien race. The spewing hatred of Luther, quoted above, in the mid-16th century gives evidence of the tenuous condition of the *Ashkenazim*. Throughout this period the conditions of the Jews in the eastern Germanic and western Slavic domains (Bohemia/Prague) were more stable.

Aufklärung

By the first half of the 18th century, a flood of Jews were entering the Germanies, especially Prussia from the east, to participate in the new knowledge, personal freedom, and wealth that was being accumulated. Chief Rabbis in Frankfurt, Hamburg, were all Polish. Many had *Schutzbriefe*, letters of protection from local princes. Their conservatism within the rabbinate was maintained throughout the century, in Germany. Moses Mendelssohn, originally from Dessau in the east of Germany, led the Berlin *Aufklärung* in the mid-18th century. He had arguments with local Rabbis over the fixed dates between death and burial and much greater conflict over his translation of the Pentateuch into German using Hebrew orthography. However, his various commentaries gradually led to larger demand for internal liberalization within the structure of Judaism itself. This trend eventually led to Reformed Judaism, at the same time, massive conversion to the Christianity of the nation.

There is no question but that the intellectual elite of Gentile Europe had erupted out of all the hidden crevices of European society. The continent was experiencing a torrent of social and economic change. The secular and scientific explosion of knowledge was irresistible. And with this alteration in European life, so, too, was there an impact on the Jews.

It is agreed that the firestorm of Reformation spread for reasons beyond the special corruptions of papal practice, having the purpose of filling the coffers in Rome with northern gold. The move to emancipate these northern principalities from papal control had its roots in the new economies of the Renaissance north, and the wish to explore their own political and economic futures out of control of Catholic interdict. This all occurred in the first half of the 16th century, while the horizons of European vision were expanding beyond the home continent.

For the Jews these horizons did not exist. They were to be encapsulated for two more centuries. But it must be proposed that these winds of change penetrated not merely north to the German states and west to Holland and Britain, but also into the darkness of what would be the Jewish *Pale*, 1772, the lands to the Slavic east. Thus can we partially explain the mystical, anti-Talmudic Hassidic movement that broke out among the Jews in mid-18th century (see below) This movement occurred simultaneously with both the Christian *Aufklärung* in Western Europe, and the first throbbings for political and economic emancipation for the Jews in these same western domains.

Perhaps the most significant figure among the *maskilim*, those most influenced by the Enlightenment, and most eager to translate the potential alteration in the status of the Jews, first by the reshaping of Judaism itself, into a congruency with the new world, then, to be liberated in consonance with the views of the enlightened, was the above-mentioned Moses Mendelssohn, 1729–1786. Hailing from one of the more tolerant German towns in the southeast, Dessau, educated by teachers who themselves had migrated from Poland, Mendelssohn, burdened with significant physical deformities, transcended his time.

From 1755 Mendelssohn was publishing a journal containing historic literary and philosophical articles, *Preacher of Morals*. His first efforts were in the direction of ridding Jewish education of "Talmudic casuistry," in favor of teaching the Talmud literally, teaching the Hebrew Bible and the Hebrew language, more so than Yiddish. Here he was in harmony with the Sephardic educational tradition, which for long had included secular sciences, mathematics, and vernacular language learning as part of their curriculum for all the young.

In fact, the lack of historical awareness in the traditional German and Eastern European Jewish education revealed itself in the fact that the first publishing in the north of Maimonides' *Guide of the Perplexed*, was in 1742.

The Marquis d'Argens, a French nobleman who was to become a Chamberlain to Fredrick the Great of Prussia, had been impressed with the abilities of the Sephardic Italian Jews. In the Enlightenment spirit he had written in 1737, *Lettres Juives*, arguing for their inclusion in civil society, seeing their "bad" qualities as a product of their exclusion and unjust treatment, and noting the outstanding intellect of the Sephardi-Italian Jews whose "decisions on matters of the mind are often of much greater value than those of the best academicians." To the King of Prussia, Frederick the Great, d'Argens appealed for Moses Mendelssohn to be given the status of a protected Jew and allowed to live in Berlin.

Scholars view the work of Jews such as Moses Mendelssohn, Naphtali Herz Wessely, and David Friedlander as assisting in the task of bringing the Jews into the mainstream of German and Enlightenment society.[5] This was part of a movement that was penetrating into the heart and minds of progressive intellectuals of the time. John Locke, in 1689 had written *Letter Concerning Toleration*, which argued for Jews to be allowed the civil rights of residents, along with the maintenance of their synagogues. John Tolland as earlier noted had translated Luzzatto's *Discourse on the Status of Jews*, c. 1660, and had subsequently published anonymously in 1714, his own, *Reasons for Naturalizing the Jews of Great Britain and Ireland*. . . ." The British Parliament passed the *Jew Bill*, 1753, allowing for the naturalization of the Jews, but popular outcry caused its immediate repeal.[6]

This antagonism against Jewish emancipation was not merely a response from the anxious masses, afraid of and thus hateful of a foreign element being added to the new national stew. Voltaire, in Volume VII of his Historical Writings (Geneva 1756) on the Jews: ". . . raging fanaticism would someday become deadly to the human race."[7] Voltaire: The bad moral condition of the Jews, gave rise to cruel, fanatical, cannibalism, unrestrained barbarism. The Jews were given to atrocities and sexual immorality, intercourse with animals. They sold their own sons and daughters into slavery, they were dishonest and greedy, strove for dominance over the whole world. Even the biblical writings, Voltaire felt, were plagiarisms from the Greeks (1771).[8]

Montesquieu, in his *Lettres Persanes* (1721), thought to have had an image of the Jew more positive than Voltaire, Holbach, and Diderot, the other French Enlightenment savants, still proclaimed: "Wherever there is money there are the Jews."[9] Also, the writings of the Rabbis representing the spirit of slaves, fashioned the continuing low taste and low character of the Jews, Montesquieu, here writing prior to 1748.[10]

Although a friend of Moses Mendelssohn, even Immanuel Kant, 1725–1804, the greatest philosopher of the 18th century and the personification of the Enlightenment worship of the scientific ethos of Isaac Newton, still, in his late 18th-century writings, could find little in the contemporary Jew to justify his membership in the national state. He makes a distinction between the rational and the crafty man. Kant's example of craftiness, cunning and slyness, made of the Jews, a "nation of deceivers" who use their special command of language for their economic advantage. Kant associates little or no virtue with the image of the eastern (Polish) Jew. Indeed, the Eastern Jew becomes the model for the rapaciousness and destructiveness of the Jew. The language of the Jews in this context becomes the measure of their craftiness, not their intelligence.[11]

The opposition to the assimilation of the Jews went deep. Immanuel Kant, as noted above, was among the doubters: "All separatists, that is, those who subject themselves not only to the general laws of the country but also to a special sectarian law, are exposed through their eccentricity and alleged chosen-ness to the attention and criticism of the community, and thus cannot relax in their self-control for intoxication, which deprives one of cautiousness, would be a scandal for them."[12]

Again, Kant on the Jews: Judaism consisted of laws and rituals whereas true religion was based on morality alone. "Pure moral religion means the death of Judaism." Michael Meyer explains Kant's Enlightenment perspective: "If Jews wanted to be genuinely religious, as a modern philosopher understood religion, they would have to leave Judaism behind, for it was inseparable from its laws, which rendered it necessarily heteronymous, eliminating the moral freedom which Kant regarded as essential to an enlightened faith."[13]

Mendelssohn's Task

Moses Mendelssohn was well aware of this hateful opposition to the emancipation of the Jews. Thus, in his introduction to his German translation of Manasseh Israel's *Vindiciae Judaeorum* (1656):

It is remarkable to observe how prejudice has taken on the shape of all centuries in order to oppress us and to place difficulties in the way of our civil acceptance. In those superstitious times it was the sacra which {they said} we wantonly desecrated, crucifixes which we pierced through and made bleed; children whom we secretly circumcised, and tore apart for the delight of the eyes; Christian blood which we needed for sacrificial feasts, wells which we poisoned, etc.; unbelief, stubbornness, secret arts and devilishness of which we were accused and because of which we were tortured, robbed of our property, driven into misery, even when not actually executed—Now {that} times have changed, those calumnies no longer make the desired impression. Now it is precisely superstition and stupidity which are attributed to us; lack of moral sentiment, of taste and refined manners, inability in the arts, sciences, and useful crafts, especially those in the service of war and the state, unconquerable inclination to cheating, usury, and lawlessness, which took the place of those cruder accusations, in order to exclude us from the number of useful citizens and to push us away from the motherly bosom of the state.[14]

One of Mendelssohn's first, if controversial, achievements as a leader of the German Jewish community had been the above-noted translation into German of the Pentateuch. The German was written in Hebrew script, with Hebrew commentary. One of his last writings was a plea for the granting of rights to Jews in the name of tolerance and the secularity of the state: *Jerusalem, Or, On Ecclesiastical Authority and Judaism*, 1783: Berlin.

In 1763 Moses Mendelssohn won the Berlin Academy prize for an essay on the application of mathematical proofs to metaphysics. Two of his competitors were Abt and Immanuel Kant. In Oct. 1763 Frederick the Great granted Mendelssohn the official title of "Schutzjude," giving him the right to live in Berlin. From c. 1750 Frederick the Great of Prussia had become more flexible in giving economic freedom to Jews. Complete political and religious equality was not yet rendered.

Mendelssohn's *Jerusalem*, 1783, was a plea for freedom of conscience. The state must stay out of citizen's affairs as regards their religious choices. Immanuel Kant described it as "an irrefutable book . . . the proclamation of a great reform, which, however, will be slow in its manifestation and in progress, and which will affect not only your people but others as well."

Perhaps the most succinct evaluation of the revolutionary character of Moses Mendelssohn's revision of Judaism, by Israel Abraham: "Judaism is not a revealed religion, but a revealed law."[15] Alexander Altman saw Mendelssohn as a disciple of Maimonides as well as the Enlightenment rationalists.[16]

Naphtali Herz Wessely (1725–1805), of Sephardic Portuguese origins, now from Copenhagen and a follower of the Italian scientific Talmudist, Joseph Delmedigo, 1591–1655, was a sympathizer of the Mendelssohnian program. Wessely wrote in Hebrew, *Words of Peace and Truth* (1782-Berlin). It consisted of a new scientific course of study for Jewish youth. The Sephardic Jewish world, the Portuguese Jews of Trieste in Italy, Italian rabbis of Venice and Ferrara responded positively. Wessely however, was condemned by Polish and German rabbis, especially for his endorsement of Hapsburg Emperor, Joseph II's pending "Toleranzpatent" proposals, 1782, for Jewish integration in the Austrian domains. Here, the mandate involved compulsory education including secular subjects for all Jewish children, all a part of the assimilation program.[17]

Assimilation?

A pivotal event in this transition of the Jews from the emancipation of ghetto life to the full intellectual, political, and economic freedom, came with Napoleon's radical reforms, now in early-19th-century, Paris, 1806–1807: here was gathered an Assembly of Jewish Notables and the Grand Sanhedrin of Jewish religious leaders in France. Decided for all Jews were a set of principles setting forth a new relationship between the Jews and the state: here, a general accommodation between non-Jew and Jew, in equality of treatment. But also mandated was the Jewish commitment to the laws of the state or nation. The state would validate the exception of religious sanctification or blessing of intermarriage between Jew and Gentile.

Solomon Maimon, 1754–1800, came out of Polish Lithuania, even there sensing the winds of intellectual change. First dabbling in Hassidic mysticism, this impoverished student was soon studying the Latin alphabet. Hungry to learn German, eager to abandon Yiddish, his goal was to immerse himself in the knowledge of the Enlightenment. In Maimon's words, in this he was: "... like starving persons suddenly treated to a delicious meal." He soon traveled to Berlin to study medicine. There he was influenced by Mendelssohn and Kant, then to become the greatest Kantian critic of the century. Kant himself acknowledged Maimon's achievements. Maimon and Moses Mendelssohn's own associate, David Friedlander, became converts to Christianity. Similarly, in Mainz the parents of Karl Marx opportunistically switched religion; they descended from a long line of rabbis. So too writers such Ludwig Borne, Eduard Gans and Heinrich Heine abandoned their Jewish faith in favor of the hope for full assimilation into what they perceived to be a dynamic universal, if Christian civilization.

During this late 18th-century time frame, the Lithuanian Jewish Council sent representatives and money to Warsaw to forestall the approaching dangers to halakhic Judaism that the *Haskala* represented.[18] From c. 1775, this opposition from the orthodox grew increasingly passionate as the *maskilim* increased in number and broke down the membrane of Judaic separatism. These East-European opponents of the Berlin *Haskala*, however, did not necessarily want to exclude scientific education. Why? Perhaps it was because they were even then protecting their intellectual Talmudic heritage from an upsurge of Hassidic emotional communalism spreading among the lowliest Jews.

Exemplars: (1) Ezekiel Landau, 1713–1793, Chief Rabbi of Prague and Bohemia, opposed Mendelssohn's translation of the Bible into German, Wessely's view of Jewish education, and the Berlin "rabble" in general. (2) Eliyyahu ben Zalman, Gaon of Vilna, 1720–1797: not a rabbi, advocated science; he hated the Hasidim, and opposed the Berlin *Haskala* and its philosophy, which he felt threatened Judaism. (3) Rabbi Moses Sofer (Schreiber) of Pressburg/Bratislava, 1762–1839, whose Talmudic and moral status in Europe was at that time, the highest, advocated a program of Jewish education in which the youth would learn the sciences, astronomy, anatomy, even modern music. But, he emphasized, "do not mingle with the Gentiles, for a people dwelling alone can always sanctify and cleanse itself from the defilement of intermingling."

In the Russian domains, after the 1770's division of Poland between Russia, Austria, and Prussia, all assimilationist writings were condemned by the Talmudic schools, here, especially by Rabbi Herschel Josefowicz of Chelm. Life for the Jews, however, showed no betterment in the East European expansion of the powers of the czars. The trickle of Jews migrating east to west grew into a flood.

No question but that there were tangible material enticements for the Western European Jew to join into . . . "enlightenment, emancipation, assimilation." Mendelssohn himself, becoming a partner in his sponsor Bernhard's silk business, became wealthy, before his untimely death in 1786. From the 1780s, Jews, many including the loyal if dissident Moses Mendelssohn having stayed true to their faith, gradually began to publicly show their new-found wealth in the salons of their majestic homes: Berlin banker family names included Bleichroder, Ephraim; Itzig; Cohen; Mayer; Mendelssohn; Herz; Warburg, Seligman, Worms, Erlanger, von Arnstein (Vienna); von Eskeles(Vienna); Varnhagen (Berlin); Lippmann (Vienna); Koenigswarter (Vienna-Paris); Rothschild (Frankfurt-Paris); Straus (Paris). All of the women of these families ran famous intellectual and artistic salons, but many of them became converts.

Four out of Moses Mendelssohn's six children converted to Christianity, as did all of the grandchildren, including Felix Mendelssohn, the composer, and Philip Veit, the portraitist. Mendelssohn's daughter Dorothea married the Christian German writer Schlegel. These assimilating elite Jews now became part of a new integrated German salon of intellectuals, including such famous Christians as Schleiermacher and the Humboldts. Jews such as Henrietta Herz, Rachel Levin Varnhagen, including the above Dorothea Mendelssohn Schlegel led movements encouraging German literary and intellectual creativity, again, nearly all of them converting to Christianity.

The general public response throughout Europe at the end of the 18th century to this emerging 'haskalah' of Jewish liberation, intellectualism and wealth and ultimately entrance into this modernizing world, is given in the words of Johann Gottlieb Fichte (1762–1814), the great idealistic philosophical follower of Kant. He would assert in 1793, that he was against granting Jews emancipation. Jewish ideas, he asserted were as obnoxious as French ideas. A little later, 1808, he would modify slightly these thoughts. The only way in which he could concede giving rights to Jews would be "to cut off all their heads in one night, and to set new ones on their shoulders, which should not contain a single Jewish idea."[19]

European Reform

Up until the early to mid-19th century when the Jews of Europe were officially given the rights of Christians living in their respective nations, there was a recognition of the externality of the Jewish community by the ruling elect. Thus in Germany especially the so-called *Gemeinde*, community leadership, represented the traditional orthodox Talmudic synagogues as they entered the modernizing world. The Jews were "apart," yet deeply impacted even by a partial dissolution of the membrane of separation. The first conflicts within the Jewish communities began to occur in mid-18th century Germany with the writings of Moses Mendelssohn and those Jews and Christians who were magnetically attracted to the *haskalah*. They began to look beyond the ancient meanings of what it meant to be a Jew in an alien world.

> ... the man of Nazareth wrought a double kindness to the world. On the one hand he fully supported the Torah of Moses ... for not one of our Sages spoke more fervently about the eternal duty to fulfill the Law. On the other hand he brought much good to the gentiles. ... For he (the man of Nazareth) forbade idol worship and removed the image deities, and he held the people responsible for the seven commandments ... he sought to perfect them with ethical qualities that are much more rigorous even than those of the Law of Moses. (Rabbi Jacob Emden, Hamburg, 1757)[20]

Adath Jeshurun, 1797, a congregation of liberal Jews attempted to separate themselves from the orthodox Jewish council of synagogues. It made a variety of "reforms" in the services, burial procedures, moral themes in its sermons. It was forced to rejoin the orthodox community a decade later.[21] Westphalia, 1808, rabbis, including Mendel Steinhardt, under the leadership of financier Israel Jacobson attempted a series of reforms in the services and ritual. As Prussian rule expanded such reforms were prohibited, revealing the influence of the orthodox community, 1823. Between 1817–1819, in the independent Hanseatic city of Hamburg, the New Temple Association was inaugurated. It included a modernized liturgy, prayer book, and confirmation practices, also allowing for lay preachers.[22]

Abraham Geiger, 1810–1874, a rabbi, influenced by the poet Herder, and the *haskalah* movement, saw Judaism as an evolving historical entity, long advocating a rational ethical monotheism as against the Christian trinitarianism. Geiger became a rabbi to the influential Jewish community of Breslau.

Samuel Holdheim, 1806–1860, a "Reform" rabbi, believed that services should be held on Sunday. He allowed for little of the Hebrew ceremonial and liturgical traditions and had moralistic sermons in his reform Berlin synagogue. He advocated the radical reshaping of Judaism into a modern messianic, universalist outlook consonant with the present and not the past, e.g., Torah and Talmud.

Conferences in 1844–46 by now German university-educated and younger rabbis attempted to solidify the reform movement. However, Zacharias Frankel 1801–1875, of Dresden, broke with Geiger, Holdheim and the reformers, to argue for the centrality of Hebrew in the service and the need to retain the primacy of rabbinical law. He was subsequently appointed to head a new rabbinical seminary in Breslau, 1854. While arguing for an adaptation to modernity, Frankel believed that Judaism needed to maintain its traditions and ritual continuity. Here we note the beginnings of Conservative Judaism. Rabbi Heinrich Graetz, d. 1891, the eminent historian of Judaism, graduated from this seminary.

Leopold Zunz, 1794–1886, originated the Society for the Culture and Science of Judaism in 1819. It was an attempt to advocate the secular scientific study of Judaism. His writings on Jewish religion and history spread and stimulated a Europe-wide secular study of Jewish history and culture, including Heinrich Graetz' multi-volume history of the Jews, first publication, 1853. In 1872, in Berlin, Abraham Geiger inaugurated the University for the Science of Judaism, inspired by Zunz. Leo Baeck, 1873–1956, rabbi, philosopher and theologian was a later graduate of this institution.

Within the orthodox community, two 19th-century thinkers stand out: (1) the Hungarian Rabbi Mosheh Sofer (Hatam Sofer), 1762–1839, author of a 7-volume "response" to Halakhic questions continued the German orthodox tradition of the late 18th-early 19th century allowing for secular education for utilitarian reasons, but strictly adhering to Talmudic traditions of orthodox ritual in synagogue and home. (2) Samuel Raphael Hirsch, mid-19th century, Frankfurt am Main: "a divine order revealed in nature, but also revealed in the Torah for Jews." Jews could participate in the secular world. Hirsch battled both reform as well as conservative Jews. He stimulated the establishment of schools, religious and secular seminaries. Yes, emancipation and culture are fine, but his advocacy was for strong traditionalism in all aspects of Jewish life and belief. The secular world is separate but not equal. He tried to resign from the Frankfurt "gemeinde" and form a separate synagogue organization.

However, even Hirsch's moves were too radical for Rabbi Seligman Ber Bamberger, Wurtzburg, 1807–1878. A great Talmudic scholar, he fought against the modernizing rationalizations of Hirsch. Bamberger, using Halakhic analysis attempted to refute Hirsch's own Talmudic reasoning in insisting on Jews remaining within the over-all jurisdiction of Jewish community regulation.

Two European forces: one lured by the seeming openness of the Christian political establishment, and the universal secular culture, abandoned Judaism for the opportunities of power, while considering Judaism a derelict intellectual/religious institution. The second group desperately attempted to re-shape Talmudic/Rabbinic Judaism so that it could remain palatable to the emancipatory lures of the new knowledge.

American Leadership

The transition of leadership of the international Jewish community to the United States began to take place in the mid-19th century. The United States alone among the modern Western nations of the world had no history of religious repression. It came into being with an explicit constitutional secular political structure, viewing religion as being separate from public political life, the "separation of church and state." As such, Jews were welcome to pursue their religious commitments or not as they pleased. No Jewish "gemeinde" could with governmental support restrict the fluid evolution of an individual or a group's religious allegiances.

The revolutionary environment of 1848 stimulated large-scale German Jewish immigration to the United States. From 1842, in Baltimore, under Rabbi David Einhorn, 1809–1879, the reform movement picked up in the United States, stressed the priestly mission of the Jewish people, opposed mixed marriage, saw little value in Jewish ceremonials, and believed in the progress of Judaism beyond the ancient sacred texts. A conference of reform rabbis was held in Philadelphia, in 1869, and in the German language, rejected the oral law of bodily resurrection in favor of "the immortality of the soul." By comparison Hebrew Union College, a Reform institution was founded in Cincinnati, 1875.[23]

Isaac Meyer Wise (1819-1900) along with Einhorn, was a powerful administrative architect of the American reform movement in Judaism. Einhorn initiated in his own synagogue in Albany, N.Y, the practice of mixed choirs and family pews during services, echoing the polemics of Abraham Geiger, in Germany. Wise was founder of Hebrew Union College in Cincinnati, 1875.[24] In 1907, under the auspices of Reform Jews, Dropsie College in Philadelphia was founded, devoted to post-graduate training in Hebrew and cognate learning. It was to evolve as a non-sectarian institution awarding doctoral degrees in appropriate disciplines.

Isaac Leeser (1806–1868) an inspirer of the Conservative Jewish movement, was unwilling to give up many of the traditions of Jewish synagogue ritual worship, use of Hebrew, *kashrut*, and Sabbath practices. Leeser was the first translator of the Hebrew Bible into English. He founded an ill-fated Maimonides College for rabbinical studies in Philadelphia. Rabbis Alexander Kohut and Sabato Morais founded the Jewish Theological Seminary in N.Y.C. for the preservation of historical Judaism, the Torah, Talmud, 1886.[25]

Felix Adler (1851–1933), was a rabbi educated at the Temple Emanuel, American Hebrew College to train rabbis in N.Y.C., this under the auspices of his father Rabbi Samuel Adler. Given scholarship funds to train further in higher education abroad, he attended Heidelberg University. On returning Felix Adler spurned his reform Judaic background and founded in 1876, the Society for Ethical Culture, a secular interdenominational fellowship.[26]

Solomon Schechter (1847–1915), a Rumanian-born, German-educated British professor, strongly Zionist, in contrast to Reform Judaism, became head of Jewish Theological Seminary in 1902, beginning its ascent into one of the foremost institutions of Judaic studies and synagogue practice, aiding in the flourishing of Conservative Judaism. Schechter continued the philosophy of Zacharias Frankel, who in 1845 had made the first move away from the German Reform movement in his quest to retain more of historic Jewish tradition in rites and belief in this balancing with modernity.

Orthodox Judaism began its American institutional transformation from a scattered series of independent, storefront synagogues, mostly serving new immigrants from Eastern Europe, at the end of the 19th century. The Rabbi Isaac Elchanan Theological Seminary opened up its doors in the lower east side on Henry Street, N.Y.C., in 1896, named after a renowned Lithuanian rabbi. It was mostly devoted to training students in the study of the Oral Torah, the Talmudic writings, not in creating rabbis. Dr. Bernard Revel, (1885–1940) born in Eastern Europe but educated in the United States, was made head of the institution in 1915. He pursued the transformation of the Elchanan Theological Seminary into Yeshiva College-University in 1928, having both a secular curriculum and rabbinical studies, eventually leading to the establishment of a distinguished medical school within its educational structure.[27]

Accommodation with Modernity

World War II was the great transformational event of institutional Judaism. Foremost was the *Holocaust* in Europe, which in essence destroyed Jewish life on that continent. The remnants in Eastern Europe were absorbed and veritably neutered by the communization of these nations and the secular atheism which became part of the official belief system, as it installed a new God/dictator in Josef Stalin and his cohorts.

The West, in an act of penance for the horrific crime of Christian Europe, allowed for the establishment of Israel as a homeland for the Jews. The Jews of Israel however were on their own in defending themselves against continuing military and terrorist attacks from the surrounding Muslim nations. In the fulfilling of a long-standing Zionist dream, the reality of Israel's "being," including its ability to defend itself, there evolved a changed outlook by institutional Judaism throughout the world. The modernity of Israel as a secular political entity also had an impact on congregational Judaism, especially in America, the homeland of the now vast majority of Jews in the *ha golah*, the exile.

> Traditional {orthodox} Judaism knows only one standard of faithfulness to God: loyalty to God's law as expounded in the Torah, especially the oral law in its continuing development by contemporary sages. The Torah has absolute primacy. Modernity can come into Judaism only as the Torah allows. Hence the lives of believing orthodox Jews display religious continuity more than religious change.[28]

Since the end of WW II, orthodoxy both in the United States and Israel has evolved in a number of different directions. What unites them all is their commitments to both Torah study of *halakhic* law and Talmudic oral law. Thus prayer, diet (*kashrut*), Sabbath and festival observance bring these groups together. In the traditional West European traditions of orthodoxy, the observance of Saadia's twofold truth, the laws of God, and the experiences of secular life bring these orthodox into the mainstream of public affairs. They can be businessmen, public servants, financiers, professors in secular institutions, medical doctors in the Maimonidean tradition, even chemists. But they also adhere to the traditional separation, if not subservience of women both in religious life and in their secular legal position.

The Conservative movement attempting to balance modernity with tradition has grown to be a powerful religious force in the United States. The Jewish Theological Seminary in New York City, while not attempting to mimic the orthodoxies "twofold truth" in maintaining a rabbinical seminary alongside a secular university, Yeshiva, has brought together a distinguished group of scholars having a diversity of views on the maintenance of the ancient traditions. Early on it was pro-Zionist, in contradistinction to the original theses of the Reform movement. And it also brought women into the rabbinate.

Yet in its approach to the revelatory aspects of Torah, and the rabbinical pharisaic and Talmudic positions on personal salvation, they have remained "conservative." Marriage and divorce laws were nuanced to harmonize with civil law. Dietary and festival observances were diluted from orthodox practice to accommodate with life in a non-Jewish community. Driving an auto on the Sabbath and the use of electricity on the Sabbath were granted. Its dynamic leadership in recruiting Jewish youth to its programs educational and cultural within this accommodation of historicity to modernity has given the Conservative movement, both in the United States and The World Council of Synagogues, its international organization, much influence in world Jewry.

However broad the Conservative umbrella for the inclusion of tradition and modernity within synagogue Judaism, there were bound to be schismatics. Thus was born the "reconstructionist" movement led by the scholarly rabbi, Mordecai Kaplan (1881–1983), a distinguished member of the faculty of the Jewish Theological Seminary. In his *Judaism as a Civilization*, 1933, he spelled out in detail his concern with the historic literality that Conservative, Orthodox, and Reform Judaism had taken.[29]

Kaplan's views were to the left of the more traditional positions of the scholarly President of Jewish Theological seminary, Louis Finkelstein, but more to the right of the Reform Judaism of the Hebrew Union College in Cincinnati. Kaplan: "We should analyze the Jewish conception of God in order to learn how it functioned in the life of the Jewish people. . . . To some people the elimination of the theurgic element from the God idea is equivalent to the abandonment of the belief in God, and an act which must lead to the disintegration of the Jewish social heritage. . . . (W)e must realize that it {the theurgic element} does not function by itself, but through that pattern of emotional, volitional, and ideational reactions which may be described as religious behavior."[30]

Kaplan thus attempted to maintain the architecture of such concepts as the revealed truth of the Torah, personal salvation, and prayer, but gave them an entirely new interpretation in his conception of Judaism as not merely a religion but as a historic moral way of life. Even the divine election of the Jews as the chosen people was radically reinterpreted by Kaplan so as not to exclude other religious groups.

While Kaplan maintained his position at the Jewish Theological Seminary, even while inspiring the formation of a secessionist grouping of synagogues and patterns of worship, this in spite of the overwhelming intellectual hostility of his faculty. He was condemned by the Union of Orthodox Rabbis. In 1945 they convened a meeting to burn the Reconstructionist prayer book and to excommunicate Kaplan.[31]

With every decade of the 20th century the dynamics of radical reform away from the rituals and traditions of Orthodox Talmudic Judaism continued to attenuate the Jewish community's relation with the synagogue. The incorporation of women and then female rabbis in the synagogue, the addition of music and choral song continued the attempt to lure back secularizing Jews. Yiddish never was reinstituted, as also with the Conservative congregations, more Hebrew entered the liturgy. As of 1937, "The *kiddush*, the lighting of the candles, the traditional Sabbath melodies were reinstated,

Hannukah and Purim, virtually non-existent in Reform practice, were introduced, the public *Seder* gave new meaning to the Passover, the Shofar was heard again on High Holy Day service, Sukkot was reestablished as a consecration festival."[32]

From 1935 to the time of the *Holocaust*, the position of Reform Judaism toward Zionism, radically changed. Earlier in their quest to create a universal Judaism, not located in Europe, Palestine, or the United States, there was serious opposition to the Zionist movement, especially the attempts of some religious Zionists to render the life and beliefs of Jews outside of Jerusalem irrelevant and antithetical to the true vocation and destiny of the Jewish people. It is clear that except for a minority of radical ultraorthodox Jews who reviled the existence of a Jewish polity in Palestine prior to the arrival of the *Messiah*, virtually the entire Jewish community took on the creation and sustenance of the state of Israel as one if not the most important secular commitment of Jewry.

Stability among the three most dominant and established wings of modern synagogue Judaism also connotes stasis, as all three groups were ready to admit to the steady erosion of membership in the respective synagogue groups, as well as the loss of unaffiliated Jews to the religion through intermarriage. In 2010 the intermarriage rate among Jews was almost 50%. This was in addition to the explicit falling away of many Jews from a recognition of their Judaic origins.

The exception to this are the so-called ultraorthodox, the Hassidic orthodoxy. Their commitment to the literal Talmudic traditions of East Europe, their political power within Israel itself, has kept their numbers and public recognition as the true representatives of Judaism today, high on the Gentile scale of awareness. The semi romantic/nostalgic writings about modern Hassidism by Shalom Asch, Martin Buber, and Elie Wiesel have also brought their practices to the modern consciousness just as they themselves attempt to remove themselves from the modern world, to whatever extent possible.[33]

Hasidism

The origin of the Ḥasidism is rooted in the East European mystic tendencies, including the Russian dissenting sects. It was founded by (Israel ben Eliezer) Ba'al Shem Tov, (Besht), in the mid-18th century, in Podolia and Volhynia, Poland. Raphael Patai glorifies the movement, as a *dionysian* response to the Talmudic elite which dominated the *Kahals*, the Jewish community governments set up by the Polish nobility—Poland from the 15th century occupied large portions of White Russia, Ukraine, Lithuania, this until the 1772 partition by the great powers.[34]

> Hasidism represents one of the most significant and most original phenomena not only in the history of Judaism, but also in the history of the development of religions in

general . . . It did not aim at the improvement of the tenets of the faith or at a reform of religious practices; what it endeavored was something greater and deeper: the perfection of the *soul*. By means of exerting a powerful psychological influence Hasidism succeeded in creating a type of *believer* which valued the ardor of feeling higher than the observance of rites, piety and religious fervor, higher than speculation and *Torah*-study.[35]

Hasidism's most influential innovation was the promotion of a new elite that differed both from the traditional rabbinic scholars and the medieval Sephardic qabbalistic ascetics. The Hassidic *tsadiq* forged a link between the qabbalistic master and the Jewish masses by emphasizing his communal responsibilities . . . by 1800 close to one half the Jews of Eastern Europe flocked to its banner.[36]

Habad Hasidism today represents the more intellectual branch; Satmar Hasids argue that the state of Israel prevents the coming of the Messiah. Their belief is that the Nazi *Holocaust* was punishment of the Jews for their Zionist secular aspirations.

The Lubavitcher Rabbi Joseph Isaac Schneerson came to the United States in 1940, to give great stimuli to the growth of Hasidic Orthodox Judaism. Women dress in simple non-modern clothes. They are believers in having many children as advocated in Torah. They speak Yiddish as their vernacular home speech, reserving Hebrew for the sacramental. In Israel they are largely supported by the state, do not serve in the army, refuse to defend the state, except to fight Arabs and the government in defending their outpost communities in Samaria. The women are more likely to work to put bread on the table while the men study Torah, Talmud, and prayer books. They are a powerful centripetal Judaic force, who in their rejection of assimilation into modernity attempt to maintain the purity of the ancient rabbinic faith.[37]

Demographic Accounting

In 1800, the world population was c. 800 million. There were approximately 2 million Jews on our planet. The American and English Jewish Yearbook, 1910, estimated that approximately 11.5 million Jews inhabited our world. At that time, 1910, the world population was c. 1.8 billion. In 1930, the Jewish population of our world was c. 16 million. The world population was c. 2.2 billion persons. The *Holocaust*, 1940–1945, saw the butchering of 6 million Jews in Europe. In 2011 the world population was c. 7 billion. The number of Jews in the world was c. 15 million.

The Jews have survived into the modern world, barely. The survival is a testament to something intrinsically powerful in the Jewish soul. However, as a diminished community in a world of proliferating belief, the future has to be in doubt.

We shall next examine this paradox, first to look back at the visionary elements of survival over these many thousands of years of revolutionary adaptation. Then we will examine the diminishing sources of institutional and moral vigor in contemporary Judaism.

CHAPTER SEVEN

Our Judaic Heritage

Context of Survival

The Jews and Judaism have survived because they have adapted to historic changes, especially when they were "losers." We have an ancient evolutionary principle at work, albeit on the sociohistorical level: those creatures/groups who are outliers, on the perimeter of historic dominance, often, if they adapt defensively to their circumstances, in the turn of history, can often return to the fore. The dominant creatures/groups of one epoch in biological time are dominant because they have made the most of their momentary opportunistic adaptation to external events.

These propitious externalities along with the internal morphological or behavioral inheritances from their past have allowed them to catapult to dominance. By virtue of this dominance and its biological opportunities, they tend to specialize, to wring that last bit of "juice" out their inadvertent opening. But alas, the world does change. Nature is not concerned with the fortunes of one successful species/social group. The larger forces of evolution create their own dynamic of change, and the once powerful can quickly fall from favor, often to become extinct.

Thus the Jews, by dint of their ability to change with the winds of history have been able to hang on and gain successive moment in the light of day. That is, when their leadership has/had the presence of mind and the visionary outlook to persuade the Jewish community to bend with time and survive until another day. This ability over a time span of three thousand years, owes its reality to certain basic cultural/civilizational attributes buried deep within the Judaic mind and soul. To extract such meaning from the depths of the Jewish experience, to adapt it to the dangers facing the Jews today, constitutes the real test of Judaism into the next generations.

National Defense and the Temple Cult

It is the interaction of a concept, an idea, within the ongoing flow of historic events that has defined the Judaic experience and brought it to its present critical confrontation with events. In the beginning, in the period before 1000 BCE, the then-forces of modernity, large national movements in the Near East and Egypt pushed the various tribal configurations of what is present-day Israel to face the reality that the days of free tribal movements were over. Already, in Canaan a large element of sedentary agricultural life was in existence. The old city-state configurations, which previously in the 14th and 13th centuries BCE had depended upon the protection of the Egyptians against the predatory Habiru and Shasu tribes, was under stress. The Egyptians who had finally absorbed the Hyksos invaders, 17th-16th century BCE, and simultaneously ousted their leadership, the Joseph epic in the Old Testament, were soon threatened by new Hittite advances from the north. In addition, the roaming sea peoples from the Mycenaean Aegean, long a presence in the area, the Philistines, now exerted an ever-stronger challenge to both Egyptian hegemony and the existing tribal groups, as these Hellenes moved from the coast toward the hill country.

The actual events which brought these tribal peoples together are still wrapped in mystery, however hinted at in the book of Judges. But it is clear from the historic move toward nationhood under Samuel and Saul, c. 1030 BCE, that the coming of the stragglers from Egypt under the mythological leadership of Moses and Aaron provided the precipitating element in giving that sense of defensive fragility the necessary intellectual and religious glue for nationhood.

Three groups have been identified as coming under this moral and monotheistic canopy of unification. First, the original Habiru tribes of northern Israel, under the ancient Semitic godhead of Elohim, (El). Second, the wandering Sinitic, northern Arabia and desert tribes east of the Jordan, the Shasu, under the fiery redemptive godhead of Yahweh. These latter tribal elements became the core of the Judaic tribes, Caleb and then David. Third, the incoming mixed ethnic stragglers from Egypt carrying with them the probable remembrances of the one god monotheism of the Pharaoh Akhenaton, now under Moses, of probable Egyptian heritage. They adopted the Yahwist semantic of the Sinai allies, Midian and Edom, on their way to entering Canaan.

Writing had long become a core element in the intellectual skills of the scholarly classes. And as we have pointed out in Chapter 3, there was already a rich epic literature preserved by these scribes upon which to base the historical and theological integrative vision of nationhood, peoplehood, which appears in the earliest versions of the Holy Bible, J and E. The writers of the J and E versions of the Pentateuch represent the heritage of the northern tribes, E, and the schismatic breakaway of Israel from the unified kingdom under Jeroboam, as well as J, Judah, and its King, Jeroboam, the son of Solomon, c. 925 BCE, and later.

In the Pentateuch these historic memories and theophoric moral injunctions appear in Genesis, Exodus, and Numbers, with the later inclusions and emendations of the various redacting schools. In spite of much patriotic mythological rhetoric there is a frank core of not so elevating stories and memories which give a quasitragic element of truth about the weaknesses of humans, Israelites included. Indeed, one can say, even of the later scriptural additions, that the writers were deeply aware of the weaknesses of humans and their easy potential to fall into disorderly and evil behavior, here the leaders, be they prophets or kings as well as the *am ha aretz*, the people of the land, and the towns.

Overriding the need to assign the glue of history to a people heretofore constantly on the move and in constant conflict, is the inchoate recognition of the unique power of one moral God that exists transcendentally as a moral judge of a people and a nation. The monotheistic principle enters the Judaic system of religious beliefs as an awareness of a logical purity that sets them apart, their chosenness and obligation to live according to the highest ethical discipline, *or else*. It is the scribes, Levites, priests who take on the responsibility to inject into the national conscience this higher vision, both intellectual and behavioral.

And of course the record of achievement of these Mosaic religio/moral defensive goals of a people, now if not in flight and aspiration, the Exodus, but in process of defensive nation building, is indeed spotty. From the time of Kings Saul, David and Solomon of the unified nation, the virtues of these leaders, as the Old Testament vividly records, are highly blemished. The weakness of the flesh, the tendency to revert in religious worship to the scattered polytheistic, orgiastic rites of worship to the pillars, the Asherah on the high places, continued.

Thus we can understand the reforms that indeed stem from the priests of the original Temple of David and especially Solomon in Jerusalem. It becomes a bulwark for the unity of the people, the nation. As such the reforms of Hezekiah, 727–698 BCE, which reveal themselves throughout the Pentateuch, especially in Leviticus, are created to organize in a systematic way the worshipful and social behavior of the people. Recall that this was an era of great fragility for the two nations, Israel and Judah. The Assyrians, on the march from the north were then dismembering Israel, sending the ten tribes into an exile of oblivion, and threatening to overwhelm Jerusalem.

The changing face of power, the diminished influence of Egypt and the expansionist drive of the Mesopotamian groupings eventually had its impact on Judah. Josiah 639–609, ruler of Judah, attempted to steer his nation around the various contending powers, Egypt, Assyria, Chaldea (from south Mesopotamia). In the process he lost his life to an Egyptian arrow. Before this however he had his priests "discover" a supposedly lost and holy document from the past. This document, now Deuteronomy, was to be a summation and interpretation of the earlier historical recording of Israel's destiny in the world. Using the voice of Moses it attempts to elaborate on his Torah, and offer guide to the Israelites in the form of giving greater amplitude to the "Commandments," in a sense modernizing the Law of God for this more international period of Judaic life. Originally it was to be a separate historic summary and injunction. Later it was probably grafted on to the holy books to become the fifth and final book of the Torah.

Most historians now see Deuteronomy as a more ecumenical coming together of the differing strands of belief and practice in the Israelite experience, then over 400 years in the making. The initial separation after the death of Solomon revealed in J and E, the vestiges of a duality of heritage and belief of these people, was by then reified into permanent political separation. With the elimination of the nation of Israel and its holy sites in the towns of Bethel, Shiloh, Shechem, and the holy mountains of Ebal and Gerizim, as compared with Jerusalem and its Mt. Zion, a more ecumenical return is hinted in Deuteronomy. After all, the nation of Israel no longer existed, but devoted remnants could still study and pray in these towns and sites and join with the people and leaders of Judah in the preservation of the commitments of mind and soul to this elect religious vision. It is also presumed that in the time of Josiah, the Deuteronomic historical writings, Joshua to 2 Kings, and beyond were added to the Israelite self-consciousness as a people.

During this long period of history another force was to be reckoned with in the two nations. These were the prophets who wandered up and down the highway and byways of both nations. These were times of much looser governmental controls and powers over the mind in this part of the Near East, and a much more fluid sense of orthodoxy. The names: Amos, Hosea, Elijah, Elisha, Micah, Isaiah, Jeremiah, constitute the external goad for the reforms that the occasionally morally and politically sensitive rulers such as Hezekiah and Josiah attempted to institute. The urgings, writings of these prophets and their followers were directed at rulers and ruled. The theme of their prophetic utterances was inevitably directed at the falling away from the Mosaic vision, one might say the constitutional imperatives of moral and ritual purity in fulfilling the defensive life. These were austere sensibilities, disciplined and aware of the diminutive presence of humans in the face of the powers of nature as expressed in divinity, the judgments of Yahweh.

It is probable that such a monotheistic and moral conception of life and reality could not have developed within the scope of the great nations. Akhenaton's vision of the one sun god ruling Egypt and the nations, abstracted away from the reigning polytheistic animal pantheon of the Egyptian religious establishment lasted only in his lifetime. The priesthood retook Egypt, and animals once more ruled the mind. Other nations gave hints of a monotheistic vision, a hierarchy of gods leading up one that was preeminent. But none ever fought against "graven images" as did the followers of Moses.

The evolution of the religion of the Jews during this historic time period, c. 1200–587 BCE can be seen as the evolution of a religion defining a people and a nation. Invoking this historic/mythic heritage, the early books of the "historians" J and E created the ground explanation for the needs of nationhood. The second phase takes place with the maturity of the two nations Israel and Judah. Here is reflected the need for reform and emphasis on the unity of the cult and its disciplinary focus on ritual and moral behavior. Thus we understand the new and indeed revolutionary character of P, the priestly writers in Jerusalem and then the broader scholarly and moral summation as exemplified in D, the Deuteronomic writers under Josiah. Finally, we again note the writers of Kings, along with Joshua, Judges, and Samuel, which in themselves were a modernized historic perspective. No hold barred, this Deuteronomic tradition told the dramatic story of an evolution of a people and its faith.

The religion of the Jews here exemplified in the now expanded Pentateuch, and the prophetic and historical writings were already a product of new external circumstances as well as the evolution of nationhood, and the human behavior promulgating its political and social evolution.

A People of the Book

When the intellectual leaders of Judah were exiled to Babylon by the Chaldean conquerors of Jerusalem, 597–582 BCE, they took with them a rich heritage of precious and holy scrolls. In the lushness and tolerance of the Euphrates valley they reconsidered this heritage. With the defeat of the Chaldeans by the Persian Cyrus, and his edict of permission, 539 BCE, for the Israelites to return to their holy city, Jerusalem, and rebuild it and the Temple, a few started to trickle back from this new land of wine and honey to the destroyed but revered and holy homeland, now the Yehud, a province in the Persian protectorate. Alongside Jerusalem now existed Samaria, a rival Judaic province with a large non-Israelite immigrant population, but now professing the ancient faith of the land.

It took about one hundred years, amid many new prophetic writings and reconsiderations, for the assertions by Ezra and Nehemiah, c. 450 BCE, both high Judaic officials in the Persian hegemon, but inspired to revive the ancient but true faith. And it was at this time that the fully formed Pentateuch was presented by them to a mostly unenthusiastic and tainted population, the children and grandchildren of Levites and priests included. But now we were at least six hundred years removed from the contexts of the original inspiration for the Mosaic Law and ritual as well as its contextual social underpinnings. The Torah had to be taught anew to these puzzled "moderns," and with explanation.

Here too as we enter an era of great enlightenment and sophistication, the golden age of Pericles. The *am ha arez* had to be retaught the metaphysical implications of the monotheistic vision. This sole moral, if fiery and redemptive God was now envisioned in a complete new historical setting. If we could no longer be an independent nation with an official religion then we must become a people with a living and portable heritage of writings, our new Temple the symbol of this vision.

This period of a Torah which needed modernistic explanation was part of the gradual internationalization of culture. The Persians allowed for commercial relations with the expanding Greeks, since many of the Greek city states had been allied with Persia in their incursion into the European homeland. The openness of the Greeks to the new, had its impact throughout the Mediterranean and into Asia itself. Literacy even in a backwater state such as Palestine began to be a necessity. And the scribes often active far from the Temple boundaries, in lands distant, often had to interpret for their constituency the ancient and stringent rules of faith.

Thus there grew the rationale for new institutions within the ancient Judaic framework. The Pharisees evolved from this scribal tradition, and with it the "Oral Law." Two hundred relatively placid years of Persian rule gave way to the revolutionary conquests of Alexander and the *tsunami* of Hellenistic civilization. While the Greeks at first did not impose their religious and cultural views on the indigenous Judeans, just their presence and the explosive openness of thought and cultural behavior of the Greek mentality was enough to break open the old configurations of the eastern mind.

The conquest of Mesopotamia and much of the Near East by the Indo-European-speaking Persians, and then their adoption of Zoroastrianism, modestly monotheistic, as the official religion of the Persian people constituted the first full displacement of the ancient Sumerian/Semitic pantheon. Then, following the Alexandrian Greek conquests, the Judean peasantry and townsfolk were in reality left with no religious alternatives but their own now historic religious world. The Persians certainly viewed the temples in Jerusalem or on Mt. Gerizim as buttressing the peace of occupation. Thus they supported the Temple priesthood and the religious consultations of the *Soferim* (scribes) and the other forms of the established cult.

But as in the earlier period the straight line of orthodoxy away from the precincts of the Temple, was constantly askew. Also the opening of communication with the outside world, the constant flow of mercenary Jewish soldiers to the various rivals dispersed a large proportion of the population of the Yehud. A large Jewish population now remained in Babylon. Many of these Jews followed the Persian and then Alexander's legions in the perpetual search for greener pastures of milk and honey.

The Maccabean revolt against the Seleucids highlights the general disaffection of the simple Jewish farmer or craftsmen with the sophisticated artistic and philosophical culture of the Greeks. Only the aristocratic Temple bureaucracy was attracted to the new way of life. The gymnasium with athletic exercises undertaken in the nude disgusted traditional Jewish attitudes, the Saducean elite in Jerusalem being deeply infatuated with this "enlightened" world of apollonian extrovertism.

The attitude of the Saducees in so far as the relationship between Torah beliefs and behavior and Hellenism was to make of this a "twofold truth" distinction. Their holy life was caught up with the cultish practices of the Temple, including animal sacrifice. On the other hand their secular behavior was very much caught up with Greek attitudes and enthusiasms. Clearly, this explains the growing practice out in the countryside of the need for explanations of the Torah in terms of modern-life decisions toward the powerful. Essentially this became a "Platonic lie of words," the "Oral Law," supposedly given to Moses on Mt. Sinai by Yahweh, now most often referred to as the "Almighty" or "God most high."

The translation of the Torah, c. 280–260 BCE, and then the other prophetic writings into Greek for the large Alexandrian Jewish community and then the larger Hellenistic Diaspora opened up a two-way level of communication between the Greek and Jewish *intelligentsia*. By now there was a large literate Jewish population throughout the Greco-Roman world. The conflicts within the Jewish hierarchy during the post-Maccabean Hasmonian rule over Judea weakened the centralized equilibrium of the 2nd temple. A wide variety of Jewish sects began to be formed within their various disoriented constituencies both within Judea and without.

Thus we see the formation of the *Synagogue* and the *Proseuch* (Greek terms for the study halls and prayer rooms) that the faithful created first in Alexandria and the Diaspora and then within Judea itself. The *Soferim* (scribes) transformed into Pharisees, now contended with the ruling Temple Sadducees and their secular Greek pretensions. It was the Pharisees who adopted the now pervasive Eastern mystery religion belief in personal salvation by a higher god, then a judgment of what life was to be for the individual after death. But such personal redemption first required the coming of a savior, a Messiah. No longer was there the centrality of judgment by God of the morality of the community of Israelites as a people and their nation. Even in Judea, there existed a now-alienated mass searching for personal hope in the hereafter.

Yet in this ecumenical coming together for mystical redemption, the concept of one higher force in the universe was an attractive counter to the polytheism of both the Greek and Roman divinities of place. The Greek followers of Alexander found in the Jewish almighty God a philosophical resemblance to Aristotle's *Theos*, the unmoved mover, an abstract and logical explanation for the ordering of the confusing particularities of experience. Hecateaus, c. 320–312 BCE, called the Jews "a philosophical race." Clearchus and Theophrastus of the Aristotelian school positively emphasized this highly powerful conception. Hermippus of Smyrna, c. 220 BCE, is said to have attributed the Pythagorean philosophy to Jewish thinkers, (Josephus, *Contra Apion*). Many Jewish writers of this era joined in an ecumenical search for wisdom in the spirit of Greek philosophy. The Torah became *nomos*, the law, to the Greeks.

The Roman conquests, in Judea, the corrupt and cruel rule of the converted Jew, Herod, 37–4 BCE, gave greater impetus to the disintegration of orthodoxy. We note along with the Pharisees and Sadducees, the Essenes, the Qumran community in the desert, the Samaritans, later the Sicarii, and Zealots, all leading toward what eventually became the most successful dissident Jewish group, the Christians. Yet within the context of all this religious and social chaos, the attractiveness of Judaism as an alternative mystery religion was enormous. These were the millions of "god fearers," attracted by the drive for moral purity demanded by the Mosaic Torah, and then the prophets and wisdom writers, this amid Hellenistic permissiveness and degeneracy, especially at the top.

It can fairly be said that Judaism reached its apogee in this period 100 BCE to 100 CE. There are many claims for percentages as high as 10% of the Roman world being Jews, affiliated in one way or anther with the people of the "one God, upon high." True, the affiliations with the Jewish institutions were fluid and often weak, the strict Sabbath prohibitions, dietary rules, and circumcision becoming barriers to conversion. Paul took advantage of this "turning off" of the masses to dissolve this very high bar.

Above all, the moral rigor of Judaic law, the abstract nature of their God, the prohibition against graven images, catapulted Judaism to the forefront as a belief and behavioral system that could now rival and potentially defeat the now decrepit Hellenic and Hellenistic vision which had originally created this powerful civilization. The Jews were part of this dynamic. Note the writings of Josephus, a Pharisee c. 37–95 CE, who like many of his confreres had made peace with Rome. Also, the philosopher Philo in Alexandria, 15 BCE–54 CE, was a symbol of a devout Hellenic Jew.

It could not be. The three wars described earlier (Chapter 4), destroyed the symbol of unity, the Temple, and then Jerusalem itself, and with it the dissolution of the Sadducees, Essenes and the other dissident groups. The Pharisees survived through an accommodation with Rome and made their hasty pilgrimage to Yavneh, c. 70–100CE, to order the heritage of writings and bring the Old Testament into its present configuration. Christianity simultaneously took up the torch of a new extrapolation of Judaism under the brilliant proselytizing of Paul, (executed in Rome, c. 62 CE), he the Pharisaic student of the elder Rabbi Gamaliel, the latter a student of Rabbi Hillel. By the year 135 CE all hope for a Jewish homeland dissolved. Rabbi Akiba's vision of the coming of the Messiah, now represented by the revolutionary warrior Bar Kokhba was concluded with the death of both men at the hands of Roman Emperor Hadrian. And with their demise, came the obliteration of Jerusalem. The Jews moved on. Their holy center was now portable.

Four Judaisms: A Summary

In order for a people to progress with time and thus to protect their very existence, and this includes their religious heritage, they must properly understand their past. Thus it is incumbent for today's Jews, so that they can evolve and survive into the next generations, to understand who they were as a people. But they must do this undogmatically, separate their thinking from those who are the momentary Judaic beneficiaries of power and influence; they who write about and control this history

Up to the final destruction, first of the 2nd Temple, and then the city of Jerusalem, by Rome, this a part of the destruction of revolting Jewish communities throughout this Roman Empire, the Jews had four times re-invented themselves as a religion, a way of moral living, as well as religious sanctification. We see Judaism as a continuum of peoplehood and belief at least three thousand years of authenticated history. Yet there were decisive changes in the holy documentation, in the relationship of a citizen Israelite with his king and temple, and with the sacred documents which underpinned worship, beliefs, and behaviors.

> 1. The epic writings of J and E which form the core around which the nationhood and belief systems of the United Kingdom and its divided successors. These writings were clearly accumulative over the generations appearing shortly after 1000 BCE. They are the epic explanation of this people's unique journey and destiny. The writings were the achievement of intellectuals but had little impact on the lives of the people and the behaviors of the ruling classes. These writings created what today we call Genesis, Exodus, and Numbers, as part of the Pentateuch.

2. Three hundred years later under the rule of King Hezekiah, c, 700 BCE, during the crisis which saw the obliteration of the Kingdom of Israel under the Assyrian spear, reform was attempted in Judah. This was the attempt to extirpate the ecstatic worship on high, the corrupt worship of idols and gods of other religions. Hezekiah attempted to give the priests of the Temple unconditional powers in Jerusalem. The critical innovations as they have come down to us were the changes and amplifications made by this priestly and scholarly class to the original documents of religious and national incorporation. Thus the three earlier books were completely redrafted and redacted, the so-called P strand, and a new book, Leviticus, written and wholly incorporated. The religion now had a deeply constraining set of cultic regulations for life as a citizen of Judah. Probably at this time, possibly even earlier the two separate versions of the original epoch, J and E were combined.

Several generations later, c. 625 BCE, King Josiah had the so-called Deuteronomic historians create a series of writings, histories from their current perspective of the past. The Pentateuchal Deuteronomy and the prophetic books of Samuel and Kings, were written, perhaps even Joshua and Judges were redacted. At this time as before, under Hezekiah, many prophetic writings were in circulation for the literate minority. But in both cases the intent of the scholars, scribes, Levites under these two kings, was to tighten the circle of belief to the rites and powers of the priests of the First Temple. No longer could the political structure allow for the casual centrifugal luxury of picking out one's own venue and site for celebrating the ancient calendric and fertility festivals of the nomadic and agricultural past.

3. The work of the scholars, Levites, priests in exile in Babylon, as well as the integrating and redacting efforts of the later leadership under Ezra and Nehemiah, c. 550–450 BCE. The Temple of Solomon had been destroyed. Judah was now the Yehud, a province in the greater Persian Empire. The Torah needed to be redacted and brought before the people of Moses, as a completed document of worship and obedience. "These books are now your holy testament to whom you are and what you are as a people." But alas, much of these writings were already five to six hundred years old. Much of the moral and social behavioral strictures were no longer applicable, literally understood for these times.

This historic period c. 450 BCE was a time of increasing literacy. Expanding empires were in intercommunication as well as at war. Thus the Torah needed to be recited in prayer, had to be obeyed, but now with interpretation. Here, a new practice among the people in which king and priest were no longer in ascendancy in the homeland, when so many Jews now lived outside the Yehud. These documents and the contemporary interpretive understandings would keep the people together for their *chosen* mission on earth.

4. The writings have multiplied. The Jews weak in armor, powerful in their moral and intellectual vision of monotheism have met up with new materially powerful empires, as well as an intellectual culture of great wisdom. They have learned much from the Greeks in terms of the power of intellect, beyond their own defensive moral aspirations. But the wars for independence and equality of condition with both the Greeks and Rome have ended in disaster. Five hundred more years have gone by, and the Jews now have a great and powerful literature, created in Yavneh by the Pharisees turned Rabbis. In c. 95 CE the Old Testament was completed, TaNaK, Torah (Law), Nevi'im (Prophets), Kituvim (Writings). Within the entirety, these were now considered holy writings, with special emphasis on the word of God, Torah.

One could say at this point in time that the Jews now had a portable literary heritage which they could carry with them wherever. It did not matter that in certain minor areas of the wisdom writings, the Alexandrian Jews, in their supplements to the *Septuagint*, would create differences. To this day, for example, the various Christian sects have differing versions of the Holy Bible than the later Masoretic version redacted during the Talmudic period. But certainly Judaism as it evolved in the 1st century BCE and into the modern world was a different faith as compared to the earlier periods.

The Gift of Talmudism

The Pharisaic Rabbis of the period 100 BCE to 100 CE, when a new transition took place were highly educated. It was they who went beyond the rejection by the Sadducees and the Samaritans of any writings beyond the five books of the Torah as Holy Writ. They perhaps unconsciously realized that the Jews needed a rich store of understandings to round out a conception of holiness and morality. And while the scientific writings of the Greeks did not touch them in terms of a value for the Jewish community, they were not insensitive to the needs of this people for a literature that had to deepen our human mental needs.

The kind of objectivity that Josephus sought in his historical research, or the attempts by Philo to make the ancient Jewish laws compatible with then modern philosophical thinking, was brushed aside. But it did not make them insensitive to the need for further explanation of the Holy Writ for the survival of the people. Thus the Talmudic writings were accumulated and integrated as a way of explaining the now long written and lived history of the Jews. These writings and the populist educational efforts that now went beyond the strong literate orientation of the Jewish intellectuals symbolized the fact that the efforts to proselytize, to accommodate the millions of "god fearers" would be largely abandoned. The bar of entrance would remain high.

For over 1500 years the rabbinical Talmudic reshaping of the Jewish community would be maintained come "hell or high water," that is until a more powerful intellectual challenge to Judaism would arise. In the history of the West no other religious worldview, not Christianity in its powerful secular advance into political power, nor Islam gaining its universal position through the force of arms, could compete, intellectually, with the Judaic system.

There had arisen intellectual challenges to Judaic thinking during this period. The rediscovery of the Greek philosophical writings, first in Babylon as answered by Saadia, then in Spain, here integrated into a new vision of Judaism by Maimonides, a migrant to Egypt. Jewish thinkers in Spain, as we have noted (in Chapter 5), were particularly able in that at-times-benign political climate, to emerge from the cocoon of the Jewish community to engage in poetic, literary, philosophical and even scientific enquiry of a more universal nature. But it was the Talmudic setting that remained the intellectual, moral and communitarian glue that held the Jews together. Whether it was Christian or Islamic power that towered over them, the Jews were still largely anathema, and their existence remained in jeopardy. They could not emerge too tendentiously without being hammered back.

For the larger community of Jews, the Talmudic writings, the debates of the Kallah in Babylon, the Talmudic academies and yeshivahs in Europe maintained their ultimate defense and intellectual joy. The mysteries of the holy writings needed analysis for the life of the times. The level of literacy and intellectual gymnastics required to win the prize were nonmaterial in nature, recognition and community status alone were awesome and then democratically awarded. If the Jews in these impoverished *stetls* in Europe could understand in the larger sense what they were doing they could have written a great scientific treatise as to how they were releasing a powerful human trait, literate abstract analysis, to be valued and shared in this community, no matter the material rewards that would later be realized.

For, in this intense literate Talmudic dialectic, they were giving acknowledgment to a deep element in human nature, the search of the educated mind for knowledge and understanding. It was like a chess game, played for its intrinsic challenge to the mind. In some mysterious way the first acknowledgment of the relationship between one morally demanding God on high, in that first phase of historical search, J and E, and the role of the prophet Moses in receiving the commandments from God, opened up a succession of acts and behaviors, which eventually would be translated into recognition of their being a people of the book, a "nation of philosophers." Circumstance forced them away from secular power into marginalization. But still, their self-denominated obligation as a people, chosen, was ever unchallenged by those who could hold the sword of power.

Thus they remained apart, devoted to Talmudic expiation and dialectic of the moral rules of life but always in intellectual discourse and participated in by the entire community. As many have noted, Talmudic writing was more than mere inquiry into law, *halakah*. "Prose mingles with poetry, wit with wisdom, the good with the bad ... it makes the Talmud a somewhat rambling compilation ... it is almost an encyclopaedia in its scope, a storehouse reproducing the knowledge and thought of the first few centuries of the Christian era."[1] But the evolution of the Talmud was ongoing, with each generation of scholar rabbis adding commentary and criticism.

Even amid the disdain and repugnance of the Christian world toward the Jew, here and there in the debates that were proposed by the feudal aristocracy at the urging of the clergy, the Jews held their own, even with the playing field of the debates so skewed that the result for the "winners" was often the glory of burning the holy scriptures of the Jews, also the accumulated Talmudic writings. Yet here and there a glimmer of reality intruded into Christian thinking. Opining on the feudal practice of primogeniture, the waste of human resources, eldest sons inheriting the estate, other sons farmed out to be warriors or itinerant scholars or confined under the thumb of the eldest: "A Jew, however poor, if he has ten sons, will put them all to letters, not for gain as Christians do, but for the understanding of God's law—and not only his sons but his daughters too" (School of Abelard, c. 1150 CE).[2]

What is significant about the Talmudic regimen in keeping the Jewish communities alive intellectually and socially was this endeavor toward the universal education of their young and at the same time allowing for their meritocratic advancement through Talmudic dialectic. Unlike Christian scholasticism, these "winners" were never bound by celibacy and in contrast were obliged to follow the biblical injunction, here reinforced by the rabbis to reproduce and bring more talented children into the defensive fold. And at the same time given the material constraints imposed upon them by the dominant hostile "weltanschauung" of both Muslim and Christian warrior and clerical oppression, there were few material acknowledgments for individual attainment, merely the fame thereby achieved within the community, perhaps marriage to the daughters of successful entrepreneurs. And here such fortuitous arrangements rarely allowed for more than continued study and procreation.

While the Jewish communities under Muslim overseership stagnated from the 12th century, in part due to the continued importation of slave workers and the gradual decline of their cultural, economic and eventually, military power, the Sephardim and Ashkenazim maintained their independence and cultural integrity. The relative success of the Jews in Spain, first under the Moors and later also in Spain and Portugal, under the Christian warlords, both ruling groups needing the skills of Jewish intellectualism, this relative success eventually led to the agitation of the friars and the relatively unskilled Christian populations, to the expulsion of the

Jews. Their subsequent success in the Mediterranean lands, Muslim and Christian, and then in tolerant Holland established them as an elite minority community in the changing world of the 16th and subsequent centuries, viz Baruch Spinoza.

For the Ashkenazim it was a slower process. Talmudism held its sway over the Jewish masses until the mid-18th century in the West and until the late 19th century in Eastern Europe. The test of the impact of this 1500-year defensive cultural regimen under the rabbis came as the Jews were allowed to leave this socio-political "ghetto" starting in the 18th century. The *Aufklärung* allowed the Jews to gradually emerge into the light of a new Western civilization in the making. Upon release, the general Judaic reaction to the *haskalah*, was a sneering rejection of Talmudic education and rule by many of their intellectual elite, here similar to the Christian intellectual's antipathy toward the scholastic rule of the church.

Bailing Out the Ship

And thus a new Judaism was demanded by history. There is no question but that of all the competing and daughter religions of Judaism, the impact of this religion, the materially weakest of them all, was the most morally powerful. It created out of this people the intellectual potential which quickly showed itself from the mid-18th century as the Jews were emancipated. They roared out of their ghettos, competing on at least equal footing with the most advanced educationally, culturally, and economically of their Christian brethren.

But because Christianity was still embedded in the political and cultural fabric, in spite of the weakening power of institutionalized religion, a mass exit of Jews from Judaism occurred among this new elite. They quickly shed their Judaic heritage, either converting to Christianity or pretending that their Jewishness never existed. The demand of the secular authorities came quickly. Powerfully exemplified in the Napoleonic reforms, rabbinical law would no longer have priority in the allegiance of the Jews within the state

The Enlightenment had opened up the new knowledge that had been brewing in the Renaissance rediscovery of the ancient Greek vision of the natural world. Next came scientific inquiry and the secular philosophical study of the physical and human worlds. The new science and the industry and technology that it promoted were a mental aphrodisiac that few intellectual Jews could put aside. The process gradually moved from West to East. But by the end of the 19th century the entire world of the Ashkenazim was aflame with this secular vision.

What we consequently observed, as related in earlier chapters, was the desperate attempt by the rabbinic leadership at all levels of thinking, to reconcile the synagogue and the basic theological elements of Judaism with this new knowledge. Is it fair to say that the situation facing Judaism by the early 19th century was similar to that which occurred in the period between 100 BCE and 100 CE when, as also noted above we saw the splintering of Judaism into many sects? And of course, out of that chaos came Rabbinical Talmudism and its miracle-working concept of "the lie of words," the Oral Law.

Judaism is still in crisis, none of the current attempts to bail out the floundering ship has resulted in a movement to bring about a new orthodoxy, Reform, Conservative, Reconstructionist, Humanist synagogue Judaism to the contrary. The process of assimilation and loss to the Jewish community continues and at an alarming rate. The most reactionary groups, Hasidim/Haredim, in the sense that they attempt to return to a more ancient version of the faith, partially Talmudic, partially emotional messianic and rejectionist in terms of modernity, have modestly increased in numbers by virtue of their Torah and Talmudic pursuit of large families.[3]

If we ask, what kind of Judaism exists at the turn of the 21st century, in comparison with the general nature of religious affiliation in our world, we can only respond in sadness. Ironically, the great achievement of the Talmudic 1500 years of defensive intellectual study has contributed to this current malaise of decline and stagnancy. The greatest minds of the modern world that the Jews have produced have largely abandoned overt membership in the Jewish community as represented in synagogue affiliation. The new worldview of science and national citizenship has given the modern Jew a new worldview for his strivings, both intellectual and moral. But its human center no longer affiliates with institutional Judaism.

As Mordicai Kaplan articulated, Jewish belief must evolve beyond supernaturalism. But to where? Few Jews today truly act as though they believe literally in the laws of Moses as given to him by Yahweh. The very philosophical ordering of the nature of our physical and social worlds has irrevocably changed from what existed three centuries ago. The great Jewish creative achievements of the last three hundred years have not emanated from the Talmudic Rabbinate. Those Jews who we most admire are exemplified in the learning and outlook of Sigmund Freud, Albert Einstein and the apostate Karl Marx. Few rabbis today could defend even to their congregations the reality of divine revelation and personal salvation. And indeed, the high intellectual achievement of the Jewish community does not lend itself to the fear mongering, the psychological dependency and educational debasement of the masses, currently witnessed in their obeisance to church or mosque.

The Jewish heritage remains a fragile treasure. There as yet does not exist a pathway for making Judaism once more a vital contributor to the destiny of the civilized world. Judaism, to survive from being a mere cult devoted to ritual celebration or mourning, must look forward. Especially and importantly it must, as it did in the great movement of inclusion of the "god fearers" of the Hellenistic world, begin to not merely ingather those many Jews who have fallen by the wayside. Judaism must also bring together within its broad moral and intellectual tent, the many "goyem" that likewise search for a center of progressive, rational, moral commitment.

In the next chapter we shall explain in terrifying terms the critical need for Judaism to look beyond cult and create a larger imprint on the future of our species. The *Holocaust* demonstrated how alone Jews are in the world. Two generations beyond this inexplicable event the Jews are no more secure, and the fate of humanity is also, less so.

CHAPTER EIGHT

Holocaust: A Message for the Jews

Significance

It is difficult to assess the relative status of the *Holocaust* as an event in the history of a long-suffering people such as the Jews. To this writer, as with many others of the generation that saw so many of their own loved ones destroyed in this horrific event, it was the greatest tragedy ever suffered by the Jewish people. Whether or not the outside world sees the *Holocaust*, as do so many Jews, as the most barbarous event in human history, especially given the advanced cultural and historical conditions of the perpetrators, it is critical that the Jewish people learn truth from this horror.

It is a fact that the state of Israel constitutes an admission, a confession by the international community. There is a powerful element of expiation here for its guilt in allowing the *Holocaust* to have occurred. And this has been a good, for Israel has taught the world how a nation can exist in liberty and democracy, even as it has been militarily attacked many times, its very existence threatened every day by terrorists.

But there is an additional lesson for the Jewish people in general about the origins and perpetration of the *Holocaust* that must be learned. This is especially true for the Diaspora, since one suspects that the Israelis have learned this truth, at the least implicitly. In this chapter we shall elucidate our argument as to the real meaning of the *Holocaust*, one that has been repressed within the teachings of the Jewish community. This repression is due to a misplaced fear of what this understanding might do to inflaming the world, once more against the Jews.

European Anti-Semitism: Retrospect

We have noted above the great activity in the various synagogue movements in the 19th century to absorb the growing flood of Jews not merely arriving on American shores in search of opportunity, economic and social, but also fleeing the anti-Semitism especially rooted in the ruling ethos of the East European nations. The synagogue establishments not only had to deal with an impoverished clientele, but also with the growing social and political enlightenment of these masses, in Europe and the United States, increasingly attuned to the secular voice of science and its impact on economic and social forms of life.

Europe, seen from across the Atlantic was of course retrograde in opening its political and economic doors to the Jews. But they were opening, and the Jews had been rushing in since the mid-eighteenth century. By the beginning of the twentieth century even Eastern Europe and Russia were astir in gradually giving rights to its Jewish minority. Yes the masses kept flowing into the United States, very often establishing as their locus of institutional allegiance, political and fraternal organizations outside of the synagogue. This threat of assimilation, intermarriage, and secularism alarmed the rabbinate, and pushed them hard to bring the various congregational associations in line with a modernity that could remain in balance with Torah and Talmudic teachings.

The germination of the Zionist movement at the end of the nineteenth century, especially in the Germanic states did not move the American institutions. Reform Judaism was explicitly opposed to Zionism, for it saw the renaissance of Judaic life as being part of an international religious movement encompassing Europe as well as the Americas. There were elements in orthodoxy which always revered the Holy Land as a source from which the Messiah might one day arrive. In general however, it is agreed that Zionism as it began to attract adherents from all over Europe, was basically a secular political and sociological movement meant to extricate the European Jews from what was then an increasingly hostile anti-Semitic cacophony that grew louder with each official liberal political enactment in the respective nations that gave the Jews equal rights.

As the governments of Europe increasingly became exposed to scientific progress, as exemplified in industrial, technological, and medical advances, they feared for the existing system of social hierarchies. As the burgeoning masses of proletarian workers increasingly were being seduced by socialistic and communistic ideas, and overseas an America with open doors and open political and social opportunities was gaining in strength, the Jews were beginning to demonstrate the significance of their inheritance from the segregated past and Talmudic defensive education.

As we advanced into the middle of the nineteenth century the anti-Semitic chorus became ever less an objection to the bizarre appearance, odor, and parochial ways of living of Jews apart from the center of Christian social patterns. Recall the concerns of a Kant and the more hateful remarks of a Fichte, cited in Chapter 6. No, the Jews were now rapidly learning how to "make it," assimilating and joining the establishment elite, in business, academia, and the classical arts, often even while maintaining their allegiance to the liberalized or orthodox synagogue.

A hint of what was soon to become a chorus of subtle defamation could be seen in the early and infamous anti-Semitic comments of Martin Luther, cited earlier. Here we had in the sixteenth-century Reformation awakening in the German north his peasantlike expatiation on the power of the few Jews in his midst. In reality his diatribe was an early warning that the few emancipated Jews were already showing their Talmudic *bona fides* in being able to compete with their German brethren when given the chance. More contextually Luther's diatribe reflected what one sees today in the Islamic world, the deep regret that even one Jew could arise from the confines of the ghetto and participate successfully with his non-Jewish brethren

By the end of the nineteenth century the awareness of Jewish civilizational dominance grew wholly out of proportion to its numbers, and with many more panting at the gates in Eastern Europe, began to arouse widespread fears mainly but not solely in Germany. Note that the Jewish medical tradition stretches back deep into the Muslim era, e.g., Maimonides, d. 1204 CE. In 1881, when Freud was beginning his medical career, Jews already made up sixty percent of Vienna's doctors. By 1900 a majority of university clinical chairs and medical directorships of city hospitals were in Jewish hands. Jewish researchers: Bela Schick, Josef Breuer, Emil Zuckerkandl, Sigmund Freud, Alfred Adler, Otto Rank, Karl Abraham, Heinrich von Neumann, Karl Landsteiner, Oscar Lowi.

The chorus of hatred was renewed. In Germany, Wilhelm Marr (1819–1904) became the epitome of the classic anti-Semite and raw loathing without end; he authored *The Victory of the Jews over the Germans*, 1879. This book went through twelve editions. Simply, wrote Marr, the Jews were trying to dominate the Germans; they should be driven out. His sub-theme: "The Way to Victory of Germanism over Judaism."[1] Ironically, Marr was the son of a Jewish actor.

Theodore Fritsch, 1852–1933, *Handbook of Anti-Semitism*, 1896, an enormous success, was developed from his earlier, *The Riddle of the Jewish Success*, 1887.[2] Fritsch's theme espoused the purification of the *Volk*, the return of the German people to the ancient rural German ethic. His writings and persona strongly influenced both Himmler and Hitler, to the point of stimulating them to incorporate special rituals for the Hitler youth and the SS, intent on bringing back the ancient glories of the Teuton/Nordic heritage. A typical phraseology of Fritsch: "The crooked thinking" of the Hebrew whose "brain is a provocation-machine with a perverse way of thinking . . . the born bacillus of decomposition," echoes the Nazi rhetoric to come.[3]

L. Woltmann, a follower of Gobineau, in 1904, offered a different kind of "appreciation" of Jewish intellect and power, one with which many democratic liberals would agree long into the 20th century: ". . . the substantially higher percentage of Jews in institutions of higher education cannot be accounted for by superior ability, but can be explained by the 'family hot-house culture.' Jewish pseudo-intellectualism is a sign of the collapse of the race under the strain of the modern." Woltmann certainly was early echoed by modern environmentalists who attribute omnipotence to family culture.[4]

One of the great influences in Germany was the writing of Houston Stewart Chamberlain, especially his *Foundations of the Nineteenth Century*, 1900. Chamberlain wrote that Germans would lose their greatness if they did not protect themselves against the Jews, for the Jews were using their unique racial qualities to destroy and conquer the Aryan world.[5]

A preeminent German intellectual at the turn of the 20th century, the sociologist Werner Sombart, was the author of *The Jew and Modern Capitalism*. Sombart hesitated in attributing Jewish economic hegemony over the Christians from the Middle Ages to the early 20th century as due to their higher intelligence. For him, as for Woltmann, this dominance could be laid at the door of tradition, "the pathological qualities of mind required for adaptation to a foreign milieu."[6] The Jewish eugenicist Nathaniel Weyl saw Sombart as highly complementary of Jewish intellect in his earlier writings, c. 1911, even though in the end he became "an apologist for the Nazis.[7]

The theme of Jewish parasitism was enunciated by Herman Ahlwardt, a member of the Reichstag, in 1896. His views had many prior and then enthusiastic contemporary advocates, and throughout European society. In theory, Jewish dominance and power in the abstract disciplines of trade, banking, philosophy, science, medicine, literature, the arts, seemed to argue for "their non-participation in good hard work." This point of view was epitomized in Otto Boeckel's (1859–1923) view of the Jews as exploiters of the rural peasantry (1922, *Die Deutsche Volksage*). This position became the political rallying cry in the Austrian march toward Nazism. In fact, at the anti-Semitic demonstrations in 1923 in Austria, speakers claimed that Jews owned seventy-five percent of the apartment houses in Vienna, and that workers had to surrender three-quarters of their earnings to the Jewish bankers.

Julius Streicher of Nuremberg spoke at these rallies urging Austrians to attack any woman who dated a Jew.[8]

Jewish Self-hatred and Zionism

The intermarriage rate in both Berlin and Vienna in 1900 was approximately 15 percent. Between 1868 and 1903, 9,000 Austrian Jews renounced Judaism. Naturally most of these converts were the Jewish elite eager to obtain positions of power, wealth and influence in their respective professions. Gustav Mahler is reported to have converted when, after being considered for the position of music director of the Vienna State Opera, Wagner's widow objected to a Jew conducting her late husband's work. Also converting were Arnold Schoenberg; Karl Kraus, the journalist; Alfred Adler, psychologist; Victor Adler, head of the Social Democratic Party; Edmund Husserl, philosopher, and the industrialist Karl Wittgenstein and all of his children who converted to one or another Christian faith, in Austria, almost always, Catholicism.[9]

While the conversions had been and were continuing to take place, many Jews reacted to this spewing hatred by accepting its premise. Arthur Schnitzler: "Anti-Semitism became popular in the early 1880s in Vienna only when the Jews themselves took it up."[10]

"Franz Kafka's friend Felix Weltsch wrote in the Zionist journal *Self-Defense*, that the Jews must 'shed our heavy stress on intellectual preeminence . . . and our excessive nervousness, a heritage of the ghetto . . . We spend all too much of our time debating, and not enough time in play and gymnastics . . . What makes a man a man is not his mouth, nor his mind, nor yet his morals, but discipline . . . What we need is manliness."[11]

T. Lessing, 1930, presented his list of Jewish anti-Semites: Paul Ree, Otto Weininger, Arthur Trebitsch, Max Steiner, Walter Cale, and Maximilian Harden.[12] Also, included were Wilhelm Marr and G.R von Schőnerer. Much later, in our own day, Isaiah Berlin analyzed the special and egregious cases of Jewish self-hate exemplified in Karl Marx and Benjamin Disraeli. He also included in this list of self-denying Jews, Walter Rathenau (Chancellor of Weimar Germany), assassinated, 1922; and Simone Weil (1909–1943), philosophical mystic, who converted to Catholicism in 1938; she became a fighter against fascism.[13]

Scholar of Jewish history and life, Raphael Patai reports on his own observing of a march of the Histradut, Labor Organization's celebration in Tel Aviv, in 1933: Printed on their banners of parade: "A parasitic people had become a people of workers."[14]

Centralverein deutscher Staatsburger judischer Glaubens (CV), 1893, was the leadership institution which increasingly defended the Jewish community.

The CV leadership: Max Bodenheimer, Franz Oppenheimer, Theodor Herzl. The First Zionist Congress was held in 1897.[15] The Zionist argument could be said to be based on its potential for improving the Jewish psychological handicaps of the past: To Theodor Herzl the primary goal was to eliminate Jewish servility, opportunism, lack of dignity, the ghetto mentality. Others leading the movement were Richard Lichtheim, Kurt Blumenfeld, Sigfried Kanowitz, Adolf Friedmann, and also philosopher, Martin Buber.

Here was a powerful movement, Zionism, incubating in the German speaking nations but quickly spreading throughout Europe. It was completely divorced from the ongoing institutional synagogue search for religious revival. Critical to its explosive resonance in the Jewish soul was the writing and advocacy of an enigmatic and perplexing young eminence, Theodore Herzl.

Theodor Herzl was born in Budapest, 1860, of a religiously liberal Jewish family. He preferred Nordic-looking women, sang Christmas carols at Christmas, and fell into a bad marriage; he did not have his son circumcised. He wrote in his diary "If there is one thing I would like to be, is a member of the Prussian nobility." He saw the problem of being a Jew, and his own solution, Zionism, out of his vain attempt to leave Judaism behind. However, he would not convert in order to turn his legal education into a judicial position. He remained a member of the Jewish *Gemeinde*, even though he was not religious. He saw anti-Semitism being turned into a racial phenomenon, ". . . the modern petrol."

Herzl himself paid for the publication of his revolutionary book, *The Jewish State*, 1896. At the time he was literary editor of the *Neue Freie Presse*, perhaps the most liberal newspaper in Vienna. He was also a frustrated playwright. However, he was always respectful of the religious orthodoxy of many of his members. Herzl had to shift early Zionist conferences from Vienna to Munich because Vienna had no kosher restaurant. After his sudden death in 1904, at the age of 44, the Zionist movement was headquartered in Berlin.[16]

But of course Palestine was part of the Muslim Ottoman Empire at that time, and it was only surreptitiously and circuitously that Jews were able to make their way to Palestine. This was the situation until the end of the First World War and thus the dissolution of the Ottomans. Then, when under the British Mandate, 1919, a recognition of the Jewish presence in their ancient land was made by the West.

What was important for the flourishing of the Zionist dream of a land of their own for the Jews, was that it was not assimilationist. Nor was it exclusionary, in its secularity and independence from the synagogue. A variety of Jewish minds here could come together to envision the forthcoming catastrophe that was brewing in Central Europe for the Jewish people, but even here without a means of self-defense against this brewing conflagration. The hope was for refuge as well as renewal, perhaps in Zion, even at some point independence as a people, politically.

Dawning Light: Recognition

A defender, Friedrich Nietzsche, *Human, All Too Human*: "The Jews have produced the noblest human being (Christ), the purest sage (Spinoza), the mightiest book and the most efficacious moral code in the world . . . In the darkest periods of the Middle Ages, when the cloud banks of Asia had settled low over Europe, it was the Jewish free thinkers, scholars, and physicians who, under the harshest personal constraint, held firmly to the banner of enlightenment and intellectual independence and defended Europe against Asia."[17]

Ernst Kretchmer, a non-Jew, who did research into the national/racial profile of Germans with respect to their high talents, did not include Jews specifically in his study. However, one prescient comment slipped out in this 1919 research. "There is a kernel of truth about claims of genius, even one would suppose, about claims regarding Jewish superior intelligence."[18]

Hans Guenther, later one of Hitler's favorite scientists, in 1930, tried to explain Jewish success in the modern world by the Jews' need to struggle to survive using their abilities in areas like commerce and finance and urban skills that were reserved for them when barred from traditional agricultural and social/political ways of life. The parasitism thus forced upon them, their need to learn to get along with majorities formed their ethnic character. This circumstance of living as a minority among foreign peoples, thus to adapt and survive, produced their prudent demeanor, adroit speech, versatile calculations, a special intelligence required in predominantly urban environments, trading in merchandise, and money transactions. Thus is explained "the considerable average intelligence which distinguishes the Jewish people."[19]

Fritz Lenz was the lead author of the most influential textbook on heredity and eugenics, translated into English, 1931, to be used in American colleges. It was later used in the *Third Reich*. His book had a very odd perspective on Jewish intelligence for one to be favored by the Nazis. ". . . Next to the Teutonic, the Jewish spirit is the chief motive force of modern Western Civilization. The emancipation of the Jews has had an effect like that of one of the waves of Nordic blood upon the Indo-Germanic civilization. Were it merely through the diffusion of Christianity as one of the main roots of western civilization, the Jewish spirit has been decisively effective in universal history . . . .Jews and Teutons are alike distinguished by great powers of understanding and by remarkable strength of will; Jews and Teutons resemble each other in having a large measure of self-confidence, an enterprising spirit, and a strong desire to get their own way—the difference being that the Teuton is inclined to seek his ends by force, the Jew rather by cunning."[20]

As with the above German scholars, there were others interested in the phenomenon of explosive Jewish talent. Many were objective inquirers outside of the anti-Semitic hatred of the street "populists," here included is the Catholic venom which precipitated the Dreyfus trials in France. Scientific minds with modern research methodologies could now scientifically examine the puzzling issue of the existence of so many "smart Jews." How should one evaluate their rise in society and their possible national influence?

That debate was taking place in France towards the end of the 19th century over the rising influence of Jews on French culture. It was epitomized by an unusual question set forth by Anatole Leroy-Beaulieu {a non-Jew} ". . . whether there is a Jewish genius or spirit, that is to say, whether in letters, science, or politics the Jew is characterized by a national genius or a national spirit different from that of the nations among whom he lives."[21] . . . "I have heard Germans urge this intellectual precocity of the Jews as a reason for debarring their children from the schools and colleges attended by other children, 'The struggle' they {the Germans} said 'between the sons of the North, the pale Germans with their blond hair and sluggish intellects, and these sons of the Orient with their black eyes and alert minds, is an unequal one."[22]

Francis Galton (1822–1911), first cousin of Charles Darwin (Erasmus Darwin was his grandfather), also, an eminent scientific mind in his own right, had the typical upper class prejudices against non-English intruders into "their island empire." In 1869, Galton had commented on the presence of genius in Jews and Italians, "both of whom appear to be rich in families of high intellectual interest." Galton, on his decades-later photographic trip to Bell Lane School in London: Jews: ". . . children of poor parents, dirty little fellows individually, but wonderfully beautiful, as I think, in these composites". . . in the adjoining Jewish quarter, "cold scanning gaze of man, woman, and child. . . . There was no sign of diffidence in any of their looks, nor of surprise at the unwonted intrusion. I felt, rightly or wrongly, that every one of them was coolly appraising me at market value, without the slightest interest of any other kind."[23]

This, with all of his scientific dispassion, Galton could not yet throw off his own colloquial prejudice against the Jews. So similar was this public view of Jews to that of the apostate Jewish Londoner, Karl Marx. What other curiosity could a Jew have of status Englishmen, other than a pecuniary one?

Hitler: Rationale for the *Holocaust*

Hitler, a minor non-commissioned officer on the losing end of WW I, and with deep and imagined resentments against Viennese Jews, was asked on September 16, 1919, by his commander, Captain Karl Meyer, in Munich, to write a critique of 'anti-Semitism.' Hitler wrote to distinguish between an anti-Semitism that was "emotional, leading to the chaos of a pogrom and an anti-Semitism of reason/ *Vernunft* . . . which in the hands of a powerful government could lead to planned measures against the Jews and, in the end could bring about their complete elimination (*Entfernung*)."[24]

This was the beginning of Hitler's expressed malignant hatred of the Jews. His activist and demagogic political crusades put him in a Weimar jail during the mid-1920s. It was there that he wrote out this expressed hatred, of course fueled by the now deep anti-Semitism building in the masses for the rise in Jewish accomplishment and leadership, the participation product of the two German nationalities having opened their gates.

Hitler's *Mein Kampf*:

> The fact that nine-tenths of all literary filth, artistic trash, and theatrical idiocy can be set to the account of a people constituting hardly one-hundredth of all the country's inhabitants, could simply not be talked away, it was the plain truth." (p. 58)

> And when I learned to look for the Jew in all branches of cultural and artistic life and its various manifestations, I suddenly encountered him in a new place where I would least have expected to find him. When I recognized the Jew as the leader of the Social Democracy, {Walter Rathenau}, the scales dropped from my eyes. (p. 60)

> Today he passes as 'smart' and this in a certain sense he has been at all times. (p. 300)

> Finance and commerce have become his complete monopoly. (p. 309)

> With his deftness, or rather unscrupulousness, in all money matters he is able to squeeze, yes, to grind, more and more money out of the plundered subjects, who in shorter and shorter intervals go the way of all flesh. (p. 311)

> By way of stock shares he pushes his way into the circuit of national production which he turns into purchasable or rather tradable objects, thus robbing the enterprise of the foundation of a personal ownership . . . .Finally, the Jewish influence on economic affairs grows with terrifying speed through the stock exchange. He becomes the owner, or at least the controller of the national labor force. (p. 314)

> . . . {T}he Jewish people, despite all apparent intellectual qualities, is without any true culture, and especially without any culture of its own. For what sham culture the Jew today possesses is the property of other people, and for the most part is ruined in his hands.[25]

The hatred of the intellectual and his free expression of ideas and enterprise is reflected at the earliest point of this gaining of totalitarian power in Germany. Joseph Goebbels, Hitler's minister of National Enlightenment and Propaganda, announced a book-burning day (Jewish and communist authors), May 10, 1933.

For Goebbels, this event was supposed to celebrate for the German people the end of "an age of exaggerated Jewish intellectualism."[26]

Four months later Goebbels rationalized this act to the outside world. In a statement published on September 29, 1933, in the *New York Times*: "The Jews were absolute and unlimited masters of the press, literature, the theatre, and the motion pictures, and in large cities such as Berlin, 75 percent of the medical and legal profession are Jews; . . . they made public opinion, exercised a decisive influence on the Stock Exchange, and were the rulers of Parliament and its parties."[27]

The desire to destroy the Jews, to rid Europe of this "stain," was ongoing both before and after Hitler gained power. Of course, to the German masses this image of Jewish power and exploitation was a great magnet to secure the votes that established his control over Germany. The scapegoating of the Jew was the precipitating element for victory. The terrible economic conditions of Germany during the Weimar Republic, the tribute wealth that was extracted from Germany by the Allied powers following the German/Austrian defeat and the latter's dismemberment largely contributed to the underlying *malaise*.

But there was a further need both for a political/philosophical rationale, a cover, to be able to commit this hoped-for genocide, but with a minimum danger for politico/military reprisals. There existed such a model, a historical stimuli. The former philosophical/scientific opportunity was given by the growth of the eugenics movement amongst the liberal intelligentsia, given the scientific support, then well established by the intelligence-testing tradition (psychometrics), and also the numerous medical advances that linked social malfunction with genetics.

Another path-breaking exemplification of the conscious destruction of populations was first exhibited in the chaotic genocide committed under the dying Ottoman Empires of the Christian Armenian population; c. 1915. Also Stalin's vast genocide of opposition populations, intellectuals, kulaks, Ukrainian peasantry, took place all the while Hitler was consolidating his power over Germany, 1930–1940.

Note that the theme of a powerful Jewish moneyed conspiracy as the cause of all that was evil never left these warped minds until they were utterly destroyed militarily. Hitler's final statement, April 29, 1945:

> It is untrue that I or anyone else in Germany wanted the war in 1939. It was desired and instigated by those international statesmen who were either of Jewish descent or worked with Jewish interests. . . . {T}he nations of Europe were once more to be regarded as mere chattel to be bought and sold by these international conspirators in money and finance, then that race, Jewry, which is the real criminal of this murderous struggle will be saddled with the responsibility. . . . {T}he real criminal {the Jews} would also have atoned for his guilt, even by more humane means {gas chambers}. . . . I do not wish to fall into the hands of an enemy who would require a new spectacle organized by the Jews for the amusement of their hysterical masses. . . .

Holocaust: Teaching the Jews

What were Hitler and the Nazis telling us about the Jews? Indeed, the spewing of poisonous hatred is clear. But beyond the fog of propaganda, there was and is a message that at the very least the Jews themselves ought to take notice of. For this message is still swirling around the globe. Today, the Arab and Islamic world is full of the same invective, the Jewish conspiracy to take over the world. No Jew is therefore safe physically in any corner of this world where this miasma of hatred gains legitimacy.

The message simply: *You are too smart, Jew. You use your smartness to gain educational access, and then to gain a place in the power structure of the advanced world. You become business men, financiers, doctors of medicine, scientists and then entrepreneurs of the most advanced research and technologies, professors in the universities, leaders in the arts and communications, in publishing and the mass media. Clearly, you are getting ahead of us, you are outdistancing everyone else, including ourselves. You are small in numbers. How dare you become so influential, so powerful, even so wealthy. For this you will suffer. No pain is sufficient, except the complete eradication of your genetic imprint on this planet.*

This is not the classic anti-Semitism directed against the synagogue and the rabbi. This is not the anti-Semitism which sees the Jews as incorrigible outsiders and ugly misfits, never wanting in to join the majority, never fulfilling the larger group's obligations of citizenship to protect the commonwealth.

No, this is a relatively new anti-Semitism, traced back a mere one hundred years before the *Holocaust*. It reared its poisonous head when the Jews revealed their Talmudic heritage of literacy, dialectic and high educational potency. The Jews then roared into all those positions in modern civilization which required the talents of the abstract mind.

Jews, don't suppress this truth! Suppression, censorship will not get for you the kindly friendship of the Gentile. All the while you still have to express what is your basic nature as a thinking, creative, highly capable minority. Tell the truth. Tell it so that others, beyond the Chinese, Japanese, and Koreans, who are also highly educationally gifted latecomers, can join this potentially universal club. Teach them about the Jewish heritage, how defense and intellect were achieved in suffering, sacrifice and a holding to ancient moral and religious values, here protecting those basic integrities that mark humans as destined for civilizational life.

A Look Back

The first exemplification of the Jewish affinity for the intellectual values of reason and philosophy came during the Hellenistic occupation of Judea and its influence on the Jewish minorities in this far flung empire. Alexandria, a totally new city quickly became a magnet for Jews fleeing the then-chaos of the Holy Land. Philo and Josephus were merely the peak examples of thinkers deeply interested in adapting Judaism to this modern world.

But even at that remote period, when the Jews were by themselves, with their powerful moral and theistic writings, magnets for these cosmopolitan populations, the "god fearers," the Jewish masses were rapidly becoming a literate people in addition to their holy writings reflecting them as being a "nation of philosophers." Had not their national political yearnings been crushed by Rome, an entirely new history of the Jews could have written. In the two centuries 100 BCE–100 CE, the Pharisees and their rabbinical successors had been strenuously acquainting the Jewish population at home and in the Diaspora, with their literary and religious heritage. It seems bizarre that Rabbi Gamaliel II, who was the controversial leader of the new rabbinical academy in Yavneh, c. 90–110 CE, reportedly was at the same time the sponsor of a parallel academy for the study of "Greek Wisdom."[28]

And as we have noted, Talmudic governance during the period of its fluorescence, c. 250–1750 CE, constituted a defensive political/social regimen undergirded by a commitment to intellectual study and Socratic dialectic. It is ironic that the classical Hellenic intellectual vision was eventually overrun, first by Rome, then by Christianity, and finally by the Muslim Turks. But the Jews, given that they were the religious roots of both Christianity and Islam remained inviolate, even as they were universally oppressed and sometimes bloodied by their daughter religions.

This intellectuality reinforced by a social regimen which demanded that every Jew male or female stand by the redoubts, in defense of the "Books," required literacy and intelligence, disciplined poverty. This took place over a period of 65 generations, (c. 25 years to a generation), and throughout the various Jewish communities scattered about the civilized world.

On the way there were hints of this general tendency toward the intellectual. Saadia came from Egypt to Baghdad to absorb the ancient philosophical fragments being uncovered in the early 10th century. He proposed the twofold truths of philosophy and science in parallel with the truths of religious and supernatural teachings. Two centuries later Maimonides, 12th century, came from Spain to Egypt to promulgate a more unified full blown Aristotelian rationalistic interpretation of Holy Writ. In between and after, in spite of the fragile conditions of life among the Jews, countless thinkers, poets, and theologians contributed to the evolving European civilization. Only at the cusp of the dissolution of the ghetto, did a Jewish outcast, Baruch Spinoza, reveal the new modern vision of secular moral law, that would soon draw in the most creative members of the Jewish family.

Today?

Today there is knowledge. Among the scientific community and intellectuals in general there is an awareness of the special, if fatal gift, that the Sephardic and Ashkenazic communities have carried with them into the modern world. The masses do not know nor do they understand this reality. Suppression and censorship still commands our reality. In spite of Hitler's attempt to wipe the Jews off the face of this earth, 15 million still exist. And they do command the respect of those who appreciate their contributions to our Western civilization, then and now.

There are public criteria by which Jews themselves and their confreres in the intellectual world can measure this contribution. It has been done by a recitation of the famous Jews in all levels of professions and occupations. We will here mostly demur.

However, by 1985, when one could argue that much of Jewish potential had been placed before the world, in terms of the betterment of all of human existence, the Jews, as noted above, then about 15 million in total world population, out of the six billion plus humans on the planet, had won 16.8 percent of awarded Nobel Prizes, 91 out of 540. Of the total awarding of Nobel Prizes, here given by Christian authorities, there is a consensus that many more German Jews (*conversos*) would have been discovered had their ethnic heritage been more closely analyzed. One example, Lise Meitner, a *converso* to Christianity, who fled the Nazis, was later overlooked for her work in nuclear fission, in favor of colleague, Otto Hahn, who quietly remained in Germany during the Nazi period.[29]

The intelligence-testing movement in worldwide use to discover educational and vocational talent, or to predict potential failure, has revealed that full-blown Ashkenazi Jews score at a full standard deviation above the European Caucasian mean of I.Q. 100. This translates into a mean I.Q. among Jews of about 115, some authorities even arguing that it ranges as high as an I.Q. 117–118, perhaps higher.[30]

This higher average in intellectual potential has the result of throwing off a much larger proportion of "geniuses." One scientist, in recent years, argued that the majority of European-origin Caucasians in the United States, mid-1970s, then, c. 176 million would produce as many 160 I.Q. individuals as would the 4+ million Jews. This, because the Jews already had a one-plus standard deviation advantage (15–18 points) over the established Caucasoid mean I.Q., 100.[31] And of course, the observed consequent prediction is that extremely high I.Q. scores lead to high achievements in every area of importance to civilization.

This fact revealed itself powerfully in the war against Nazism and Fascism. Among the few refugees from the Nazis and Fascists to the free West were the following luminaries, in one way or another involved as Jews or with Judaism: A. Einstein; H. Bethe; N. Bohr; L. Szilard; F. Haber; M. von Laue; B. Pontecorvo;

H. Bondi; L. Meitner; M. Born; V. Weiskopf; R. Courant; M. Delbruck; W. Pauli; W. Feldberg; H. Krebs; E. Wigner; O. Frisch; R. Peierls; E. Teller; J. von Neumann.

Most of the above were Jews, others *conversos*, half-Jews, often married to Jews. They were able to get out of Central Europe between 1933 and 1939, before the jaws of Fascism firmly closed. Many subsequently worked on the atomic bomb project; all added to the weight of allied intellectual predominance that made inevitable the obliteration of Hitler, Mussolini, and their Japanese allies.[32]

Can it be denied that the flourishing of the West in the half century after WW II was due in significant part to that remnant of Judaism that either escaped the *Holocaust* or was secure in the refuges that were England, the United States. Also, we must include those remnants that were rescued by the Red Army of the Soviet Union. But in addition, a new reality has since been born, the State of Israel. Here the world powers agreed for but a moment that the destruction of the European Jews was not merely a singular exemplification of Nazi bestiality. All of Europe even, America itself, was in part responsible, a complicity and a negligence that facilitated and allowed for this historic human horror.

Our responsibility as Jews and human beings is to understand the hellish character of the 20th century as prelude to our own. Indeed, Israel was given back to the Jews, a grant by the world community, compensation for its malfeasance. We will next examine the historic nature of what has befallen both humankind and the Jews in this modernity, what it augurs for the future and requires of us, if this world-wide community is to survive as a civilization.

CHAPTER NINE

Israel, Judaism: Our Contemporary World Malaise

History Warns Us

By the close of the 19th century there were many Jews in the developed nations of Europe, especially Germany and Austria, who felt the impending dangers of the gross anti-Semitic hate rhetoric that was filling the minds of these nations. A tiny minority of Jews lived in Germany, a larger minority in the Austrian Empire, mostly the impoverished of the Slavic domains. The Zionists predicted what was to come. A few made their way to Palestine, then under Turkish rule. Most of the poor and still persecuted Jews in Eastern Europe saw the torch of the Statue of Liberty in their minds and attempted to head for the Atlantic ports.

There was not much that the Zionist few could do or persuade to do for their Germanic cultured brethren. Franz Joseph was benign. The German elite saw the Jews as a provider of strength and wealth with their high educational yearnings. The masses below, the petit bourgeoisie, would be exploited by the Nazis and the European fascists for their hatred of the Jew, who was "getting ahead."

But first the growth in wealth and modernization which in part buffered the Jews in their assimilationist endeavors, had to end. And of course, it did. The defeat of the Central Powers, the two German nations, the humiliating Versailles terms of trade and restitution opened the doors to over a decade of political and economic turmoil. Oddly enough, during this period stimulated by much Jewish creativity, the arts and sciences in the Germanies blossomed freely.

Behind the curtain of innovation and leadership among the elite, the groundswell of anger from the masses below grew exponentially. In 1923, Hitler attempted his Munich Beer Hall Putsch, which landed him in jail. This is when he started to write his *Mein Kampf*. The political center increasingly was diminished by the nutcracker press of the left, Communists and Socialists, and the Fascist right. Most Jews were unperturbed. They could not conceive of such irrational political movements coming into control of a highly civilized Germany, or even a now-diminished Austria. As full-fledged members of the middle class the Jews loved their German culture, felt fully assimilated, regularly intermarrying with this Christian elite.

No one could have realized that the 20th century had now created new industrial and technological conditions for war and mass murder. These were now joined to the new power of the national state now determined to survive even if by reaping its grim "rewards" of ethnic and social-class demonization. The hatred for economic and social success, the "Judaization of capital" as it was accumulated in the wild lurch forward in knowledge, finance, and industrial/technological/scientific power, created a dark *golem*, the accusation that those who had ostensibly acquired their wealth and power were illegitimate. They had gained wealth through the exploitation of their fellows.

While the classical Marxists pointed the finger at a social class, increasingly the powers that controlled the national state saw that their own illegitimacy in gaining power could be masked by a counterattack on vulnerable ethnic, religious minorities. This began in the mass murders of the Christian Armenian minority in the last gasps of the Ottoman Empire. Stalin in the Soviet Union saw his opportunity for unlimited power by destroying his intellectual class, and then the independent Ukrainian *kulaks*, farmers.

The Armenian toll was in the one-to-two-million range, of hapless farmers, business people, craftsmen, and many in the upper economic levels of Turkish society. But they were not rich or domineering exploiters. They were Christians. Stalin's toll was in the range of ten to twenty million victims, assisted by government inspired starvation, and the Siberian *gulag*. The ideological cover for these genocidal atrocities as stated, was the supposed illegitimate garnering of wealth and power by these groups.

But these minorities, also the Jews under Hitler, while personally in advance of the mean economic levels of their respective societies did not really control the means of production and consumption so as to fit the Marxist model. They were convenient scapegoats for the dominant powers to cover up their nefarious intentions. Why, because they were highly intelligent and productive people, that which a nation needed desperately to survive. And indeed these genocidal horrors did have their impact on the survival of the respective societies, always to a negative result.

Even in the post-WW II period of reconsideration and reflection on the horrors of these genocides of the elite, it continued. Indeed, we can also turn to Pol Pot and the Cambodian genocide of the indigenous middle class, earlier to Mao's horrific genocide of the "landlord" class, which eventually took the lives of over 40 million of his most talented citizens through government-induced starvation and state-supervised killings.[1] It also happened in Bosnia, with the urban Muslims falling victim to Christian Serbs and Croats.

Genocide of the supposed elites also occurred in Africa, the Christian Igbo of Nigeria in the 1960s, and more recently to the Amharic-speaking Tutsi of Rwanda and Burundi. This is not to discount genocides of more vulnerable peoples such as has recently occurred in the southern parts of the Sudan. In the main the great genocides of the developed and developing nation-states of our modern world have been directed at the educated, seemingly economically advanced minorities.

Today, the Jews are small in number, a prosperous and elite group, truly expecting that as before, the storm clouds are momentary. They will blow away. Serenity will once more come to the synagogue, the prosperous Kibbutzim, the Hillel schools, the beautiful beaches of Tel Aviv.

A Serious Future

Does it sound familiar? And is this not the contemporary situation of the Jews in the still-flourishing lands, of freedom, c. 2013, the United Kingdom, France, and the United States? But are these nations really flourishing? True, there are the beautiful Harvard grads at the top. They and their Princeton siblings rushing into financial cornucopias still have great wealth and power in spite of the economic crashes of 2008–10. Within this elite social class are many prominent Jews, politicians serving the powers in Washington, London, and Paris. The financial sector of this world economy has at its richly bonused management, a disproportionate number of Jews. Do we have to note the symbolic significance of Bernard Madoff? The masses are already beginning to howl at the financial exploiters, the systemic unemployment, the destruction of their formerly vaunted and credit-subsidized standard of living.

In France the large Muslim population is largely dependent on the welfare support of the state. The level of anti-Semitic attacks grows exponentially. Muthathir Mohammed, the Muslim former prime minister of Malaysia, said it very openly. Simply, he blamed the ills of the world and the pitiable condition of the Islamic masses in particular, on the thrust for worldwide domination by the

Jews, all 15 million of them in a world of 7 billion humans, including 1.4 billion Muslims. Heard this before?

What will happen when this as yet inchoate anger coalesces into an organized political movement? Who will then be the scapegoat for the international economic and social malaise?

These questions should not be seen as mere abstract concerns originating in a longstanding level of fear, part of the Jewish inheritance. There are truly serious and ominous social conditions lurking in our conjoint human futures which could make the position of the Jews truly fragile.

The Jews flourished in Europe from the time of the Enlightenment emancipation because of the expansion of resources, economic wealth. These were a product of scientific and technological innovations which allowed for the discovery by Europeans of new continents for trade and mercantile exploitation. The Jews had the knowledge capacities to help in this expansion of opportunity. The industrial revolution which itself started in the days of Moses Mendelssohn in Germany was itself furthered by the discoveries in the use of coking coal, the invention of the steam engine and the explosion of technological control over our physical environment which followed into the 19th and then the 20th century.

Historians are agreed that the "motor" of this advance, which scientific medicine also exploded in terms of demography, was the utilization of cheap energy resources, first coal, then petroleum. As populations rose from, c. three hundred million in 1 CE, to close to one billion in 1804; two billion, 1927; three billion in 1960, then exploded to 6.2 billion in 2000, the explanation has to lie in the progress of scientific medicine in holding down death rates, and the availability of cheap oil and gasoline in providing the fuel for the expansion of wealth through the exploitation of the agricultural and mineral resources of the world. Here the key has been the scientific method and the scientific mentality in dealing with the basic elements of our physical existence.

This explosion of populations in the 19th century and then into the early 20th century took place mostly in Europe, East Asia, and North America. But from the end of WW II, when the West endeavored to right the wrongs of colonialism and extend aid to the undeveloped world, Africa, parts of Asia, South and Central America, and the Islamic world, the explosion has taken place among the poorest peoples of the world. As long as the resources were available the vast transfers of wealth that were available into the first decade of the 21st century continued.

The great worldwide recession of 2008–2010 has revealed some potentially frightening trends. Much of the prosperity of the final decades of the 20th century indeed still depended on the availability of cheap natural resources and available food production and water. From 2000 to 2010 the world has added c. 600 million people, the world population c. 1700. But the prosperity was also based on the ephemeral printing of paper fiat money, extended to poor and rich alike. The essential productivity did not exist to support the mountain of debt that fed this last surge of pseudoprosperity.

And as the world economy crashed there came a realization that the poverty still existing in many parts of the world concomitant with this vast explosion of humans might not be capable of being diminished, rescuing these masses from their fate. Lurking in the not-to-obscure background was the reality that cheap oil which had powered this expansion was running out. Petroleum still existed under ground and under the oceans, but it was scarcer and getting more expensive and rarer with each year, *peak oil*.[2]

Not only were the projections for the free availability of petroleum worrisome, but also water was less and less available for agriculture and life sustenance for these exploding billions of humans. Rational United Nations projections for population growth, mostly in the poorer nations saw a world population of nine to ten billion humans less than two generations into our future.

In 1800 with about one billion people in the world, there were approximately two million Jews. In 1910, with approximately 1.7 billion people on this earth, there were 11.5 million Jews. In 1930 with a bit over two billion people on earth, there were 16 million Jews. We can say that the Jewish population increase in those time periods was not inconsistent with world population increases. Today, after the *Holocaust*, which wiped out six million Jews, there are still c. 15 million. The world population as noted above is now 7 billion.

Statistics of several current world religious populations, as noted in Chapter 1 show that there are: 2,173,184,000 Christians of all denominations; 1,335,964,000 Muslims; 872,000,000 Hindus; 382,542,000 Buddhists; 26,000,000 Sikhs; 7,801,000 Bahai; and 180,300 Zoroastrians. Naturally these figures show ostensible membership, and a number of these religions, Hinduism, for example, are national ethnic religions.

As an international religion such as Christianity and Islam, Judaism has fewer adherents than the Sikh who are basically a subset Indian observance. When the population of the world in 2050 touches the 9.5 billion mark, will there be more than 13–15 million Jews at the current rate of increase in the world Jewish population, considering how many are lost through intermarriage and indifference?

The Jews must plan for the worst, taking Joseph's advice to the Egyptians. We see today the beginning of what tomorrow's realities will be. As even the wealthy nations become poorer sliding back from their most roseate expectation of prosperity and middle-class comfort, *triage* may become the theme of the world at large. The natural resources out of which wealth is created will diminish, the number human competitors for these resources will increase. Already we see the reverberations of unreason.

Is it fair to say that demagogues will search for the scapegoats of this ever-pressing impoverization of the many while the comparative few who make the world function scientifically and socially diminish in number? Already we see the relatively few highly educated acquiring out of proportion to their numbers, the emoluments of power and wealth. Before us already is the ideology of terrorism and quasireligious emotional crusades against reason. Soon, under what ideological or religious flag will they come after the Jews?

Can democracy exist under such conditions? Will there not be demands for saviorlike dictators, a Chavez-like military takeover, perhaps religious leaders, Ahmadinejad, the Mullahs in Iran, and their Nazi-like Revolutionary Guard/Basij storm troopers? The terrorists of Hamas and Hezbollah are clear exemplars of the hate that can universally await us. Remember the Jews have today arrived everywhere in the world as a seemingly privileged minority, privileged by their competence, education, and intelligence, to take leading positions in all walks of life that demand these civilizational human attributes. Can the Jewish people avoid being targeted in the vengeful search for revenge, here a still visible and vulnerable minority?

In times of prosperity all boats are lifted. In times of want and chaos, irrationality and ideology rule. Inevitably there will be a search for the cause of the malaise. Examine the situation today of the nation of Israel. Here we will learn more about the need and the means for survival of this ancient and noble human faith.

Israel's Destiny

In the beginning the vision of the settlers in Ottoman Palestine and then the British Mandate was both religious and utopian. Jerusalem was the ancient capital of Israel. Here was where the two Temples were built, and where Jews worshipped under the tutelage of priests, Levites, prophets, and even Pharisees. Throughout Palestine were scattered holy places for worship and study. Safed in the Galilee during the Middle Ages was one example.

The Zionists, however, for the most part were secular. They envisioned the Jews going back to basics, away from the cities, the ghetto mentality, back to the land, so long forbidden to them. The Kibbutzim thus engaged the future aspirations for a new Israel, socialistic, productive, and democratically egalitarian in nature. This is where idealism was focused at the time of the founding of the state of Israel under the auspices of the United Nations, in 1948. Almost immediately it was attacked from all sides by a number of Arab nations intent on not allowing such a modernistic thorn to be created into the body of medieval autocracy.

The Israelis fought and won their freedom. But it was only the first of continuing wars and the struggle to survive: 1956, 1967, and 1973. After the Arab nations realized they could not defeat Israel in conventional wars, they attempted several *intifadas*. The suicide bombers came from all sides of the Palestinian territories, Gaza, the West Bank, also Lebanon, even from the Arab population living in Israel itself.

Gradually it was realized within Israel, that long-term survival depended on Israel becoming a modern, sophisticated nation on the model of the United States. The people of Israel eventually discovered that they could not survive militarily and economically in the modernizing post-WW II-world based on religious tourism and a kibbutz-based economy. An opportunity occurred when the Soviet state dissolved and close to a million highly educated Jews from the various Soviet republics arrived. Israel gradually loosened the socialistic agronomist model and became a free-wheeling entrepreneurial society not too different from the old European Jewish urban model from which the Zionist founders had hoped to flee.

The explosion of innovative frontier technologies and corporate productivity of Israel's 7+ million population, 80% Jews, has impressed the free world. "Tel Aviv has become one of the world's foremost entrepreneurial hot spots. Israel has more high-tech startups per capita than any other nation on earth, by far. It leads the world in civilian research and development spending per capita. It ranks third behind the U.S. and China in the number of companies listed on the Nasdaq. Israel attracts as much venture capital as France and Germany combined. Analysts at Barclay's write that Israel is "the strongest recovery story in Europe, the Middle East and Africa."[3]

In the most recent year, 2007, for which we have statistics, the percentage of research and development in relation to GDP in the international community, was led by Israel, with 4.9%. Here R&D usually refers to scientific, technological, and industrial research and development. Naturally, smaller developed nations would tend to lead here. For example, Sweden was second with 3.7% of its GDP devoted to R&D. The U.S was listed at c. 2.8%. But then, Israel had to devote much of its GDP to military preparedness and still suffered from rocket and terrorist attacks emanating from Gaza, the West Bank, and Lebanon.

It is clear that in a climate of peaceful coexistence with its neighbors and the Islamic world in general, Israel would prosper and survive, just as Jews have done since the destruction of Jerusalem by the Roman Emperor Hadrian in 135 CE. By then the Jews were literate, armed with their Torah, and their Holy Scriptures, plus a vast arsenal/library of moral, theological, historical, literary writings upon which the Talmud would soon build into the future of this *ethne*.

Out of sweat and much blood the Jews in Israel have built a momentary haven from the real and incipient anti-Semitism in the world, the hatred for modern Judaism's educational, intellectual, political, economic and cultural accomplishments. To understand the destiny of the Jews we must come to the realization that it is a destiny that is integrated into modern Western civilization. In a sense the Jewish people and this momentarily, historically given Jewish state represents the paradigm of the modern scientific, secular in vision, society, leading the world forward onto a democratic, creative entrepreneurial pathway.

A Socio/Scientific Exemplar

The character of a nation such as Israel is shaped by its response to modern dilemmas in science and ethics, in the social and political character of such decisions. Because of Israel's place in the hearts and minds of world Jewry, such social policies are defining.

The American society is today torn apart over sociobiomedical issues such as abortion, stem cell research, and a realm of profound philosophical and ethical issues as to the nature of human life. At the so-called extreme right wing of Christian political activism there exists a large political chorus which views all human life as beginning with the fertilized egg. Abortion thus becomes linked to the killing of human life.

There is here no concomitant negative political expression against military killings both by our own military as well as the tragedy of Americans being killed in war. These views as to our biosocial nature are in part shaped by theological commitments among Catholic authorities as well as by fundamentalist Protestant groups. American Jews have largely distanced themselves from such antiabortion political activity, especially in the light of the medical fact that Ashkenazi Jews carry with them a heritage of inbreeding. With the advance of medical knowledge there is now an understanding of the role of genetics in the appearance of fatal diseases in the newly born such as Tay-Sachs.

It is difficult to point to the initiating dynamic that has placed Israel in the forefront of research in neonatal and other human biomedical areas research. Jews including the late 19th-century Italian-Jewish scholar Cesare Lombroso were among the leading proponents of applying the new sciences of evolution and genetics to the improvement of humankind.[4]

Here is another early Jewish exemplar of this progressive thinking about human destiny. Harold Laski: "The science of Eugenics has been ably defined as the study of those social agencies that may improve or impair the mental and physical characteristics of the race. It is at once a study of national deterioration and of national progress . . . Society will work out its own destiny without eugenics, but with its aid can accomplish its salvation."[5] The above was written in England, in 1910 by a 17-year-old Jewish prodigy, Harold Lasky. Lasky was later to become the leading spokesman for British socialism and the future Labor Party in that nation.

Many of the earlier immigrants to Palestine/Israel in the 1930s were medical doctors educated in the Kretchmer, Guenther, Lenz German eugenic tradition, (see Chapter 8) and carried these values with them as they became the founders of Israeli medicine in the 40s. Thus they did not associate Nazism with eugenic practice, and in fact saw the perpetuation of the *Holocaust* as a vast dysgenic destruction of human talent in Europe.

This Israeli/Jewish-Torah/Talmudic tradition had no religious or ideological qualifications that work against modern neonatal research. Likewise they have enthusiastically endorsed a wide variety of cell-therapy, stem cell research and other reproductive and therapeutic approaches to improve life itself. Thus in contradistinction to the above-mentioned sometimes extremely restrictive Christian views on abortion and research utilizing embryonic materials, the Israelis follow the most progressive approaches of the major scientific research institutions of the world.

The Jews, among others of various religious, philosophical, or scientific persuasions, deny the fertilized egg to be nascent life, and therefore endowed with the legal and moral rights of a fully formed neonate. In fact Orthodox Jews, following the teachings of Torah and Talmud, would not endow the neonate with such rights until thirty days *after* birth. This reservation is enacted to examine whether the neonate is indeed normal in physical and mental health, fully able to participate with family and community in the obligations and benefits of social life. The rule is epitomized in the phrase "*a life worth living.*"

Jewish religious and now secular governmental law in Israel argues that the foetus is part of the mother's body, has no independent human standing until birth, and then for the 30 days after birth when viability and normality are ascertained by medical authority. Israel has probably the most scientifically and medically tolerant approach to the entire reproductive conundrum of any nation.

The rabbis look down upon abortion for frivolous reasons, yet now argue, as redefined through Talmudic analysis of the Old Testament condemnation of "the spilling of the seed," for the principle of the moral and social good of the normal healthy life outlook of the neonate, as noted above, "a life worthy of living." Thus they are intense in their biogenetic search for parents of healthy genetic heritage and possibility, down to the point of genetic scrutiny, if necessary and when possible, of an embryo's destiny {Hashiloni-Dolev}.[6]

The results of this several generation effort to improve the condition of individual life, as well as lessen the burden for family and community of weakened life, has been the great reduction of birth origin disabilities. This has occurred in a nation that has suffered grievous human losses in young people at the prime of their lives, in the defense of their nation.

For example, Tay-Sachs disease kills most children before the age of five. It is transmitted genetically to a greater extent by Ashkenazi Jews. Modern medical genetic screening and the availability for abortions in both the United States and Israel, has since the 1970s eliminated by 95% the number of such births in the United States, and virtually 100% in Israel. Now the scientific medical community in both nations is attempting to identify and eliminate the incidence of other genetically transmitted diseases prevalent in Jews and others: cystic fibrosis, Canavan, and Goucher.[7]

In general one can say that Israel, in spite of living under the threat of the sword has been able to maintain its democratic and rational secular vision of what a Jewish society should be like, philosophically and politically

Will Israel Survive?

Israel has attempted to come to a peaceful resolution of historic differences with its neighbors, mainly through the surrender of land to the Egyptians, and a generally conciliatory policy towards Jordan, both of these nations, as is Israel, are dependent on the United States for both military and civilian aid. There is also some movement towards a military and economic truce with the West Bank leadership of Fattah. Critical has been the ostensible belief of all groups that Israel given the above economic advances, and the Muslim inability to destroy Israel by traditional and untraditional military means.

But this is for the short term. No doubt the suppressed hatred of Muslim for prosperous Jew will not soon disappear. Yasser Arafat, former leader of Fattah had encouraged the Palestinians, in the territories as well as Israel itself, to reproduce, to allow demography to create its own facts on the ground and thus to nudge the Israelis into the sea. And indeed the facts do argue for the Palestinian demographic fulfillment of his program.

Consider the figures. Israel, as of 2008 had a population of c. 6,427,000, living on 8019 sq. miles of land of which 76% of the population were Jews. The rest were mostly Muslim Arabs. In Israel population growth shows a 3.2% increase per year among the Arab population as compared to a 1.8% increase of the Jewish population. This shows a birth rate of 2.9 children per Jewish female in Israel, compared to 3.7 children per female among Arabs. Extrapolating forward, the Arab population in Israel is expected to reach a proportion of at least 30–33% by 2050.

In the territories, the West Bank and Gaza, the demographic contrast is even greater. Gaza has a population of 1,483,000, living on 139 sq. miles. The West Bank has a population of 2,536,000 living on 2,263 sq. miles of land. In Gaza the rate of birth is 5.19 children per female. In the West Bank the rate is approximately 4.1 children per female.[8]

Some optimistic diplomats have pointed to the great economic and social disparities as allowing Israel to act as Singapore does to its less developed neighbors. Here its trade would be to "offshore" less technical manufacturing to these peoples and nations, and thus engage in a mutually advantageous economic relationship leading to stronger political and social ties, and thus furthering the hopes for long-term peace between these neighbors.

In order for such trade to be seen as developmentally advantageous to the Arab peoples and Arab nations there has to be the expectation, as with Singapore's neighbors that they were on the same arc of high valued economic development, only the neighbors progressing on a somewhat slower pathway. Such trade seen as a very long-term or even permanent condition could be considered colonial in nature, and thus be hardly acceptable to the neighbors.

The question then must relate to the possible dissipation of hatred as the Palestinian territories, Egypt, Jordan, Syria, and even Saudi Arabia, the one wealthy nation of possible military competence, rise up in modern scientific productive and social capabilities.

The evidence for such a possibility is not thrilling. Recently a committee of Islamic scholars and diplomats issued a report sponsored by the United Nations. This committee noted that 280 million Arabs lived in 22 nations. All of these nations translated as many foreign books into Arabic as Greece translated books into their own language. Greece is a nation of 11 million.[9]

Among the nine leading Arab economies, several hundred million people, having tremendous amounts of oil revenues to support higher education, between 1980 and 1999, almost twenty years, only 370 new patents were registered with the U.S. Patent Office. In the same period South Korea, with a much smaller demographic profile, 45 million, registered 16,328 patents for inventions.[10]

Between 1980 and 2000, Egyptians, population 80 million, registered 77 patents in the United States. Saudi Arabia with a population of c. 28 million, registered 171, (mostly by resident foreign technologists working for the Saudis.) Israel with a population of 6.5 million registered 7652.[11]

Clearly, such a record of modernization cannot auger rapid progress towards becoming a modern scientific society in the reasonable future, competing with the likes of China or Korea, no less Israel in the production of the fruits of modern technological innovation. On the other hand the demographics of the adjoining Arab world are frightening. Medical knowledge and practice provided by the outside world has led to a diminished death rate from disease and poor sanitation. Poverty rates rise along with seething anger at their own leadership, itself eager to transfer this hatred to Israel, *naturally* the cause of all the troubles in the Islamic world!

The question often asked as to the cause of this retrogression usually results in the conclusion that it is adherence to ancient Muslim tribal traditions that keep the people in backwardness, cause the brutalization of women, and in general has led the Islamic world to turn their backs on science and modernization. It is just as rational to argue that it is their incapacity to deal with the complexities of modern education, science, mathematics, and the organization of modern information-structured societies that lead them back into the primitiveness of mindless obeisance to rote teachings and consequent subservience to religious authority.

Yet, there is no doubt that provided with modern weapons, as was Hamas in Gaza when they unleashed barrage after barrage of rockets at southern Israel, that they can aim ever more deadly missiles into the Israeli heartland. Iran is happy to so provide, and North Korea and China believers in free trade with the oil rich Arab states, will be happy to fund these purchases. And of course, the teeming millions external to Israel, who already dwarf Jewish numbers will not tolerate a wealthy Israel competing with Japan or China, or even the United States for the technological leadership and thus economic wealth in our international marketplace.

Indeed the international community might come to Israel's aid were such threats, including a tactical atomic bomb smuggled into Israel by Hezbollah or Hamas via Lebanon or Syria with friendly regards from Iran. Considering the growing chorus of anti-Israeli, pro-Palestinian sentiment in Europe today, even this hypothesis could be questioned. To prosper Israel needs peace. We have seen in the past, at the hands of the Chaldean Babylonians, the Seleucid Macedonians, the Romans, how the lands of Israel have emptied out as a result of these military incursions. All those high-tech companies now listed on the Nasdaq might be quick to run even under the mere threat of such aggression.

For the future it is fair to say to the Jews of the world: do your best to help Israel to survive and prosper. It is a model of modern Judaism, and a lesson for the world at large. But do not put all of your Judaic eggs in one basket.

The Path Forward

A writer declaims to the world: "Jews make up two-tenths of one percent (0.2%) of the world population, but contributed 54% of the world's chess champions, 27% of the Nobel Laureates in physics, and 31% of the medicine laureates."

Further: "Jews now make up only 2% of the population of the United States, but 21% of the Ivy League student bodies, 26% of the Kennedy Center honorees; 37% of the Academy Award winning directors, 38 % of a *Business Week* list of leading philanthropists, and 51% of Pulitzer Prize winners for non-fiction."[12]

This is the image of the Jew today in the civilized world of the West. The traditional synagogue and the cult of ritual, the dominance over the shrinking Jewish community by rabbinic law is the past. Once, long ago, the synagogue, a Greek word meaning, "coming together" became a place of literate study and debate about the moral and intellectual destiny of the Jewish Diaspora. Philo, of Alexandria, became the exemplar of intellectual Judaism. He was essentially a Jewish philosopher hoping to acclimate the Judaic faith to Greek rationalism. The Talmudists in Palestine and then in Babylonia ignored his work and his brethren in this lost community. Today, in Egypt, they are probably part of the heritage of the harried Christian Copts.

Centuries later it was the Egyptian Jew Saadia in 10th-century Baghdad, who first felt the impact of the rediscovery of Greek rationalist thought, along with his Muslim contemporaries. Later in 12th-century Egypt it was Maimonides, the Spanish Jew who fully absorbed the secular philosophy of Aristotle and tried to join it to the law of Holy Scripture and Talmudic dialectic. The European Talmudists more or less ignored the writings of Saadia and Maimonides.

Then, in the seventeenth century came Spinoza, of Portugese heritage who tried to introduce another reality, modern scientific thought to his Netherlander refugee Jewish confreres. He was rejected in fear. Finally in the 18th-century Enlightenment came Solomon Maimon and Moses Mendelssohn, Ashkenazi Jews coming west to Germany, the former leaving Poland and Judaism in repulsion for its denial of the modern world, the latter welcomed to Berlin, and arguing for a new way forward for the Jewish people, balancing the heritage as a deep historical cultural value with his vision of the future of the Jewish people as joining the world of scientific and secular knowledge.

The Jews can no longer remain an isolated religious sect, turning its back on the reality of knowledge and leadership. It is one of the smallest religious groups demographically. The prosperous minority position of the Jews places them in renewed danger. Still, Judaism carries within its tradition and heritage the most modern vision of what humans could be. No, not necessarily the Talmudic tradition of rabbinic rule. Although the Talmud will always remain a rich repository of wisdom, and should be consulted and studied, it cannot be the formative guide for the creative Jewish mind into the international congregation of humanity in the future.

The flood of Roman and Greek "god-fearers" who once poured into Jewish meeting halls and prayer rooms to take part in Jewish learning and ritual can once more be duplicated in a modern setting. The Jews need not fear such a new infusion of humans desiring to drink from this historic cup and apply this rich wine of moral knowledge to the real lives of humans in our fragile times. The doors of Judaism should swing open to welcome those who want to become part of this tradition of knowledge, rationality, for a belief in science and a heritage of moral defensive discipline. This is what created the modern Jew.

The challenge for Judaism in the 21st century is twofold. The first is to open the doors to those who might want to partake of this heritage and become part of a critical religious fellowship of debate, scholarship learning, and above all futurity. The world needs alternatives to the political totalitarian ideological mentality. The world needs forward-looking grouping of thought and purposeful rational thinking, and outside the political press of unification and conformity.

But Judaism does need numbers, though not masses of uneducated true believers, but those who see the need to integrate the moral with the intellectual. Without the heft of numerous Jews the world will not give a flick of interest as it is pressed to force Judaism into oblivion. That two-tenths of one percent of the world population could disappear in a blink. But consider, a world population of several hundred million alert nay-saying Jews against the irrationality of a globe gone mad. Here, at last, a resistance point.

Second, Judaism must recast itself from the inside. It has over the past two centuries been abandoned by some of its most eminent thinkers. Clearly the Judaism of the current synagogue, a theology appropriate for the 10th century BCE perhaps even the 14th century CE, has since the 17th century gone down the road toward irrelevancy. One has only to look at the roster of great Jewish minds who either converted to Christianity or else left the community because of the Mishnah's matriarchal principle's definition of Jewishness. There are yet millions of secular Jews who still so define themselves in terms of heritage, tradition and intellectual allegiance.

Judaism over the past several thousand years has given itself ever-renewed opportunities for relevancy for its devotees by harkening to the events of the world outside. Talmudic Judaism and the synagogue are themselves products of one of the great Judaic intellectual and social revolutions. Today after a horrific century for the fate of millions of Jews, yet marked by great Jewish achievement, we are obligated to look forward, and plan for those inevitable "seven" tensile years of want.

In sadness we must report the obvious. Synagogue Judaism looks back. It has little to offer a Judaism that wants to survive and prosper. The only forward route that Judaism can follow to survive is one that embraces and utilizes the true power of Judaism, the Jewish creative and intellectual mind. But this mentality is universal, existing in all ethnic groups. It is only Judaism, of all the contemporary religions, and indeed it was the rabbinic and Talmudic traditions, which created the conditions for its efflorescence, that can now contribute a secular moral envisionment for our world civilization.

Here is where a Judaic revival must begin. And as it reforms itself to encompass the values of the modern international intellectual, scientific community, it must take this heritage of Torah, Holy Scriptures, Talmud, as well as the historic struggle of its people, and in a revolutionary manner, as it has done so many times in the past, look to a defensive future of combat against human immorality and irrationality. We must welcome the world to this vision of reason and the good; create a new leadership, transform the existing and ossified institutions; recreate Judaism as the magnet for a great international movement.

Next we will look at historic Judaism, but with modern eyes. We can discern in all the traditional building stones of Judaic thought, ritual and moral commitment elements of the universal. In terms of humanity, here there are eternal verities, ever relevant and capable of adaptation to the new.

CHAPTER TEN

Understanding Historical Judaism

Monotheism

The radical nature of Moses' vision and gift to Judaism and the civilized world was an inner recognition of the unitary nature of the human world of things, powers, and human existence. The evidence argues that the Moses persona was but a few generations beyond the reign of Pharaoh Akhenaton, c. 1350 BCE. Moses lived together with the other Semite corvée laborers in the Delta of the Nile under the rule of Ramses II, c. 1270 BCE. By then the monotheism of the sun god Aton which Akhenaton tried to impose over the traditional priesthood and onto the Egyptian masses was a fading memory. Yet there could have been a residue of believers in this intellectually more powerful construction.

At any rate this conception of one ruling principle in the universe was joined to the powerful war god Yahweh believed in by the Bedouin tribesman, in this case the Midianites of the Sinai, the Arabian and Negeb deserts. We should not think of the monotheism of Moses and the Israelite leadership fleeing Egypt as a primeval religious vision. Let us put a tentative date of c. 1200 BCE on the events of the Exodus. Literacy and the writing down of the various religious myths of the Near East go back to c. 3000 BCE. Much intellectual effort had already gone into varied attempts at understanding the structure of material and social life that we humans had come to inherit in the natural world.

The very fact there had been attempted in a conservative culture such as Egypt to impose a revolutionary religio/intellectual regime testifies to the search by humans even in that long ago realm of urban life, of the need to intellectually purify our vision of reality. This attempt by Akhenaton to disestablish animal and polytheistic worship failed. But it did probably lead in the Decalogue of Moses to the injunction to the Israelites not to engage in the making of graven images, and of course his consequent destruction of the golden calf, puzzlingly encouraged in its fabrication by Moses' brother Aaron from the Egyptian loot confiscated by the fleeing Israelites {Exodus 32:25–29}.

The Shasu Bedouins of the Sinai and northwest Arabia were often mentioned by early Egyptian texts, 15th century BCE. It should be noted however, that subsequent to the attempt by Akhenaton to establish his sun god Aton, monotheism, c. 1350 BCE, reports out of Egypt in the days of Ramses II, c. 1270 BCE refer to them as "Shasu land-Yahweh" indicating a possibly parallel worship of the one preeminent god of the sky.

Many centuries later Aristotle himself would break with the Hellenic worship of many gods to emphasize the philosophical principle of the 'unmoved mover,' an abstract non-corporeal *god* here emphasizing the logical necessity of envisioning a first and abstract cause of the diversity of human experience and knowledge. The *mushites* understood this inchoately. The very mobility of these desert tribal groups allowed for few fixed temples and sacraments, just a fiery disciplinary principle of favor or retribution.

The fact of the various Sashu and Apiru tribes in and around Canaan taking up this allegiance to Yahweh and his demanding laws for living argues for the resonance of the logical power of one abstract principle and its power, unity, and reality. Living on high, unseen, if on occasion descending in discourse with his flock; giving guidance but also much pain when the weakness of humans revealed itself in their immoral behavior; here was a dominating God dispensing blessings or curses. The dominance of Yahweh as the one God to these tribal wanderers could be attributed to the fact that the Israelites and the semi-migratory Bedouin tribes needed only one god in a nondifferentiated economy of animal husbandry and nonurban, nonagricultural migratory patterns of life.[1]

The tribal admixtures in the land of Canaan and the adjoining Bedouin lands were many. Often the gods were as interchangeable as the fate of these migratory peoples. The Pharaoh Menerptah's stele, c. 1207 BCE; states: "Israel is laid waste and his seed is not." The Shasu/Yahweh are also illustrated in a Rameses III stele, c. 1150 BCE, as lightly bearded warriors wearing a "sea people"-like feathered headdress. King David almost one hundred fifty years later is stated to have hired warrior Cherethites from the desert. Earlier they apparently were immigrant sea people from Crete. Well paid, they fought for him {1 Samuel 30:1}.

The hypothesis is that Moses led his people out of the Egyptian Delta in the time of Ramses II, c. 1270 BCE, and purposely avoided the Philistine areas of Canaan {Exodus 13:17–19}. In {Judges 18:30} Jonathon, the grandson of Moses is said to have accompanied the Danites (Danaoi, Denyen, Danuna—these Aegean peoples) in their northern migration from the coast near the Philistines (Samson in Yavneh). The Danites might originally have been descendants of the sea people invasions {Judges 5}.

The archaic Hebrew evidenced in the Song of Deborah {Judges 5}, she a heroic Yahwist, Kenite (Cain the nomad) a tribe related to Moses' wife Zipporah argues for the ancient penetration into Canaan of the cult of Yahweh. Here in a war consisting on one side, of a confederation of Israelite tribes, not all would commit, plus Amalekites, Kenites, Midianites, Edomites, they engage in northern Israel, far from their presumed grazing grounds, an alliance of Canaanite Indo-Europeans (Hittites, Horites, Hivites, Perizzites Jebusites) and Philistines. Yahweh smiled down upon this Semite confederation in their victory over the enemy charioteers.

We are thus in a puzzling context for the introduction of the monotheistic principle among the allied Israelite/Judean tribes. The writings of J & E based on an already ancient literary tradition in the area, this presumably in existence before the arrival of the Mosaic immigrants, c. 1200 BCE, plus J & E the earliest stratum of the Holy Scriptures, set down c. 900 BCE, argues for great fluidity in the chronological systematization found in these two proto-documents, here also applying to the Deuteronomic historical books of Joshua and Judges.

Thus the appearance in Genesis, Exodus and Numbers of highly anthropomorphic renderings of the One God, either as a person conferring with Moses, Aaron, or Joshua, mostly in the J versions, else as a cloud, or from an angelic messenger, these found in the Elohistic (El=on high) version from northern Israel, they, influenced by ancient Babylonian traditions, should not obscure the originating intellectual and psychological powers of the basic nonimagistic vision of a higher authority both moral as well as metaphysical. The struggle against such personifications of Yahweh and the introduction from external tribal traditions of gods such Ashtorath, Chemosh (Samson) and Baal to commemorate the various orgiastic agricultural naturalistic traditions of the Near East was a continual work in progress by the Israelite intellectual class, Levites, priests, and scribes. King Solomon himself surrendered to this recurring syncretic degenerative polytheism.

Circumcision {Genesis 17:9–14}

To further support the above-stated relationship of Moses to the Egyptians is the manner in which the daughters of Ruel/Jethro the Midianite relate Moses' kindness, to their priest father, "An Egyptian helped us against the shepherds" {Exodus 2:19—J-source}. This Midianite Priest, Jethro, invites Moses, the "Egyptian," into his home and subsequently gives him one of his seven daughters, Zipporah, in marriage. In time, she bears him a son, Gershom ("an alien there" or "drove them away") {Exodus 2:22—J-source}. Jethro, in Judges 4, is identified as being a Kenite, as noted above, traceable to the nomadic destiny of Cain, and at that later time a group also related to the Edomites, descendants of Esau, Jacob's twin brother.[2]

These southern tribes seem to be inextricably intertwined with the destiny of the Israelites on their return through the wilderness into Canaan, except for the stated relationship of Joshua to Moses (Moses' assistant- {Joshua 1:1} and Joshua's northern Ephraimite heritage (Shechem).

Probably the most mysterious insight into the origin of Moses comes from the fragment of an ancient Exodus source inserted into Chapter Four of Exodus. This is the so-called bridegroom of blood episode:

"On the way, at a place where they spent the night, YHWH met him and tried to kill him. But Zipporah took a flint and cut off her son's foreskin, touched Moses' feet [genitals] with it and said 'Truly you are a bridegroom of blood to me!' So he {YHWH} let him alone. It was then she said, 'A bridegroom of blood by circumcision'" {Exodus 4:24–26—J-source}. This circumcision of Moses' son by Zipporah, the mother, constitutes an enigmatic moment in Exodus. A son who is circumcised was often called 'bridegroom of blood' in Semitic tribes. The Hebrew word for father-in-law is "one who circumcises" {Exodus 18:2–6—E-source}. In a later incident, both sons of Moses are reintroduced: Gershom and Eliezer (El northern Mesopotamian source, "my God," ezer "help").

The clear implication here is that Zipporah saved Moses' life by circumcising her son and symbolically circumcising Moses in order to deceive and ward off the wrath of YHWH. Moses had seemingly entered into marriage without himself having been circumcised![3]

The next reference to circumcision in Exodus concerns the flight from Egypt. After the Israelites arrived in Succoth, following the Passover sacrifice, which exempted them from the Tenth Plague, the killing of all the first-born of the Egyptians, YHWH gives directions to Moses and Aaron for all subsequent commemorations of the Passover. These require strict observance of the circumcision ritual for all male members of the household, including slaves and resident aliens {Exodus 12:43–49—P-source}.

The act of circumcision was a typical Yahwist/Shasu tribes-people rite. Too, it was the practice among the royalty, most likely also as a rite of initiation for the priesthood and military of Egypt, but not an Indo-European Canaanite ritual. The contemporary Arabic tradition, of descent from Abraham and Hagar,

Abraham's Egyptian slave/wife, through their son Ishmael, continues the ritual of circumcision at age thirteen. This was the age of Ishmael when Abraham and his entire male household underwent the rite at the covenant agreement with God. We have here a P-source story added to Genesis, much later in time, c. 700 BCE {Genesis 17—P-source}.

The earliest historical reference to circumcision in the Hebrew Bible occurs in {Genesis 34—J-source}. Here the brothers Simeon and Levi, full brothers of Dinah, from their mother Leah and Jacob/Israel, avenge the rape of their sister by the scion and namesake of the town of Shechem. They kill all the males of the town, still incapacitated from the mass circumcision to which they had agreed, so as to allow for the marriage of Dinah to Shechem. All the sons of Jacob had beforehand been circumcised.

Moving forward in time, the necessity to circumcise Joshua's warriors, because of the lack of opportunity to circumcise the new generation born to the stiff necked wanderers from Egypt is a tacit admission of the relationship of these peoples to Egyptian practice {Ex. 12:43–4}.

Before the army of Joshua was set to cross the Jordan and give battle to the enemy: "And it came to pass, when all the nations were circumcised, every one of them, that they abode in their places in the camp until they were whole. And the Lord said unto Joshua: 'This day have I rolled away the reproach of Egypt from you'" {Joshua 5:2–9, Masoretic text}.

Circumcision of strangers within Israel was originally optional, but not for the slave {Exodus 12:48}. Later in Priestly times it was required of resident aliens {Lev. 17:10, Numbers 9:14, 15:15, 16}.[4] The belief is thus warranted that originally circumcision was a rite of the military before battle, only later becoming required of all Israelites, then required of slaves, servants, visitors, alien residents, *gerim*, this the Priestly addition, c. 700 BCE {Exodus 12: 43–49}.[5]

Sabbath {Genesis 2:1–3; Exodus {20:8–11} and Dietary Laws {Exodus 23:14–19; 34:18, 26}

In practically all ancient, and indeed modern societies, there exist regulations encompassing the Sabbath, rest periods from labor, as well as dietary regulations, even prohibitions. In our own time these latter rules are mostly encompassed under health laws regulating the preparation of foods, their methods of cultivation, as well as the preservation and cooking of food. In the ancient world, tribal people inchoately understood the need for such discriminations. However, since the exact knowledge governing such inchoate perceptions and experiences was lacking, the substitutes were religious and ritual rules and sanctions.

In the case of the Sabbath, there were widely differentiated responses to a human need to rest from labor. In the Greek and Roman worlds strict divisions of the year were not marked with any regularity. Greek and Roman holidays and festivals were widely dispersed into the working regimen of the population. In the Middle East, and especially in Mesopotamia, the Sabbath was associated with astronomical and astrological analysis. Here the number seven gained its holy significance in that the lunar calendar utilized in Mesopotamia in this era divided the month into units of seven days. There is an element of fear of the higher powers in the establishment of a day of rest on the seventh day. This principle of Sabbath "rest" was adopted by the Israelite priesthood in {Genesis 2}, elaborated in the commandments in {Exodus 20:8–11}.[6]

The term Sabbath is related to Shabattu—the moon cult in Babylon. This is the only celestial influence on Israelite religion. So too, here is derived the sacredness of the number "7," in the Hebrew literature and cult. Shabattu also means "to swear."[7] The Legend of Jephthahs daughter in {Judges 13:34–40}, argues for an annual agricultural deity-type of yearly remembrance. In {II Kings 4:23}, there are reflections on the limitation to work on the Sabbath, but only in {Nehemiah 13:16f} is the Sabbath a day to bring all work to a halt, not merely for a day of relaxation and play. There is no attempt at astronomical correctness in the Israelite celebration of the Sabbath, and no moon cult.

The Sabbath exhortation in book of the Covenant {Exodus 23: 10–11—E} said to leave orchards and vineyard fallow every seventh year so that wild animals and the poor might taste of the free-growing fruit.[8] In {Leviticus, 25:4–7} the beneficiaries are further elucidated: owners, workers, servants, metics-*ger*, guests, animals, cattle and beasts. In Deuteronomy, the fallow fields every seventh year do not appear, instead the remission of debts is legislated.

Whereas in the J and E sections of the Pentateuch the Sabbath restrictions related to the division of labor, and the convening of a day of holiness are rare to find, the basic nomadic husbandry of these primeval Israelite groups stands forth. The great defensive circle of ritual constraint appears in the P revisions, not merely in Genesis, Exodus, and Numbers, but in the newly added book of *Leviticus*, c. 700 BCE, some 200–250 years beyond the writings of J and E. Thus the frightening stoning to death of an individual who gathers sticks on the Sabbath, demanded by the Lord, here agreed to by Moses and Aaron, is a priestly addition {Numbers 15:32–36}. No longer applying to Israelite tribal entities, we now see the extension of the Sabbath ordinance to the larger national community, here including slaves, resident aliens, the *gerim*, and servants in the home and field.

> Remember the Sabbath day to keep it holy. Six days shalt thou labour and do thy work; but the seventh day is a Sabbath unto the Lord thy God, in it thou shalt not

do any manner of work . . . for in six days the Lord made heaven and earth, the sea, and all that in them is; and rested on the seventh day; wherefore the Lord blessed the Sabbath day and hallowed it. {Exodus 20:8–11, P}[9]

In Deuteronomy, this priestly recognition of the traditional cosmological creation myth is repeated. But added is a broader historical reminder to the Israelites of the original impetus for peoplehood, Moses freeing the multitude from Egyptian servitude: ". . . And thou shalt remember that thou was a servant in the land of Egypt, and the Lord thy God brought thee thence by a mighty hand and by an outstretched arm; therefore the Lord thy God commanded thee to keep the Sabbath day" {Deuteronomy 5:15}.[10]

The general pattern of extension to the larger Israelite population during the monarchy, especially the vulnerable divided nationalities applies as well to the dietary laws. The highly elaborated distinctions between pure and "tref" is similar to all ancient cultural traditions which attempt to draw a circle of uniqueness around their way of life, the totem and taboo, the pure and impure. But these are largely later priestly regulations inserted into the early books of the Torah.

The statements by the E and J authors, {Exodus 23 14–19; Exodus 34 18, 26} concerning the festival of unleavened bread to commemorate the escape from Egypt coincides with traditional spring agricultural festivals. In remote times these plantings as well as the arrival of a new generation of calving were orgiastic meat-eating events. In this case the demand for seven days of partaking of unleavened bread symbolizes a more disciplined realization of the sacrifices humans must make in the face of possible catastrophe and hoped for deliverance.

Also here repeated twice but again in other books of the Pentateuch is the prohibition "Thou shalt not seethe a kid in its mother's milk" {Exodus. 23:19; Exodus 34:26, Masoretic text}. An ancient tribal superstition is implied here, the mammalian protectiveness of mother and young and the fear of supernatural retribution for such a primeval violation. This is the origin of the Kashrut law of modern Judaic orthodoxy to separate dairy and meat.

While it is unclear why only creatures with fins and scales in the waters may be eaten and not other food sources from the sea such as clams, shrimp or lobsters, it is probable that the prohibition against eating the pig, as unclean stems to a degree on the degree to which sedentary agricultural peoples as contrasted with the semi-nomadic herding Israelites would not utilize pigs. Certainly the Philistine enemy as well as the other settled peoples of Canaan had enclosures of pigs which they bred. Also certain non-Israelite cults had penetrated the land in their worship of the pig.[11]

The purely animal act of eating food here becomes a priestly act—a sacrament. It is one thing for these rituals and sacraments to be mildly enunciated to a people on the move, as with the J and E renderings. The more elaborate sacrificial and food restrictions in {Leviticus 11} and later repeated in {Deuteronomy 14:4–5} are emphasized as part of the priestly sacraments before and around the Temple, a way of solidifying patriotic rigor in a centripetality which demands a division of behavior between the sacred and profane.[12]

Defense: Circling the Wagons

The explanation for the elaborate ritualistic regulation that characterized the P additions to the Pentateuch as well the later Book of Deuteronomy must be understood in terms of the history of the period when these writings were produced. The P priestly writings seem to derive primarily from the rule of the Judean, Hezekiah, d. 698 BCE, and in Jerusalem at Solomon's Temple precincts. The more extensive writings of the so-called Deuteronomic historians appear early in the reign of Josiah, c. 620 BCE, perhaps one hundred years after the Priestly emendations and additions to the first four books of what would become the Torah.

The work of the Deuteronomic historians was extensive. In addition to the book of Deuteronomy itself which originally may have been the first volume of their inclusive history of the Israelites, there were also Joshua, Judges, Samuel and Kings. This very ambitious literary/historical program was probably underway in Shiloh during the tumult with Assyria. Final sections of 2 Kings were probably completed in the period after the destruction of the First Temple, 587 BCE During the period from the breakup of the unified Kingdom, literary expression had been widening in Israel, many prophets in addition to those noted in Kings were wandering the byways of the kingdoms with their followers, often echoing the concerns revealed in the historical material over Israel and Judah's material and moral fate.

On the material end of things, militarily and politically the Jewish Kingdoms were no longer in competition with such as Philistia, Ammon, Moab, Edom. Assyria was on the move as was Egypt in attempting to maintain its influence in the area. By 722 BCE Israel as an independent nation was no longer. Gobbled up by Assyria, a large proportion of its population, the ten tribes, were deported to the mists of the north. Even Judah was now under siege.

Much of Judah's southwestern precincts including the great city of Lachish were enveloped and taken as the Assyrians began their siege of Jerusalem in 701 BCE. Hebrew-speaking Assyrian officers, possibly from the former Israelite military who had latterly joined up with the Assyrian campaigns first against Egypt, attempted to sway the Judean population to surrender. Most probably a vast tribute was paid to the Assyrians who were unable to win an easy victory over this towering fortress, now with its own supply of precious water. But it did remain a vassal of Assyria. Jerusalem had now become the great center of Jewish national pride, the Temple priests supervising a vast sacrificial and tithing operation.[13]

The reign of Josiah was marked politically and militarily by the conflicts between a resurgent Egypt, a declining Assyria and an aspiring Chaldean-Babylonian movement upward from the swamps of the Tigris-Euphrates Delta. Josiah was killed by the Egyptian military in 609 BCE. Culturally and religiously the Judeans were in desperate straits to maintain the now ancient monotheistic moral tradition. The kingdom of Israel had deviated from the Mosaic straight line, massively flirting with Phoenician economics and theodicy. In reality a syncretic Judaism was growing up in both nations, as the prophets Isaiah and Jeremiah lamented in their writings.

The heavy life regulations that one finds in all the books of the Pentateuch derives from this attempt to enclose the Israelite people in a web of ritualistic subservience to the priesthood, to maintain the centripetal defensive enclosing of this people. The regulation of sacrifice, circumcision, Sabbath and dietary specifications became the means to the end. Surely the priests and the Levites were sympathetic with the prophetic themes of the day. They were scholars and historians. But now the unending regulation of Judaic life became the key to maintaining the integrity of Judaism.

Sadly it was unavailing. The Chaldeans were the next to taste the fruits of Judean tribute. The Jews were demoralized. Ultimately their leadership contributed to the destruction of their Temple and to the continuing exile of their intellectual base.

The Oral Torah

The Oral Torah is part of what constitutes one of the great revolutions in Judaism. In a sense, Jewish thinkers turned away from the Written Torah's conception of Yahweh as the all-powerful fiery and vindictive God judging the Israelite people as a whole. The weaknesses of this people had explained to the priests and prophets the terrible disasters that happened to weak kings and the vulnerable people who supported them. It is a tale of woe and a constant reflection of the ancient trials and tribulations that Moses experienced as he led this "stiff-necked" contingent out of Egypt and toward their promised land.

Events had intervened over these many centuries to create new conditions of life and thought. The nations of Israel and Judah were no more. The momentary if century-long bump of political independence represented in the Maccabean revolution and the rule of the Hasmonian syncretists was an ethically marred interlude of priestly corruption and constant military bloodshed. It was concluded by the Idumean (Edomite) tyrant Herod (a converted Jew) and then the complete Roman occupation.

The Jews of the Yehud (Judea) had enjoyed two hundred years of peaceful and largely benevolent Persian rule. Persian expansion into Hellas, and in spite of their subsequent defeat in European Greece, extended an internationalism that allowed for the growth of the Jewish Diaspora. A consequence for their ongoing communication with the Yehud was an involvement of many Jews with this intercommunicating, international commercial environment. As always, with commerce came new intellectual and cultural influence. While the priests imperially ruled in Jerusalem the people far a field were listening to new messages. These influences grew to a torrent with the victories of Alexander and the Hellenizing of the then civilized world.

There was, generation by generation, ever less in the Pentateuchal writings that gave relevance to this new international climate and then the concerns of the people. A Jewish nation no longer existed as a political or even a cultural unit. In contrast to Mt. Zion, Samaria was going its own way on Mt. Gerizim. In Mesopotamia and Persia, as well as in the Hellenistic cities to the west, Jewish communities were growing. A large Jewish immigration to the new city of Alexandria created a new center of Jewish thought which required the translation into Greek of the Torah and then other prophetic writings for a modernizing generation.

Centuries were passing by in which literacy was a requirement for life and prosperity. When the prophet Ezra read from the Torah with explanation to the untutored Israelites at the gate in Jerusalem they already required his commentary on what they were hearing. This was approximately one hundred years after the Persians allowed for the Temple to be rebuilt and Jerusalem to once more be a Judaic center. And thus the scribes (*Soferim*) became a central factor in the education of the Jews to understand the past and to live in the present.

The Persians brought Zoroastrianism with its dualistic tension of the supernatural struggle between good and evil. Their mercenaries brought other "mystery religions," as did Alexander with his attempt to meld Hellenism with Orientalism. While the priesthood flourished in Jerusalem under the protection of Persia, the coming of Alexander unleashed an enormous flow of trade, craft, and wealth which ever more poured into the coffers of the Temple on Mt. Zion.

In the process Judaism fractured. Wealth and power breeds politics. And the Hellenizing Jerusalemites created a political power base called the Sadducees. The Qumran rejectionists fled to the desert with their own interpretation of the Judaic message. The Essenes, Hassidic in orientation and thriving in their mysticism among *am ha arez* also stood apart from the Saducean's odd combination of Pentateuch traditionalism (here they were congruent with the Samaritans), and Hellenic cultural intellectualism.

But it would be the *Soferim* transformed into the Pharisees that would permanently reshape Judaism into a new orthodoxy. Probably the first transformative event was the Maccabean revolt from 166 BCE, which originated in the countryside among the "Hassidim" and their Essene oriented followers. They became a challenge to what would become the Sadducean Temple elite, their traditions, rituals, animal sacrifices, "first fruits," and half-shekel donations during the many festivals, from locals as well as "pilgrimages" from the enlarging Diaspora of Hellenistic times.

The Pharisees, scribes turned scholars and holy men, turned their self-conscious awareness of serving the Jewish community into a political force counter to the Sadducees. The Pharisees took advantage of these movements in establishing their counter-creed. The establishment of synagogues (*bet am*) and prayer rooms first by the Diaspora Jewish communities to discuss not merely Torah Law but also the teachings of the prophets and the writings, became contexts within which a substitute for the Temple sacrifices and rituals could be maintained, and the laws of the Oral Torah could be quietly established as a modern guide for Jewish centripetality.

What is important to note is that the Pharisees promoted as part of their scribal heritage the study of the written Torah, in the spirit of Ezra and Nehemiah, but also the rich prophetic and scholarly literature that was infiltrating into all the Jewish communities of the Yehud and then Judea (Persia and Greece). Thus when the destruction of the Temple occurred in c. 70 CE they were ready to finalize their holy written scriptures TaNaK = Torah-Prophets-Writings in their academy in the town of Yavneh (also called Timnah-Jamnia), now-ancient home of the Judge Samson, the Nazirite.

But in addition to this seemingly conservative capturing of the ancient literature of the Israelites they followed the path of least resistance among the people, the Qumran Hassidim, and Essene dissidents. Thus the hidden revolution in the alteration of the Law of Moses in its written form gave rise to a new at first unwritten "literature" which pretended to also be descended from *Elion* on high and Moses. It constituted a method of understanding the written Torah in these new times when the old vision of YHWH and his rigorous demands no longer seemed relevant. The masses were now alone in the world run by distant and impersonal forces. They needed to become close to a savior god.[14]

An entire panoply of new symbolic meanings was being introduced, disseminated, and the Pharisees, and later the Rabbis, appropriated them with enthusiasm. It is not irrelevant that these same mystery religion elements from Mesopotamia and the Hellenistic states enfiladed themselves into Christianity as well as into Rome itself: angels, demons, the vision of a Messiah to redeem the Jews, judgment, personal resurrection after death, water libations for purification, the struggle between supernatural demons, angels and devils, and gods of good and evil.

The Pharisees, to distance themselves from the cult of Temple sacrifices, created a new sense of purity and holiness. Parush, meaning living apart in purity of ritual observance now including diet, strict Sabbath observance, and circumcision. The skills of these Pharisees originating in the interpretive guidance given by the *Soferim*, scribes, guided practice even to adjust, for example, "an eye for an eye" to more subtly nuanced retribution. They became the scholar manipulators of the old religion of Yahweh as noted above to the point of using the term *Elion*, "god on high."[15] The absolving of the supreme god on high for the fate of the Jewish people was resolved to an expectation of a Messiah, a savior to come. This was hinted at in the First and Deutero Isaiah {7:14; 53}. Both sections of Isaiah were subsequently utilized by the Christian apostles to rationalize the Christ as the true inheritor of the Davidic line.

The Isaiah of the reign of Hezekiah, c. 700 BCE: "Therefore the LORD himself will give you a sign. Behold a virgin will conceive and bear a son, and shall call his name Immanuel" (El is with us). Thus, a savior Messiah for the Jews, but a King who would again establish the glory of Israel as a nation, and all would flock to the family of Jacob. In Deutero Isaiah, written in the era of the Babylonian captivity, c. 550 BCE, the emphasis still is that out of the suffering of today the community will be redeemed {Deutero Isaiah, Chapter 53}.[16]

The issue of "resurrection" surfaced during this period, perhaps earlier reflected in Psalm 73 and 92, probably written after the Babylonian captivity, ended 539 BCE. We here have expressed the perennial need for the reaffirmation that "the prosperity of the wicked does not endure."[17] This set of beliefs entered Rabbinic Judaism, as with the expectation of the coming of the Messiah, as an integral teaching of the Oral Torah, and then the Talmud. It was also part of the absorption of Middle Eastern mystery religious values. Formerly, individual resurrection was foreign to the Jews. The woes of a people, their disasters as well as benefits were part of the judgmental beneficence or wrath of Yahweh on the Israelite nation and their leaders {Deut. 26:14}.[18]

In earlier Yahwistic periods death sacrifices-mourning customs, were frowned upon, man's relationship with God ended with personal death. Since there was no aristocratic class to create the cult of the dead there was a deep antagonism by the priesthood and prophets to such practices as in Egypt {Isaiah 28:15}. Tabooed mourning practices can be found in Amos, Isaiah, Micah and in {Leviticus 19:28} and {Deut. 14:1–2}. Yahweh resides in the mountains or in the Temple, never on earth or in the sky. Never in the Israelite scheme of things was there an agricultural god or sky deity, and never a cult of the dead. The priests and Levites of Israel feared the cult of Osiris. None of these concepts were in the original Mosaic teachings. No inherited nobility lasted long enough to motivate resurrection dreams. True, there were to be Israelite kings, but none claimed deification. Only much later, as in the book of Daniel, resurrection became popular, this after the time of the Maccabees, first adopted by the Pharisees—from folk Babylonian cults, now inserted into the Oral Law.

The Matrilineal Principle

The central statement on the matrilineal principle is found in the Mishnah, (Repetition), one of the earliest compendia of Talmudic writings, c. 200–250CE, M. Qiddushin 3:12 (see also M. Kiddusin 68b); codified in Talmud: Shuchin Aruch Even Ha Ezer 8:15; in the Jerusalem Talmud Yevanut 13a; Babylonian Talmud = Tractate Yevanut 23a.[19] Often this principle is argued to be based on {Deuteronomy 7:3–4 and Ezra 10:3}.

The Mishnah formulation is a relatively late presentation of the perennial Israelite concern about intermarriage with foreigners and the possible fate of children who might "follow and serve other gods." It marks a time of great change in the fate of the Jewish people since the heyday of Pharisee expansion and the promulgation of the Oral Law. And of course, the Mishnah as well as the bulk of the Talmudic writings to come do constitute the now-written down body of this Oral Law.

It is important to note that the Pharisees and the early Rabbinic successors were not ascetic secessionists from the affairs of the Judaic and secular world about them, as with the Qumron and Essene communities. There had been, in the period between 100 BCE and 100 CE a great movement towards Judaism. Millions of so-called god fearers found their way into the synagogues and prayer rooms of the Diaspora Jewish centers. And while most of them did not adhere to the strict ritual demands of the Pharisees/Rabbis in terms of circumcision, and dietary and Sabbath regulation they were interested hangers on, much as today's secular Jews today observe only some of the ancient disciplines.

And indeed, the Pharisees did contest for the control of power and the Temple during the later Hasmonian period. For example they allied themselves with Queen Salome Alexandra (76–67 BCE), widow of Alexander Jannaeus, of the Hasmonean dynasty, and thence engineered a slaughter of the existing Sadducean Temple aristocracy in revenge for earlier Sadducean killings of Essenes/Pharisees. So too during the first war against Rome 67–70 CE it was the Pharisees who struck a deal with Emperor Titus and secured peace for their academy in Yavneh. And it was the Judean warrior/intellectual, Josephus, a Pharisee who earlier and then after the war had gone to Rome to argue the case for Judaism.

The Romans waxed hot and cold toward the Jews in this time period. But there were enough Jews in Rome such that Rabbi Mattiah ben Herresh "could establish an advanced academy of learning" in that city, c. 130 CE {B.T. *Me 'il* 17a}. This was after the "world" uprising of the Jews against Emperor Trajan c. 115–118, and before the catastrophic war of Hadrian against Simon Bar Kohkba, Rabbi Akiba's "messiah."

By the time of the writing down of the Mishnah, in Sepphoris and Usha in the Galilee 200–250 CE, the millions of "god-fearers" had fled in large numbers from Judaism, many embracing the more mystical and less demanding Pauline ritual commitments of burgeoning Christianity.

The Mishnah setting for the matrilineal principle seems to have had no precedent in the teachings of either the Pharisees or earlier rabbis. The critical enunciation: *And any woman who does not have the potential for a valid marriage with this man (Priest, Levite, Israelite) or with other men (Priest, Levite, Israelite), the offspring is like her. And what is this? This is the offspring of a slave woman or a Gentile woman.*

The key issue is thus a valid marriage, which clearly cannot exist between a Jewish man and a slave or gentile woman. Thus their child would be a slave or *mamzer*, a product of illegal intercourse or an invalid marriage.

The problem that arises is that this enunciation in the Mishnah is now part of the Oral Law. Such stark prohibitions are difficult to find in the Torah. As a matter of fact the Pentateuch and the Prophetic writings are replete with the legitimate offspring of non-Israelite women married, ostensibly legally, with Israelite men. Thus Joseph marries an Egyptian, Azenath {Genesis 41:45}. His children out of Azenath are Mannaseh and Ephraim, both to be the tribal offspring of Jacob. Moses marries a Zipporah {Exodus 2:21} a:Midianite (Cushite); Judah marries Shua, an Adullamite, (c. 18 miles southwest of Jerusalem) {Genesis 38}.

David, his wives, and sons: A possibly non-Judean or non-Israelite wife is Maacah, daughter of King Talmai of Geshur {2 Samuel 3:2–5}. David's son, Absalom, through Maacah, was beloved of King David. The full sister of Absalom, Tamar, was raped by Amnon, her half brother. Geshur was east of the Jordan Valley, in the northern portion of today's nation, Jordan, "Geshur in Aram" (Aramaic) {2 Samuel 15:8}. Ironically there is a reported Talmudic injunction of death to those who impute impure morality to King David, as compared to King Saul.

For example, {Ruth. 1:16:} "thy people shall be my people, and thy God, my God," Ruth, the Moabite, speaks to Naomi her Jewish mother in law. In (Ruth. 4: 10–15}, she marries Boaz with the assent of the Jewish elders of Bethlehem, (Ephrathite) recognizing that Ruth was a Moabite. A child was born into this Israelite family, named Obed, father-to-be of Jesse and then, David (King), {Ruth 4:17–21}.

Certainly there are numerous imprecations against marriage with foreigners. Early on the J writer in {Exodus. 34:11–16 = J} states that Israelites should not take *their* wives daughter, etc., for they will pollute you. In Deuteronomy:

"For he {foreigner} will turn away thy son from following Me, that they may serve other gods."

In {Deuteronomy 21:10–14} there is an extended concession for the love of the female slave, who may be joined in marriage. The assumption is that her children would be Israelites. In {Judges 3:5–6} the Israelites fall into error, live among the Canaanites, Hittites, Amorites, Hivites, Perizzites, Jebusites, marry into them, give their daughters to them and take their daughters for their sons—and they worship their gods. But they were punished only for worshipping the Baals and Asherahs. As a consequence they were enslaved for breaking their covenant, by the King of "Cushan-Double wickedness," probably the Midianites {Judges 3:5–9}.

The critical issue in all of these ancient Torah and Prophetic concerns is not the ethnic or national origin of either parties to a marriage or the children produced there from but their religious commitments, keeping the covenantal faith.

Much argument is given over the prohibitions on intermarriage put forth by Ezra, c. 458 BCE, and here to the exile Levite returnees as well as the general population of the Yehud, requiring them to divorce their non-Jewish wives and to not recognize their children {Ezra 9: 4, 13–14; 10: 6, 9–16}. Was this a ban against all intermarriage with foreign women, per se, else a fear of religious contamination? Max Weber argues that it was fear that emanated from the experience of Israel, the in-migration of foreign elements that already had separated the new province of Samaria from the Yehud.[20]

Nehemiah, who later arrived in the Yehud from Persia, still was concerned that the children of these marriages spoke the language of Ashdod and not "yehudit." He also had an Israelite priest excommunicated for marrying the daughter of a Yahwist leader of Samaria, Sanballat {Nehemiah 13:28}. But the Jews had always been open to proselytism {Ezra 6:21; see also Exodus 12:49; Leviticus 19:34; Zechariah 18:23}.

> And the foreigners who join themselves in YHWH, to minister to him, to love the name of YHWH, and to be his servants, all who keep the Sabbath, and do not profane it, and hold fast to my covenant—these will I bring to my holy mountain and make them joyful in my house of prayer. . . . or my house shall be called a house of prayer for all people. . . . I will gather others to them besides his gathered one. {Trito Isaiah 56:6–8} c. 520–515 BCE

It is interesting to also note that in {2 Chronicles 8:11} the authors, c. 400–350 BCE, the time of the Second Temple, write about Solomon's marriage to the daughter of the Pharoah of Egypt. However, Solomon, worshipper of many gods besides YHWH, brings her to another house in Jerusalem to live, and not the house of "King David of Israel, for the places to which the ark of the Lord have come are holy." This marriage is presumed to be valid, as is his marriage (another of many) to the Ammonite princess who bore the next King, now of Judah, Rehoboam {2 Chronicles 9: 31}.

Rabbi Shaye Cohen in his recent and extensive survey of the literature asserts that the Matrilineal Principle was also not known in the period of the Second Temple. And that the writings in the period just prior to and after the destruction by Rome of the Second Temple, of Philo, Josephus, Paul, (Acts), show no awareness of such a position on the validity of such marriages and the children born of these relationships.[21]

How can we understand the Mishnah's ruling?[22] It was Louis Epstein who first articulated the closeness of the Mishnah ruling with existing Roman law concerning the potential validity of marriages between individuals of unequal legal status.[23] In the potential for a valid marriage the child always follows the father (*conubium/qiddushin*). When this does not occur the child follows the status of the mother. "A Roman matron impregnated by a non-citizen or a slave bears a non-citizen or a slave. A Jewish woman impregnated by a Gentile or slave bears a *mamzer*, a citizen of impaired status."[24] The child of two non-citizens or two non-Jews follows the status of the father. Without the possibility of a valid marriage legal paternity, the marriage of Jew and non-Jew, demands that the child follows the status of the mother, thus even a *mamzer* is a Jew.[25]

Such Roman laws can be traced back to the era of the Republic when Rome was expanding militarily into an international power, thus before 171 BCE. Both Cicero and Livy discuss this issue in their writings. The question raised by many Jewish scholars concerns the question, why did the Mishnah so inexplicably follow Roman law, in this period between 200–250 CE? The long-existing hatred of the Jews for Roman culture and dominance is put forth. On the other hand both the Sadducees and Pharisees had times of peaceful intercourse with Roman authority after Rome exerted its power into Judea under Herod, c. 37 BCE.

And of course the greatest hatred of Jew *vs.* Rome took place in the final of their three wars, here against Hadrian, especially his outlawing of circumcision, then his destruction of Jerusalem itself. Antoninus Pius who succeeded Hadrian as Emperor, c. 140 CE, attempted to calm the waters of Jewish nationalism. By that time Christianity was beginning to make special inroads in Rome, whereas Jewish scholars and leaders were concentrated in the Galilee, else in Parthian and then Sassanian controlled Mesopotamia, both ruling dynasties tolerant of their Jewish citizens. The Jewish community of Alexandria was in process of being destroyed, the writings of Josephus and Philo becoming anathema to the Rabbis.

But the critical element came with the rule of the Severenes in Rome. Emperor Septimus Severus c. 200 CE had traced his origins to Syria and North Africa. He and his entourage were well acquainted with Jews and Judaism. A grandson, Emperor Alexander Severus, (222–235) dabbled with Judaism as a possible state religion for Rome. He was ironically called *archisynogogus* by the citizenry of Rome, before he was killed by his own troops. Thus we are speaking of a period of at least a quarter of a century when Judaism had the wind of Rome at its back to build synagogues, to engage in the vocations as a free people.

And it was at this time that Judah Ha-Nasi (the Prince) appeared as the sponsor of the Mishnah, bringing together in written form the wisdom of prior scholars, Pharisees and Rabbis, and embarking on a new pathway of inner Judaic discipline. Judah himself was a person of great wealth, with slaves and concubines. Note that Judaism was still immersed in the ancient patterns of Eastern polygamy. However, Judah used this wealth in the Galilee to begin a great historic enterprise, but as a Helleno/Roman and not a Temple priest pursuing animal sacrifice. It is quite understandable that in erecting this compendium of Jewish practice derived from the tradition of the Oral Law, not necessarily anchored in Jerusalem or Rome, Judaism as a way of life might be maintained.

Consider also the comparable situation with the relatively wealthy elite returnees from Babylon in the days of Ezra and their non-Jewish wives (and concubines?). Could it not be that in the polygamous practices of the Middle East in this now Roman era, many Jews, now over a century beyond the memory of Jerusalem burning, could have indulged themselves with such fleshly opportunities? The Mishnah ruling could have been a foresightful remembrance of Joseph's interpretation of Pharaoh's dream. Prepare for those seven years of want. Indeed, another century would pass and officially Christian Rome would then invoke vengeful retribution upon the Jews.

Talmud: Survival

A Jew, at the same time a Hellenist philosopher, Philo in Alexandria, Egypt, at the beginning of the Common Era, could devote himself to the rationalization of the by now richly augmented literature of his people, attempting as with the contemporary Tannaim in Judea, to find in the transcendental truths of the Pentateuch and the prophets, guidance in their modern secular era. Philo was as devout as his contemporary Hillel in Jerusalem. The syncretic teachings of the pharisaic scholars in creating the Oral Law, was as intellectual an endeavor as the patently Hellenistic attempts of Philo to reconcile belief in the Jewish law with the rationalistic and secular intellectualism of Plato, the Stoics and other philosophical schools of the Greeks. The Pharisees were then bringing a protective and modernizing "mystery" system of faith to the ordinary folk. Philo was reconciling Judaism with a universal conceptualization of the mind. He still lived in an environment which saw and hoped for Judaism and the Law of Moses to become a universal covenant, for the universally "chosen" throughout the civilized Hellenistic world.

The wars and the final destruction of Jerusalem erected a great barrier for the rabbinical successors of the Pharisees to the external world about them. The dabblings of Jews such as Philo and Josephus in the Hellenistic intellectual world was drying up. Rabbi Gamaliel II could still run a school for Greek studies Yavneh at the end of the first century Common Era. But as time went on the scholars in the Galilee and then in Babylon turned inwardly to again circle the Jewish communities in defense. They were creating a new book for this people living in a new world that now included Christianity.

When in the seventh century the Middle East was reclaimed from Byzantium and Christianity by Islam, the Jews were reserved a special status, second to Muslims, but ahead of Christians. It was there that the Exilarch distributed the wealth of the enterprising Jewish community to the Caliph, he in turn providing the Jews with his personal protection. It was there that the Jewish academies nurtured the Babylonian Talmud and aspired to a high rabbinic intellectualism.

From Fayum in Egypt in the early 10th century, Saadia ben Joseph immigrated to study in the academies along the shores of the Euphrates. In 928 CE, he was appointed Gaon, or leader, educational and administrative, of the Yeshivah of Sura. He became the intellectual light of Jewish Babylon, unusually productive as a scholar, unusually polemical and controversial. He communicated in his writings the mental ferment that was then obtaining in the Islamic schools *mu'tazilah*, the boundaries of reason and faith. Although he was not a philosopher in the secular sense, his openness to reasoning, balanced by considered belief in the totality of holy writings, was a flash of light that was perceived westward across the Mediterranean.

So too in Spain, liberal Islamic rule opened up enormous realms of intellectual, religious and economic freedoms for the Jews. There would never have been a Maimonides if Spain had not already produced a Muslim physician/philosopher of the caliber of Averroes, 1126–1198 CE. But from the Jews there also came poets, mystics, and warriors. The removal of Maimonides, 1135–1204, and his family from Spain, 1148 CE, and his subsequent search for a Muslim haven in Egypt of tolerance for Jews had already been forewarned by the accusations against Averroes in Spain, of being a Judahizer.

Clearly, the differing political, and cultural contexts in which Judaism developed and diverged did not create a chasm between these Jewish communities in Lucena (Spain), Mainz (Germany), Rome, Pumbeditha (Babylon), Fustat/Cairo (Maimonides). The Babylonian, Spanish and Ashkenazi Jews were clearly three extensions of one branch. And in each context as the nail emerged from the wood to take a breath of freedom and creativity, it was eventually hammered down again into a protective cocoon.

The Jews threw themselves completely into the internal dialectics of Talmudic interpretation. In the case of the Babylonian and Galilee scholars, it was a rush to save Judaism from a foreign modernity, to create a balance with the Roman Imperium, as well as to protect from the oncoming challenge of the Christians. Later the Ashkenazim were under a continuing if varied political and national press undertaken by a universal Christian oppression. The Rabbis dug deep into the inner resources of the Jewish mind, binding the small Jewish enclaves into a religio-legalistic Talmudic embrace, for survival.

> During the Middle Ages the Jewish communities no longer contemplated battle. The medieval Hebrew poets did not celebrate the martial arts. The Jews of Europe were placing themselves under the protection of constituted authority. The reliance was legal, physical, and psychological.[26]

The city of Mainz was the center of northern Judaism during the centuries following the Carolingian invitation of the Jews into northern Europe. This peaceful coexistence with their Christian neighbors ended with the First Crusade, 1096 CE. These Jewish communities, including Speyer, Trier, and Worms, along the Rhine, were attacked. The killings and destruction dispersed the Jews; some drifted west into France. Rashi, (Shelomo ben Yitzhak, (1040–1105)) perhaps the premier Talmudic scholar among the Ashkenazim, who made his living as a seller of wine, was then teaching and developing his commentaries on the Old Testament and the Talmud for the guidance of these French communities, only recently being rediscovered. Others fled east deeper into the Germanic domains, the beginning of the tradition of Yiddish as the vernacular of European Jewry.

Earlier, about 1000 CE, during the good times, Rabbi Gershom of Mainz, head of the academy in that city, called together a conclave of rabbis from this relatively prosperous region, before the slaughter of 1096 CE. The decision was to revoke the privilege of polygyny among the Jews, and to give women the equal right to initiate divorce, more in keeping with Roman/Christian traditions. The tactic of defensive life in a potentially hostile environment required prudential actions by the vulnerable minority to institute laws for the guidance of their own behavior which would not be a red flag of remembrance to Christians that the Jews were originally from the distant Oriental east.

The one area of life that Christian authorities allowed for the Jews was self-education. The Talmud was the great purveyor of intellectual life to this people. True, at times, 1242 CE, after a debate between Jewish rabbis and scholastic philosophers, including Albertus Magnus, Louis IX in Paris had all copies of the Talmud burned. A moment of human openness to inquiry was here followed by the force of hatred and fear. Because the Talmud is often disputatious in its commentary on the ancient Law of Holy Writ, as well as containing much legal interpretation, it can be considered an ongoing encyclopedia of Jewish thinking on important contemporary issues of moral and community life. By contrast the original writings of the Torah had their origins in the often-mystifying contexts of biblical life, 15th to 10th century BCE.

Thus Jewish education in the yeshivahs of the Ashkenazim, while often rote Hebrew learning in the early stages, at the advanced secondary and higher educational stages of Talmudic analysis became a great intellectual chess game in which disputation, argument, analysis, and imaginative insinuation, all played important roles in deciding who were the intellectual "winners." These worthies gained great eminence but minimal social privilege within the Jewish community; marriage to the daughter of a middle-class merchant, else the daughter of an eminent scholar. This social hierarchy of competitive achievement could take place among the Jews, beyond the ken of the external power centers of the Christian world. It was a free enterprise race within the Jewish community with little tangible material gain.[27]

This world lived through these Talmudic "games," the stuff of their moral and social existence. These "games" created meanings and allowed for a dynamic that was internally rich in social movement and advancement, even without the tangible wealth to show for it. The saving grace for Talmudism as the center of gravity of Jewish intellectual self-absorption was that it had no rivals in the medieval world, as compared with the coming advent of the scientific revolution which left Judaism, as well as the other faiths with a now meaningless scholasticism, untouched by a world in great dynamic ascent.

The Metaphysics of Rationality

On the surface of historical experience the Jews were enacting laws they believed in consonance with their dedication to the highest principles of reality, their Lord, however titled. So too the long Talmudic interregnum, 1500 years, in which the Oral Law and its written personification, the Talmud, became a new guidance system again under the highest moral and ontological reality available. Thus they achieved a long-existing stability and survivability, even under painful material duress.

They were internally strong because the other competitive, rational systems of understanding our world were incapable of challenging theirs, metaphysically, morally, and socially. But the others had had the power of numbers, and political and military heft to keep the Jews under reign. What the Jews had going for them during this period, in spite of great suffering and blood letting, whenever the powers that be would have it, was that they were forced by circumstance, and by this inner sense of law, morality, and above all intellectuality to discipline their people in the metaphysics of rationality. They gave up their concubines, their multiple wives, thus the exploitation of the female; also gone were slave, servant, and serf. They committed to universal education, literacy, the quasideification of the scholar, the wise man. But they did not allow the best to become powerful in material ways.

Inchoately the Jewish elite, the rabbinate, understood that humans were inherently weak, without ultimate answers to the questions of the universe. Thus they needed to and were forced to tread lightly on the world stage. It is noteworthy that the worst of their experiences as Jews came towards the end of the Talmudic period. And it is noteworthy that the intellectual, nay the scholastic frenzy of Talmudic legal disputation arose towards the end of this period before the dawn of the Enlightenment heralded a new era. It is also worth examining and in a contemporary and serious manner, the inner hatred that surfaced just as the Jews entered the world of Emancipation and as full-fledged citizens of the world society of intellect and civilizational achievement. Why, once more were they struck down?

The *Holocaust*, was one additional reminder, ever more horrendous than any other historical tragedy that the Jews suffered, as Jews. Horrendous, because the means for this destruction were themselves so much more scientifically efficient. Is it not ironic in the history of civilization that these Jewish *haskalah*, civilizational achievements, the crowning jewels of the 1,500 years of Talmudic material deprivation, became the nail fated to be pounded into dust?

The Jews of the Talmud unknowingly obeyed a higher law of human existence, a metaphysical truth consonant with *Homo sapiens sapiens*' evolutionary condition for survival. They were defensive and forethoughtful of that which might allow them even seven years of meager plenty, perhaps released from perennial want. This destruction of the Jews came in a time of great ferment in the lurch for prosperity and rational modernity. Other human groups were so destroyed in the 20th century, perhaps for the same reason as the Jews. They too played the defensive game of human survival and intellectual enhancement. And they too suffered for this *crime*. Why?

To understand such human horror and debasement requires understanding as yet beyond our grasp. The most that Jews can now do to prevent another terrible moment in the course of their traversing of history, is to survive. They must not turn away from the moment. Above all they must envision the future in terms of the deepest probing of this elemental vision of humanity. Next.

CHAPTER ELEVEN

Judaism Reconstituted

The Historic Challenge

The scientific mode of thinking which began to grip the European mind in the 17th century turned into a veritable revolution in our understanding of the natural and human world. The Enlightenment which was the inevitable social and general philosophical outcome of the victory of the scientific method began to seriously impact Jewish life by the mid-eighteenth century.

What was happening to this Ashkenazic culture was unlike what had occurred almost two thousand years earlier with the spread of Hellenic and then international Hellenistic cultural throbbing. Greek philosophy opened the mind to a wholly new way of rationalistic thinking. And except for the pregnant scientific work of scientists such as Aristarchus, Eratosthenes and others in Alexandria and elsewhere in the Hellenistic world, this envelopment of rational study and analysis never quite developed the instrumentalities of thought and experiment which by contrast created the ongoing transformations of thinking and acting that the scientific method enabled.

In one great and ongoing stroke the intellectual ground of belief was undercut from all those theological incarnations of thought and social power that had undergirded Judaism, Christianity, and Islam. True for the Jews the stimulation of foreign intellectual developments was always ongoing. And as such we today recognize these great thinkers as Judaic groundbreakers, but not necessarily the Rabbis who later integrated the ancient Torah experiences with the need to survive in the hostile and dominating world about them. Here the Talmudic disciplines of ritual and moral behavior were once preeminent.

And thus we today hearken to Josephus' and Philo's Hellenistic writings, then later to the hidden rational enlightenment which influenced 9th- and 10th-century Common Era analysis to produce a Saadia. The full rediscovery of the ancient Hellenic writings influenced such as Averroes (1126–1198 CE) for the Muslim world and Thomas Aquinas (1225–1274 CE) for Christian Catholicism, but also created the greatest Jewish medieval thinker, Moses Maimonides (1137–1204 CE). A host of other seminal Jewish creative minds came out of these Spanish generations of tolerance. Then, for a moment, the fences around the Jews were torn down.

But as the world entered the modern scientific era it was Baruch, later, Benedict Spinoza (1632–1677 CE) who first and powerfully echoed the new philosophical vision and was thrown out of the Jewish community of Amsterdam for it. A century later Moses Mendelssohn (1729–1786) while tempering his Enlightenment values with a steadfast adherence to his Judaic faith, unlike his wildly aspiring younger contemporary Solomon Maimon (1754–1800), still enunciated in his philosophical quest to modernize Judaism, saw the writing on the wall. Whereas in the past the moral and supernatural sources for Judaism could only be paralleled by such as Plato and Aristotle in their perceptions of the real, and by the Epicureans and Stoics in their rational ethical searchings, the modern incarnation of rational thinking, the scientific method, brought forth a wholly different challenge.

The power of scriptural Judaism in the Hellenistic world lay in its Unitarian cohesiveness, the transcendental sources of the laws of reality joined to social and communitarian injunctions to live the good and proper moral life. There was no bifurcation in Judaism, except for the fact that the ancient Torah injunctions from God on high, in their specificity had to be modified, the Oral Law, by the Pharisees and their rabbinic successors, in this new cultural setting.

After our scientific revolution there was no possibility that the ensconced Talmudic culture of the European Jews could be so modified as to compete with this modernity and the Enlightenment values of democracy, individual liberty. This impact on the structure of society and the economics of progress did not allow for this now-ancient Talmudic and synagogue tradition to compete intellectually. And thus the Jews fled the synagogue *en masse*. And those that did not flee, stayed on, basically for the ritual and the historical connectivity which still constitutes a crucial dimension of our human cultural awareness.

This need is made particularly piquant when we observe the behavior of Karl Marx (1818–1883) towards his Jewish brethren. It is quite understandable that this raising of the prison gates from the Jews in the eighteenth century saw them searching around for the security of their material existence in a still largely hostile world. And it is no surprise that many went into public areas of finance, banking, and trading which they had surreptitiously engaged in while ensconced in the ghetto. And therefore, many of those who did abandon their Judaic identities, as well as those who remained in the synagogue, became inordinately wealthy.

The Marx family in Mainz, descended from a long line of distinguished rabbis, chose to convert to Christianity for the possible governmental employment that would be available. Karl was thus raised in a *converso* environment both of self-hatred and opportunism. He himself married a woman of the Christian lower German nobility. His hatred of the Jews and accusations of insatiable money-hungering, typical of the Christian anti-Semites of the era, must be seen in this light of embarrassment and self-denial for what he must have known to be a violation of his own historic integrity in favor of momentary personal advantage.

This one individual is a clear exemplar of the rupturing of a great historical civilizational tradition under the goad of a wholly new and powerful vision of knowledge and our conjoint human position in the universe. How to confront the new, how to manage it? Where was the synagogue?

Is There Significance?

We must do as the rabbis did in the centuries after the destruction of the Second Temple, 70 CE, and then of Jerusalem itself, 135 CE. They had to look beyond the Torah of Ezra (c. 450 BCE) and the later Septuagint (c. 280–260 BCE). They had to reconstitute a faith so that it could maintain itself in the face of enormous pressuring historical crosscurrents, a new world order of Roman power. Also, they recognized the swirling competitive search for meaning in the many mystery religions that swept over the apathetic and alienated masses. Christianity was only beginning its ascent when the intellectual and cultic Talmudic defensive efforts drew a boundary around the future of Judaism.

Now the boundaries have been dissolved, and an ever more powerful intellectual description of reality put into place. But it was not merely a new establishment of knowledge, but an instrumental reshaping of social reality as well. The almighty powers of a transcendental God, his law giver Moses, were now revealed to be embedded in a new sense of the transcendental. God was now Nature itself, its powers to be revealed not by an immortal moral prophet but by the enquiring mind of ordinary humans. Humans no longer had to obey those powerful personages who asserted that they spoke for God, in the written or oral laws given to a Moses or a Christ. The power of secular knowledge, the mysteries of nature to be revealed by this open, democratic method of thought, relegated the old mythological writings to heritage, history, identity, and "the will to believe."

What could the synagogue, the rabbis, and the Talmud offer in defense of their intellectual and social prerogatives in the face of this avalanche of knowledge and real secular power—the social opportunities for the European Jews that the emancipation had opened up? By contrast the older vision still recalled the ancient defensive specters and always, future threats. The new was also threatening in its invitation to the loneliness of separation from one's roots in a world that had lost its historic moorings.

The synagogue had always periodically trembled with the reverberations of history, pogroms, and hatred by the *goyem*. But now in this new world of even pseudo acceptance there needed to be more then this ancient canopy. As masses of Jews either converted or became secular, the search within synagogue Judaism for a correlation with the modern world has been a losing battle for over two centuries. Instead, and especially after the *Holocaust*, secular America and Israel became the central focus for the evolution of Judaism in the 20th and 21st centuries, probably even beyond.

The original purpose of the synagogue was the coming together of believers to study, to discuss the teachings of the Torah, and the prophets, the writers of wisdom. Also, there was a search to understand the relation of belief to the workings of the wider world in which humans lived. Deepest of all was the road to be taken for the moral life, the holy life, the life which God on high *Elyon* had demanded of His "chosen." That was the reality, the intellectual form within which life had to be lived. But now, in the 21st century, after so many Jews have abandoned the synagogue, often even their historic Jewish identity, these questions have become critical to the survival of Judaism. How many Jews today, even the more devout behave consonant with a belief in the existence of Yahweh, the moral Law of Moses?

Can Judaism survive only identified with a completely symbolic, metaphorical, even historical integration of this tradition? Certainly Mordicai Kaplan and Sherwin Wine, 20th-century rabbinic revolutionaries, in this respect, hoped that such a Judaic renaissance within the synagogue could come to pass, and even flourish. By leaving the supernatural behind, the basis of the ancient cult, what could then remain of Judaism as a moral and social force in human existence?

There Is Significance

As we have noted in Chapter Two, the symbolic structure of religious thinking and practice is itself an inchoate reflection of the search for meaning in an as yet undecipherable world. Yet it cannot form itself into social practice unless it makes good its metaphysical claims for truth. Religious beliefs in one way or another, cult, ritual, claims concerning moral and immoral practices, the totems and taboos of a disciplined life, all reflect our attempt to give protective behavioral and intellectual meaning to this complex world about us. It has assisted this frenetic, emotional two-legged creature in finding instrumental structure in the inchoate evolutionary progression of life forms.

Modernity Preempted. A view of the rabbinic system as a metaphor for science:

> The myth of Torah {Written & Oral} is multi-dimensional. It includes the striking detail that whatever the most recent rabbi {scholar-scientist} is destined to discover through proper exegesis of the tradition is as much a part of the way revealed to Moses as is a sentence of scripture itself. It therefore is possible to participate even in the giving of the law by appropriate logical inquiry into the law. God himself, studying and living by Torah is believed to subject himself to these same rules of logical inquiry. If an earthly court overrules the testimony, delivered through miracles, of the heavenly one, God would rejoice, crying out, 'My sons have conquered me! My sons have conquered me. . . .'
>
> Before us is a mythical religious system in which earth and heaven correspond to one another, with Torah as the nexus and model of both. The heavenly paradigm is embodied upon earth. Moses 'or rabbi' is the pattern for the ordinary sage. And God himself participates in the system, for it is his image that in the end forms that cosmic paradigm. The faithful Jew constitutes the projection of the divine on earth. Honor is due to the learned rabbi more than to the scroll of the Torah, for through his learning and logic he may alter the very content of Mosaic revelation. He is Torah not merely because he lives by it but because at his best he forms as compelling an embodiment of the heavenly model as does a Torah scroll itself.[1]

Monotheism. We have reflected on the intellectual sophistication of the monotheistic principle, the injunction against the creation of graven images purporting to represent higher deities and their secular powers. Here too is the struggle of the Jews against the barbarisms of the ancient Temple, reflecting ancient fears and superstitions, the sacrificial system. Here too the Jews were ahead of most religions in seeing these practices disappear with the destruction of the Second Temple and the Sadducean political powers, the Aaronic priesthood, all ensconced behind this primitive rite.

It is but a short segue from this one all powerful God, YHWH, and the law giver this God has chosen to represent this one moral principle, here Moses, today the human mind searching to apprehend the nature of this one all encompassing principle, causality revealed. One transcendental, eternal God now is to be understood as a universal natural principle within which we all must live. The new chosen, appears as the conjoint efforts of the intellectual mind, in all ethnic and social groups to understand in rational, experiential terms, the causal interrelationships within which we live. The universe is a unity of laws, potentially available for inquiry and practical testing.

Bur we do not have to pray to this principle. What we need do is to preserve and protect the human mind from the irrationalities of emotional obfuscation. We need to keep steadfastly to the law. This is what the prophets attempted to preach in their incisive indictments against public and monarchical malpractice, irrationality and barbarism. The Torah and its attempts to provide a system of laws for human individual and social behavior was a reflection of the fact that we must practice defensive social behavior in the face of blinding ignorance and emotion. The written and oral Torah recognized the reality that the human soul was open to reason and rationality, but also senseless emotionality and evil practices. Humans had the potential to approach the defensive injunction from nature recognizing our weakness and ignorance, but also the propensity to fall, a recognition that infused the ancient mystery religions and certainly facilitated the Christian rise to dominance.

Again, the pure and demanding monotheism of Judaism is as modern today as it was thirty-five hundred years ago. There is a "god" out there. It has no human form. That "god" is the natural laws of the universe that have created us. Our challenge, as it was to Moses and the prophets, is to understand these inner causal relationships as best we can, and for any portion of the evolutionary and historical time line that may face us. Thence we must put into place laws created by our own reason that could effectuate our survival at the highest levels of intellectual responsibility that can be socially mustered.

Sabbath. As we noted in the previous chapter the tradition of the *Sabbath* can be traced to Mesopotamian sources, cosmological and astrological traditions fearful of the gods on high. Humans need institutionalized periods away from the fields for rest, contemplation, and humane ritual. The Jews took over this principle, here also involved with the number 7. European traditions of rest, festivities in Hellenic and Roman times, were irregular in their dispensations from labor. Many more holidays and festivals were observed to break up the working periods. Here too the Jews with their plethora of traditional seasonal celebrations and observances were in the vanguard.

Today we have a mixture of the two traditions. The Christian Sabbath which followed the Jewish tradition institutionalized religious observance of this day away from labor. But as we understand it, the Sabbath, however observed and when observed regardless of the number of days of "rest" involved, recognizes a critical dimension of the human mind/body relationship. There must be time when the dross of overt labor is put to one side and humans engage their other symbolic dimensions of thought, the emotional, social consecration.

Today, when the barriers of institutional religious compulsion have dissolved, weekends are not merely for entertainment and culture, but for shopping which in a time of abundance is not merely a necessity but a festival in its own right. The question is not necessarily how long, how late, and when shops should be forced to close, also bars and liquor stores, but whether a nation, society, ethnic or religious groups can indeed encircle their own or other affiliated groups with strict Sabbath regulations. And if Sabbath disciplines cannot be enforced within any political community, are we here violating an ancient human need to surround one's culture with disciplinary, defensive boundaries, what we can or cannot do with our persons, our communities.

In the Torah, even modest Sabbath violations were considered serious desecrations and were punished by stoning unto death. The Jews lost many "god fearers" in the Hellenistic world with their strict Sabbath regulations, and the enormous time spent in prayer and observance. The Christian tradition later in history under an all powerful Church instituted similar lengthy services and restrictions. Then too the Muslims with their multifaceted prayer rooms and teachings continued an ancient desert tradition. In our modern day, the weakening of the synagogue reflects our universal modern hubris.

To many Jews such traditions seem to be senseless ritual, and they will have none of it. As each generation passes into history fewer and fewer Jews facing the problematics of modern life see their Judaic identity as compatible with the traditional Sabbath synagogue rituals. One must ask whether Judaism's survival as a potent moral and intellectual force rests only on such traditional observance. Note that the ancient sacrificial system of the temple was abandoned without major wounds to the future of Judaism. Therefore, is there a way for Judaism to survive by promoting the perennial defensive need for an observance of Sabbath rest and reflection without the heavy historical accretions of contemporary synagogue practice?

Kashrut. Few ancient societies neglected the ritual division of impure dietary practice from pure or socially acceptable diet. Such disciplines might be reserved for holiday rites, others such as with the ancient Torah injunctions maintained by a set of highly disciplined rules for what is correct and what is forbidden in terms of dietary regulation.

Now, certain rules can be traced to "reasons why." The prohibition of eating pork might be attributed to a seminomadic peoples disdain for a sedentary agricultural enemy, pigs not part of pastoral life, as are cattle and sheep. Then the Philistines were the settled and unconquered enemy. But in general it is reasonable to take an aspect of human life, *Homo*'s omnivorous ability to partake of and cook a wide variety of foods, animal and vegetable, seemingly unlimited by nature. The human mind needs to understand all experience animate and inanimate. The human mind needs to draw causal boundaries around the social experience of the group, even the most basic human activities. Certainly, from time immemorial the hunter has exercised such discipline, if not for his survival on the hunt for dangerous creatures, but also in the provision of the hunt for themselves, their loved ones and the community.

During long eons of scarcity such behavioral disciplines for survival gradually evolved into more theologically oriented values when life became more regularized and secure. Thus Jews accepted the regulations involved in the Talmudic revisions of Torah Law, these to be serious and justified modifications established for the betterment of the community. Even as such rules and regulations seem not to have the health rationalizations that are given to modern Jews, the laws of *Kashrut* symbolize that defensive commitment that marks them out as defenders of their heritage.

So how do we remain true to the spirit of *Kashrut* while at the same time freeing ourselves from its literality? How is one to remain a Jew and at the same time enjoy a BLT, a hamburger, no less shrimp salad, else a lobster roll? And of course we note that several synagogue denominations of necessity have bent over backwards to bend the rules. Are we thus condemned to dissolve such a tradition, a primeval defensive awareness that alerts us in advance that there will be times when things will be tough? Thus we shall not swerve from the principles of the pure and impure. For, without such laws disciplining our humanity, we open ourselves up to moral anarchy, behavioral chaos.

But, hold on. We do live in a world where we are constantly told the scientific dos and don'ts of rational dietary behavior. For the sake of our heart, our duodenum, our kidneys, we have now transitioned to another dimension of *Kashrut*. If these rules and regulations do not derive from the ancient Torah or Talmud, they derive from modern science, our new transcendental Torah/Talmud. The ancient Jewish sages were correct in attempting to define what was good or bad, what would work in becoming and remaining a Jew, chosen to be pure; even when it came to food gathering, cooking, and consumption. They perceived the necessity of transforming the prosaic and vulgar act into a religious and holy admonishment. Perhaps today we have a more instrumentally effective ways of disciplining our potentially anarchic, self-destructive selves. Do we explain vegetarians as covert Jews?

And of course science and medicine can be wrong. Eating several scrambled eggs a week will today not necessarily kill you, as we once feared. And that is the beauty of scientific medicine and nutrition; they are subject to altered reconsideration and recommendation if new facts come forth that contradicts the old, a true Talmudic *halakah*. Yes, sadly, dietary principles are not made in heaven. Nevertheless considering our human nature, they will always be relevant and necessary for the disciplining of human behavior, our Oral Torah.

Circumcision. In a previous chapter we have discussed the most probable origins of this practice. Originating among wandering Bedouin Semites in the desert, among the Egyptian elite, either enactments by the military as a ritual purification rite, or among the priesthood of Egypt as the entrance ritual into holy communion, it became a great Maginot line in the defensive ethnicity of the Israelites. Abandoning circumcision for the ability to proselytize among the gentiles, Pauline Christianity won over these masses from Judaism.

But in the end the Jews have triumphed. At one time it was their "calling card" of disdain towards their Philistine antagonists. Then it was a great defensive shield against Christianity. But Islam continued this ancient desert rite, even as it gradually separated itself from biblical Judaism. It has now become the great enemy of Israel for the latter's small-scaled existence among the hundreds of millions of impoverished Islamists.

Modern science, medicine, public health in all the Christian nations is now introducing circumcision into Africa and beyond. Scientific medicine now views this ancient rite as a necessary health procedure for all males everywhere. Did the ancient desert peoples, Midianites and others intuit this health need and turn it into a tribal ritual of self identification? Did the Egyptian aristocracy, the priests and soldiers want to give themselves an extra "edge" by performing circumcision, to the newborn, the adolescents as with Ishmael, or for the novitiate in war and in the Temple?

One bit of evidence comes with the general reproductive health of the Jews all during the millennial siege imposed by Church or Mosque. The Jews always brought more children to reproductive maturity then their confreres, even under a state of externally induced poverty. This especially occurred in the 19th century in Eastern Europe when the first scientific public health bits of knowledge began to be transmitted from the West. Jews did not engage in sexual activities more than their Christian counterparts. Rather, they brought the pregnancies to term more often, and the infants thereby given life, survived into reproductive maturity at a higher percentile rate than their neighbors. Circumcision was no doubt part of the equation that Talmudic teaching supported in making for the survival of this race.

Contemporary Judaic Dilemmas

It is the argument of this study that Judaism has undergone a number of revolutionary pathways over the approximate 3500 years that we can use to account for its self-awareness as a nation, a people, and a faith to bind it together. Also, the revolutionary turns in its various struggles for survival have been shaped by the contextual historical events which have impacted on this people. These were political and economic, as well as philosophical, intellectual challenges.

Change in response to challenge is the purpose of any religious ideal that can maintain its significance. Failure in this respect is why so many outlooks on life have faded into history. It is perhaps saddest to have seen from our distant perspective the disappearance of both the Hellenic and Hellenistic visions of Greco-Roman culture. There are here many causal factors. The religious outlook of both Greeks and Romans was rooted in gods of place, not too different from earliest Judaism with its centers of worship, Shiloh, Gibeah, Shechem, Bethel, Samaria, and most importantly, Jerusalem. However, by transforming Judaism from a sacrificial cult on Mt. Zion to a People of the Book, the leadership internationalized this religion, this worldview.

The Greeks and Romans could not so extend their ancient mythology. It was too rooted geographically and thus ethnically. Indeed, the Hellenes created philosophy, then science, great rational envisionments of nature and humanity. But such outlooks were elitist in nature. They did not touch the inner emotional realities of human existence. Neither Epicureanism, nor Stoicism, nor the other ethical developments of philosophical thought touched the essential mystery of human existence—those deeper elements of ethnic and ethical vulnerability. Above all, the philosophy and science of Greco-Roman culture did not change the face of economic, technological or social life. It was purely conceptual.

At all points Judaism faced front and center the deepest elements of the human psyche, especially human weaknesses, vulnerability, the violence and the volatility of social relationships. The Greeks saw this too, but in an Apollonian manner, transmuted these underground elements into drama and poetry, then into military interethnic violence. Finally their powerful rationalistic militarism precipitated a vast cultural expansionism under Alexander and his successors. The Jews were luckier. They quickly failed at such attempts. Their internecine wars culminated in a quick Assyrian and Chaldean obliteration of their national identities. The Jews had to fall back on a rich and encompassing set of Holy Writings to bring them together. This supernatural moral surety lasted throughout the ages as their response to military/political impotency.

The world has once more changed. For two hundred fifty years the old Torah/Scriptural/Talmudic institutions have attempted to hold the Jews together in an ancient embrace. During this period the world has pulsated hot and cold whether to admit the Jews to the international community. The Jews have made epochal contributions to the advance of European civilization from the eighteenth through the twentieth century. Then a horrific political and ideological cancer inspired the *Holocaust* in Europe, destroying its Jewish community—six million productive souls killed in an inexpressible brutality.

Yet there is now Israel as a nation. Once more Jerusalem is a contested center of Jewish commitment. In the United States many millions of Jews have become economically "comfortable," contributing hugely to this nation's 20th-century domination in culture as well as political and economic progress. Talmudic/Synagogue Judaism however is no longer a meaningful way of life for the vast majority of Jews. Some proclaim their ancient ethnicity in the synagogue by attending the rituals, the festivals, the great moments of passage. But such observance only constitutes a remembrance of past affiliation, historical allegiance, and the maintenance of the ethnic membrane.

Unlike Islam or Christianity, Judaism does not proselytize. If it allows new entrants, it does so with so many ifs, ands, or buts, as to remain inviolate from outside intrusions into its presumptive ethnic purity. Institutional Judaism has lost millions of its most creative members, either to conversion or alienation. It has long remained impotent in redefining itself for the future. To survive as a faith, as a way of life, and not to descend into minor cultish status, irrelevant to what is happening to the world, intellectually, philosophically, morally, or socially, a religion needs the vigor of modernity and inclusion. It is not enough to celebrate circumcisions, bar and bat mitzvahs, marriages and funerals under the holy canopies and with sacramental rituals enunciated now by professional, well-employed rabbis.

We have earlier pointed out the pathways by which synagogue Judaism has attempted to come to terms with the modern world. All these attempts are admirable. We here exclude the atavistic world of the *Haredim*, the ultraorthodox who would have to engage in serious decision making in terms of their version of Judaism, were they not supported by the welfare state. One thinks that their attractiveness as a way of life and belief to those born within and those who join voluntarily would be quite different were there another Judaic set of choices than those epitomized by the semimodernized synagogue movement of the past several centuries.

Most of the reformers, including the Cincinnati movement still hold on metaphorically to the supernatural claims of the Talmudic tradition, but now in "its progressive revelation" here the age of reason, the Enlightenment and then the Emancipation of the Jews. It is yet but one more step in this revelation of the nature of a universal God and the brotherhood of humankind. Reform Judaism thus has not broken with synagogue symbolism and ritual. And this is why so many individual Jews have committed to be Jews without the aid of the rabbis. Another and growing proportion of Jews has married outside the ethnicity, here largely abandoned by the synagogue.

True, the Reconstructionist movement initiated by the deeply intellectual rabbi, Mordicai Kaplan, has overtly done away with supernaturalism, attempting to maintain the outer corpus of the synagogue traditions. There is in Kaplan's writings an attempt to metaphorically retain much of Talmudic theology and tradition.

> The quality and quantity of life that spell Judaism must be rediscovered and reemphasized. It must be considered as nothing less than a civilization . . . As a civilization, Judaism is that dynamic pattern of life which enables the Jewish people to be a means for the salvation to the individual Jews. In the past when salvation meant attainment of bliss in the hereafter, the Jewish civilization was other-worldly in its entire outlook, content and motivation. Now when salvation depends on making the most of the opportunities presented in the world, the form of social organization, the language, literature, religion, laws, folkways and art must so function that through them the Jewish people will help to make the life of the Jew creative and capable of self-fulfillment. . . . Their hearts will then be set upon so revitalizing their social heritage, so restructuring their mode of life, so conditioning their future, that the Jewish people might become once more a source of spiritual self realization to the individual Jew.[2]

The Humanist Synagogue movement under Rabbi Sherwin Wine completely rejected theology and ritual, the outer shell of the traditional rabbinic symbolism of belief, i.e., salvation/resurrection. In his synagogues, Wine argued for a commitment to humanistic values. What these are beyond traditional secular political and cultural liberalism is not clear. However, Wine treasured the cumulative humanistic philosophical thinkers in the history of the Jews as well as non-Jews.

> For some humanistic Jews, their Jewish identity is the strongest emotional bond. For other humanistic Jews, their intellectual and moral commitment to humanism is more powerful than their ties to Jewishness. Both groups value their Jewish identity—but in differing degrees. Humanistic Judaism has room for both commitments. Humanistic Jews share a Jewish agenda with other Jews. Holidays, Israel, anti-Semitism, and the study of Jewish history are some of the items on this list of common activity. They also share a humanist agenda with other humanists. Humanist philosophy, ethical education, and the defense of the secular state are some of the items on this second list. Neither excludes the other. They are both necessary.[3]

In Humanistic Judaism we have a close approximation to the Ethical Culture movement founded in the late 19th century by Felix Adler, a rabbinical student, descended from a long line of liberal German rabbis. The Ethical Culture meeting houses, originally dominated in numbers by Jews who were alienated from traditional synagogue practices, today have a more ecumenical membership. Yet, in Ethical Culture's rejection of the traditions and symbolism of historic Judaism or Christianity, it is barely more than a liberal humanistic philosophical grouping of pragmatists, highly educated men and women, all searching for a humane, rational ethical center in a very complex and dynamic world. The deeper ethnic, historic, ritualistic symbols of affiliation and identity necessary for the maintenance of any quasireligious fellowship are here not in evidence.

Judaism in Potential

Jews are a diverse group. Their identification does not stop them from being secular or ultraorthodox, and all grades in between. What differentiates them from the standpoint of Protestantism, another wildly diverse conglomeration of sects and beliefs, is that after one leaves a Protestant denomination, one remains, as a Christian, little different than a Protestant agnostic or atheist. The Jews, by contrast have their history, ethnic identity, and the burden of worldwide antagonism and suspicion, literally thousands of years of this distinction.

As with the Protestants, Jews have no official governor of beliefs. The Protestants can vary from extreme fundamentalists in their approach to theology and behavioral restrictions, often joining with Catholics in denying evolutionary theory, or restricting birth control, abortion, or stem-cell research. The Jews join the Protestant rejection of Rome's and the Pope's authority, but do not join them in their antiscientific biases. In fact the ultraorthodox *Haredim* in Israel are as eager as the secularists in improving the life of the yet to be born by all the scientific genetic procedures available. Abortion is also sanctioned when the life of the mother or other serious impediments to the birth and sustenance of a healthy child is in doubt.

Thus the monotheism of Judaism, in its various forms does not exist as an obstacle to rational scientific progress when applied to medical and other biological facets of human living. There is very little room for supernaturalism in Judaism today. By contrast Protestantism can vary from the very socially modernistic Anglican or Unitarian forms of worship to the most antiscientific and politically/socially recidivistic forms of worship/social behavior—here without naming names. The Catholic Church with its carefully structured and officially sanctioned Trinitarianism cannot be considered a monotheistic religion. And it has with great dragging of the feet been allowed to enter the modern scientific age, but always with innumerable caveats, at sharp contrast with modern scientific-secular understanding.

Since both Catholicism and Protestantism share the Old Testament scriptures with the Jews, their various problems with modernity lie in the established New Testament theology with which they are presently burdened. One can respond with the fact that Talmudic Judaism now exerts, as we have shown in preceding chapters a heavy burden on Judaism. However, the status of Talmudic Judaism in the theological corpus of Judaism, as the Oral Law given to Moses by God on High, supervenes the Pentateuch in most of its teachings and presents an interpretive structure that can be bent and reshaped, on demand.

This the Reform and Conservative movements long ago achieved. This the Reconstructionist and Humanist rabbinical congregations are attempting to do today. Consider the fact that Jewish ethnic associations such as The Workmen's Circle (*Der Arbiter Ring*) still exist as Jewish organizations, unaffiliated with any rabbinical congregations. At one time a confederation of groups organizing cultural and linguistic (Yiddish speaking) programs, a grouping of schools intent on teaching young American Jews their heritage, both historical, biblical, and cultural and in Yiddish, the language for the past thousand years of Ashkenazi Jews, it still modestly functions.

The Workmen's Circle is a secular organization of Jews, recognized by Talmudic and Pentateuchal criteria as Jewish, committed to the circumcision of the male, the celebration of bar and bat mitzvahs, the great holidays and festivals of Jewish heritage, all those criteria by which a Jew is defined as a Jew. On all matters of scientific scrutiny, if the evidence is available certainly members of *Der Arbiter Ring* would be in harmony with the Lubevitcher Hassidim in their teachings. The secular Jews have one advantage. When the end of the welfare state eventually occurs, when the nation becomes solvent, they may have more skills to survive on than their ultraorthodox brethren.

Issues of celibacy and child molestations do not affect secular Jews, as contrasted with the scourge that is now devastating the Catholic priesthood. Most Jewish congregations have peacefully allowed for female rabbis. Responsible procreation for most Jews is now the norm, thus the alarm by Jewish leadership over the decline of gross and relative numbers among the Jews. Except for the ultraorthodox who have many children, mostly because as with their welfare-dependent brethren from other religions, the state continues to support procreation at any level, all denominations of Jews have become middle class.

Here is the great potential magnet for Judaism. The Talmudic tradition and the 1500 years of pariah status within Christianity and Islam have given the Jews an enormous defensive potential for educational civilizational advance in the modern scientific, democratic society. Here increasingly, brain supersedes brawn. Information technology, the entire structure of automated processes being created by the most highly educated humans on our planet is rapidly putting the unskilled, uneducated underclasses of the world at risk. With a population of more than seven billion humans on this earth, in contrast to the less than two billion one hundred years ago, given the capacity of 21st-century welfare programs to provide the wherewithal to support such vast population with anything but the most poverty laden forms of life-support, the Jews are an exemplar to the world.

The state of Israel is a testament to what the world would look like if it were Judaic in modern constitution. In spite of on one hand, the pressures of Arabic nihilism and anti-modernism, all rolled up in unending hatred of and lust to once more subordinate Jew to Muslim, and on the other the ultraorthodox willingness to pressure the secular Jews to institute a wide variety of ancient restrictions of their own concatenation, this is still one of the most open, progressive, democratic, scientific, free-enterprise societies in the world.

True, it has had to have shed its own and other's blood to survive. But, has any other nation in modern history responded to the level of overt aggression to its life, since its 1948 inception as a nation, and still maintained the liberal, open, institutional political and social structure. At the same time, due to the efforts of its people educationally and economically, Israel has prospered in this tough, competitive world environment.

The key, as we have noted earlier is Israel and the Jews commitment to modern scientific education, similar to that of the world's most advanced societies. The Chinese are today ramping up their scientific and technological prowess and their concomitant educational institutions. No nation threatens the existence of the Chinese communist government, only its own people from within. Few in China believe in the theological orthodoxy of the Chinese communist party, surely the leaders themselves do not.

While Israel is threatened by people surrounding it borders, and also within, those who are not Jews or believers in its philosophical and international mission, China is threatened by its own ethnic citizens, from within. Which nation will survive in its present form, and for how long, is the open question.

The world needs a belief system that reflects the Judaic civilizational experience, the struggle to fight against irrationality in belief and behavior, the experience of both the victories and defeats. As we have pointed out in earlier chapters the people of Israel, the Jews themselves are the products of this history, this struggle. The only precious historical contribution to civilization that has left us permanently, and to our memory of regret, is that of the high point of Hellenic culture. These Greeks gave us a permanent introduction to democracy, science, high intellectual art, and, of course, to secular philosophical dialectic and analysis.

The Jews sampled of this heritage. And if they were forced to walk away from the freedoms which the Hellenic opening provided, this memory came back to stimulate the great Jewish intellectuals of history alongside their Muslim and Christian confreres. It is a shared heritage. Only the Jews have firmly left behind theological intolerance of free creative thought and achievement, and have done so totally. It is only the Jews who today can open up a window of opportunity to all their confreres, Christian, Muslim, and all other religious sects, to say, join us in the secular unraveling of the depths of the moral and intellectual spirit of disciplined advance.

The World Needs Jews

There are few Jews in our world today who resist canons of the scientific mentality. This attitude, in medicine, reproductive genetics, technology, in business practice, even the practical empirical lore of cutting a diamond to pristine proportion, is universal. In a time of vast human multiplication, especially of the poor and uneducated, in a time of great irrational ideologies, who exploit our raw emotional limbic system nature, we will need reason and science to find our way forward. The Jews have the historical superstructure for a religion, a way of life that can command the best in us, in ethics, in the use of reason and science, and above all in the searching for a moral middle-class way of life for all humans, without the disabling incubus of social class warfare.

The Jews have pioneered in the creation of a classless society of the relatively poor. Now they can and must show the way for the world to achieve a classless bourgeoisie middle-class world of rational secular humans with a symbolic devotion to the historic struggle. This is a struggle for social justice and rationality, but at the same time a search for a high intellectual civilization without populist degradations.

It is very clear that the Jews will have to be, because of their present middle-class achievements *a people apart*, a minority striving for the best for the majority. For, there will be political gangsters as there were in the 20th century who saw the enormous social and technological ferment, exploding demographies, and vast disparities in economic and social conditions, for the opportunity to destroy, by working off the timeless fears and jelousies of those left behind, those who seemed ahead.

We see this in the case of Israel. Surrounding them are hundreds of millions of Muslims, disenfranchised, seduced by a barbarian version of their ancient if tribal monotheism, and pauperized in the process. Oil will one day give out, and what will they have left, engorged with human masses now without education, political experience, and hope? The hatred is there, even while their own exploiters live as medieval caliphs, on rented natural resources, while these masses wither in resentment.

The demagogues will come again, here even in the most wealthy of nations, in the early 21st century. There is danger in mass political frenzies. Some must stay aloof, to whistle the naked prince and his admirers into reality. It is going to be very difficult for any social group to remain outside the totalitarian magnet of centralization. That is why religion is critical. For, there are some things in religious commitment that are not for sale to the regnant political ideologies. The Jewish people have the heritage, the documents, the raw experience of being outside the dominant ethos, for attempting to protect the integrity of what they believe to be pure and impenetrable, by the momentary institutions of power.

But, can a few million Jews worldwide survive on a planet that will hold some nine to ten billion humans a few decades hence? It cannot be, it will not be. Simply, we need more Jews. This is critical to the survival of the fifteen million or so souls today of Jewish identification. But it is more important for a world of ten billion humans awaiting the planet not far into our future. The need then, is the recruitment, proselytizing, showing the flag to the increasingly unaffiliated, but educated. To those who hold out hope for a more rational world, a world in need of survivor's discipline, the Jewish faith is the only one that places its heritage in reason, education, and science, whose vision is democratic, egalitarian, and high in a culture of intellect. Judaism could rescue humanity from a barbarism that is displacing the human mind.

First, the Jews themselves must become aware of the growing challenge to their existence. The solutions of Reform, Conservative, Reconstructionists, Humanists, even socialist Yiddish-speaking Workmen Circleites, secular Ethical Culturists will not do the trick, no less the recidivates bowing to their dominating Tzaddiqs. What is needed is a new opening for the Jewish faith. This opening comprises the establishment of a flexible vision of an ancient heritage that incorporates its highest ethical and intellectual vision, open to all who want to enter. It means that new institutional forms need to be created which go beyond the Talmudic institutions created for a world long absent from our memory. All we need to do is to recall that these Talmudic institutions once supplanted a Judaism of animal sacrifice, forced tithing, to support priest and Temple.

A Concrete Future

What follows in the concluding chapter of this book is controversial. We will ask about the real need to have a professional, vocationally trained synagogue leadership. It is not etched in marble. Also, the question of admission to the community of Jews is raised, and the ultimate power of the rabbinate to say who is and is not a Jew, and how one "becomes" a Jew.

Further, we will raise the leadership question. What kinds of persons do we want to lead the new Jewish congregations, rabbis educated in the ritual cult or real intellectuals, the kinds of persons that have illuminated the glories of Judaism? Going even beyond these controversies is the issue of the recognition of the *Holocaust* as a supremely horrifying and epochal event in the historical sufferings of the Jews at the hands of the majority. There must be, not merely a ritualistic nod as at *Yom Kippur*, but a radical behavioral alteration that will inform the future of the Jewish people.

In essence, what have we learned from the destruction of the six million? Can we go on as a materialistic, both middle-class and wealthy ethnic minority ignoring the sacrifice of those six million who died for us. Must we not apply the same disciplines to our lives as did those ghettoized Talmudic students in the depths of the medieval age whose high intellectual achievements were subsequently released into the modern world? Most of their descendants suffered for their defensive intellectual disciplines. We few escapees have reaped the material fruits of their efforts. Will we consequently reap another whirlwind?

Important questions!

CHAPTER TWELVE

Values and the Future

"It is better to strip hides off animal carcasses than to say to other people, 'I am a great sage, I am a priest, provide me there fore with maintenance.' So did the Sages command us. Among the great sages there were hewers of wood, carriers of beams, drawers of water to irrigate gardens, and workers in iron and charcoal. They did not ask for public assistance, nor did they accept it when offered to them." [Maimonides *Mishneh Torah* "Gifts to the Poor" x, 18, (c. 1177 CE)]

A Model for the Secular

The Pharisees: "What counted was the life worthy of the world to come, the dogged trudging on the road to life eternal, the surmounting of every external and internal obstacle barring the way to the day of resurrection. The Patriarchs had lived such paradigmatic lives and they were even now with their Father in heaven; Moses had lived such a life and was even now basking in celestial bliss; the prophets had lived such lives and were even now awaiting the day of resurrection; the teachers of the twofold Law lived such lives as they yearned for the life which death could never snatch away."[1]

Leadership Choices

Judaism today represents itself to the world in three ways. One is the synagogue and the rabbi. They speak for Judaism even though they represent only a minority of Jews. The second visage of Judaism lies in its political re-creation, Israel, a secular multireligious entity that calls itself a "Jewish state." Of course this is the ancient home of the Israelites, now returned to them by the international community as recompense for the *Holocaust*. The third is the political realm. Here we have such organizations as AIPAC, the American Jewish Committee, as well as a number of organizations which are Zionist in orientation, supporting Israel to the public and the various political establishments, American and others.

In the first case the synagogue representation of Judaism looks back to the celebration of the great human moments of tradition, birth/circumcision; the bar/bat mitzvah of young adulthood; marriage; and death; the high holidays, the reading of the Torah, the Talmudic wisdom, the momentary expression of the ancient language, and much ritual, cultish observance during these critical identity events.

In the past Judaism has presented quite a different face to the world. The rituals, the laws, were all meant to secure a moral vision of human experience that differentiated Jews from others, a higher intellectuality aiming at a higher moral, familial, and community-centered vision of humanity.

There is little that differentiates a synagogue Jew today from his Gentile confreres. Yes, he may wear a skull cap or other accoutrement reminders of his/her faith. They may excuse themselves on certain days so that they might observe the Sabbath at a different time than their Christian co-workers or neighbors. So too, dietary restrictions might make for problematic meetings in the business or professional worlds. More likely even the orthodox would here modify their behavior so as to be competitive with the non-Jewish or non-orthodox.

But, is this the final meaning, the conclusive outcome of three thousand years of self-definition, the struggle to survive as a people, to overcome the ravages of barbarian hatred? The internal critics of Judaism, rabbis for the most part, themselves saw the vacuousness of the synagogue ritual, the sometime conspicuous consumption, the materialistic displays of status and wealth that went into these synagogue celebrations. No one disdains the celebratory, the fun or the joy. Is this enough to mark an important international religious denomination, a serious fellowship?

The problem of Israel, we have earlier discussed. It is a tourist magnet for observant Jews as well as cultural Jews. Not only does it contain the ancient historical monuments and events of the Holy Land within its borders. But it also represents a new face for official Judaism, a representation of Judaism that could be a worldwide model for all who would call themselves Jews. But as I have said before, don't put all your eggs in one basket. Israel in twenty or fifty years might and will be a very different political entity, merely considering demography. On one side, the ultraorthodox, on the other, the Arabs, here both within Israel itself and the surrounding sea of seething hatred.

The third, the political representation of Judaism to the outside world, is important, especially in the growing environment of anti-Semitism, often covertly accusatory of Israel's supposedly iniquitous treatment of the Palestinians. But aside from the influential cultural journal, *Commentary*, there is little of an intellectual/philosophical representation of what Judaism should stand for in the future, both to the Jewish community and the outside world.

All three dimensions of contemporary Judaism are fragile. One is dying, a cultish relic without intellectual or moral leadership. The other is a great national political, social and cultural vision, that one may not see in the same way a generation or two into the future. Israel is not a vast and powerful nation such as China, Germany, or even Brazil.

Insofar as synagogue worship is concerned, no doubt many Jews find great internal calm and satisfaction in the observance of these rituals. There is history here, ethnic identity, which all humans need. And indeed these observances and the commitment to a people and a tradition act as a great break on the universal politicization of the world with its emphasis on symbols of national patriotism, the flag, and the uniform, too often an emotional pull, a beckoning to diminished individual and community freedoms, often the call to war.

The political organizations are also fragile, in that they point to the supposed power of the Jews in the modern world, elite organizations attempting to fend off a rising tide of hostility. How much longer can they be effective considering the small demographic footprint, the minor voting blocs which are dispersed into the modern political arenas?

In the oncoming decades to follow, this human race, our modern civilization will be sorely tried by mass hysterias, emanating from the redistributive left, religious fundamentalism and the as yet inchoate fascist right. In times when the old sureties and standards of life are dissolving around us there will be many such seductions. Remember the 20th century when Fascism and Communism, nationalism, religious and ethnic hatred all sounded their respective siren calls for those millennial genocides. We will desperately need humans who will dig in their heels, as the Jews did against the Macedonian/Greeks and then the Romans. Indeed they lost. But the ongoing fight for civilization is still the key element in the struggle to attain human dignity. It is never about momentary victories or defeats.

There is still time here in the United States as elsewhere to create voluntary centers of allegiance that humans can anchor themselves to; still enunciate an institutional independence, the freedom of individuals to associate outside of the political tides. Here is where Judaism, with its emphasis on intellect, education, democracy, and independence of creative thought, should become a magnet for the likeminded of all backgrounds.

The only hope for Judaism in the near-and long-term future is to open the door to the wider intellectual community of Jews and non-Jews. That is why Rabbi Wine is so correct in emphasizing the debt Jews owe to their own literary, scientific, and philosophical leaders of the past several hundred years. These are the men and women who truly have, should, and will represent Judaism in the future, not the professional rabbinate striving within the synagogue to retain their traditional privileges and status.

The Open Door

The key question is from where will this leadership come? The era of 20th-century cultural, "yiddishkite" Judaism disappeared along with its infatuation with socialism and the language of the European ghetto, as beautiful a language as it is. The leadership Jews are yet out there in the community. Many have been alienated from the synagogue by it incomprehensible commitment to a Roman legal institution, the matriarchal principle as surreptitiously placed into the Mishnah. Over and over again, as we have attempted to describe in earlier chapters, new leadership has arisen among the Jews to allow them one more sunrise in our world, one more year to observe the principled monotheistic moral belief system, the commandments that symbolized a chosen-ness to be a holy people, a moral people.

Perhaps it will be a proselyte. Saadia Gaon (Sura, d. 942 CE), was himself accused by his Talmudic opponents as being an Egyptian proselyte. Two Jews, Jesus and Paul, created Christianity, and separated it from the Pharisees. But it is no matter from whence this new Jewish leadership comes as long as it identifies itself with the historic Jewish mission, indeed today still represented by the synagogue. For what was the synagogue in origin, but a Greek-language meeting house first established by the Alexandrian Jews c. 280–260 BCE, for the discussion and reading of the Holy Writings. It thence spread throughout the Diaspora, and into Judea itself.[2]

Napoleon in 1806, offered the Jews full citizenship if they would emerge from their Talmudic encapsulation and become French citizens while retaining their religious rights as practicing Jews, if not their separate legal institutions. Today the Jews need to open their institutional doors to those who wish to act as Jews, but at the same time want their Judaism to count in the modern world, and not shrink away as a cult. The official literature of the history of Judaism redounds in the wisdom of the Talmudic rabbis. But indeed how much more relevant to our world and the future of Judaic civilization are these writings than the writings, creative lives and thought of Baruch Spinoza, Moses Mendelssohn, Solomon Maimon, Heinrich Heine, Felix Mendelssohn, and Karl Marx. These men all belong to the Jews as well as civilizational humanity, yet only one of these men, Moses Mendelssohn, officially retained his synagogue practice. And, indeed there are many others who should be admitted through this open door.

Each potential grouping of Jewish associations, yes synagogues will have their literature of study. Here is Rabbi Sherwin Wine's list of eminent Jewish thinkers worthy of inclusion in any humanistic Jewish synagogue setting: Emile Durkheim, Salo Baron, Simon Dubnow, Theodore Gaster, I. L. Peretz, Sholem Aleichem, Chaim Zhitlowski, Ahad, Haam, Micah Berdichevsky, Theodor Herzl, Max Nordau, A.D. Gordon, Ber Borochov, Shaul Tchernikhovsky, Vladimir Jabotinsky, David Ben Gurion, Joseph Brenner, Albert Einstein, Sigmund Freud, Erich Fromm, Walter Lippman, Walter Kaufmann, Isaiah Berlin, Hannah Arendt, Horace Kallen, Yehuda Bauer, Haim Cohen, Albert Memmi, Gregorio Klimovsky, George Steiner, Yehuda Amichai, Amoz Oz, A.B. Yehoshua, Primo Levi, Franz Boas, Joseph Brenner, Jacob Bronowski, Howard Fast, Emma Goldman, Aaron David Gordon, Berl Katzenelson, Max Nordau, Hayyim Schauss, and Peretz Smolenskin.[3]

How many other artists, musicians, writers, could we add to this list? How many eminent Jews since the 18th century that have contributed to Western civilization, as earlier Jews have to the Torah, Holy Scriptures, Talmud, have been devout believers and practitioners of synagogue Judaism?

It does not matter what shape the new Jewish meeting house will take. For some, indeed the synagogue will remain a center for its symbolic architecture, for its ritual and holy days. Hopefully it could become, in addition, a place of intellectual discussion and high culture as it once was, not a place to "show off." Many Jews remember their fraternal secular cultural organizations where the holidays were tasty, the children learned about Judaism without the strictures of Talmudic law, where Judaism meant progress, the adaptation to life in the most democratic, freest environment the earth has ever known, the United States of America. Sadly, today these millions are assimilated, many intermarried, effectually lost to Judaism.

The United States can only continue to function as a democratic haven by the flourishing of independent, freely chosen, private, nongovernmental associations. This concept, the founders of the United States themselves believed to be a marker of a free society, the right to form groupings of the like-minded, religious or not, free of coercion from those temporarily ensconced in power.

Who should be welcomed within this expanding Jewish community? Certainly, no racial, ethnic, sexual, nor prior religious affiliation criterion should be invoked. Men and women, whatever their previous beliefs, who want to participate in a community of intellectuality, with a rich communitarian, historic heritage, whatever their formal educational backgrounds, should be cheered beyond the doorway into this Judaic sanctum of ideas and deep moral commitments. As Jews they will join a unique heritage, literary, philosophical, and moral. We humans need to know and feel the often painful story of humankind as it is recorded in this historic literature.

A new Talmud will here have begun, an encyclopedia of creative ventures into the meaning of our humanity, the moral and natural laws that need to be absorbed, as once the Jews accepted the laws of YHWH, through their great prophets. Today the laws of Nature's God are extrapolated from our human inquiry. The prophets who enunciate them hypothetically, the scholars and artists of our faith, will have them discussed, tested, and evaluated in terms of the oral and written ideals of the Jewish tradition.

The test of any structure of fundamental natural laws is its ultimate impact on the human condition. The human condition is always impacted by the moral law that we create to make possible our highest functionings as cultural beings. We humans want to survive as biological creatures. But our biology is now mainly enunciated through our social/cultural behavior. It is this question of the nature of the laws and injunctions that we must follow that has become the grist for the basic questions of human survival. But survival cannot be measured by the barbarian exploitation of the natural resources of our environment. The test of civilization lies in the transformation of these resources by our intellect, our emotional as well as our cortical powers.

The above issues need sober discussion, and from a variety of philosophical standpoints. However, there can be no higher power than the authority of the autonomous human mind. Never should our individual consciousness be subordinated to supernatural injunction, inevitably and always opportunistically transmitted by priest, minister, mullah or rabbi.

A Reprieve

Rabbinic Judaism had its earliest murmurings under the comfortable and relatively benign Persian hegemony and the Judean immersion in Second Temple rite. This priestly guidance crumbled under the attack by Seleucid Greek governance and the Maccabean revolt of 166 BCE. Judah Maccabee, in his struggles with Antiochus and the latter's Jewish allies revealed the theological changes which had over time gradually overtaken the Jews. The Jews had now lived for almost four hundred years under external political domination. The world had changed, the Temple and its priesthood had changed. The powerful impact of Greek thought surged throughout the Hellenistic world. In times of great uncertainty, rationality does not always offer humans serene recompense.

In {2 Maccabees 7:1–42} written c. 124 BCE there is recounted the story of the resurrection of the seven martyrs of the Maccabean struggle and their reward with eternal life, while the wicked Antiochus IV, is predicted to be punished in eternity.

This section refers to Judah's battles against the Seleucids, c. 161 BCE. Other discussion of the resurrection of the individual, in this case Judah's own warriors are related in {2 Macabees 12: 39–45}.[4] References to resurrection and eternal life, with regard to the Maccabean revolt can also be found in {Daniel 12:1–3}, c. 165 BCE.[5]

Clearly for the *am ha aretz*, the people of the land who precipitated the revolt, these mystery-religion facets of belief had already permeated their sensibilities. And the scribes and Pharisees abounded in the land to feed them this new message of the Oral Law given to Moses by God on high. In the older Pentateuchal religious tradition, now upheld by the Sadducean Aaronite/Zadokite elite, there was no personal salvation. Individual and Israel were one, the punishments took place on earth, and the dead were relegated to the dark underworld, *sheol*, and forever. In a world of alienation, the Hellenistic/Roman, created by great, distant, and untouchable power, the individual needed solace. To think of the poor and the oppressed as being given a portion of a second, happy and eternal life with the arrival of the Messiah, while the arrogant, wealthy and power laden would be relegated after death to unending suffering, became solace to the pariahs, soon to be all the Jews and the Christians themselves, who eagerly incorporated this Pharisaic teaching.

Resurrection, the awaiting of the Messiah, is a core element of fifteen hundred years of Jewish apartness, a religious balm for the suffering of the day. It was an integral part of a belief system that held them to a defensive intellectual and moral discipline. It constituted the moral center of their experiential beings. No more; we don't believe in such things. We must create a new internal discipline and the organizational and social support system ever apart from the powers that be so as not to be absorbed by them. These distant powers are looming ever threateningly whether they exist in the United States, Israel, or anywhere.

The Jews today constitute a leadership class. They are everywhere in the world participants in the seats of power. To the anti-Semite Arab or others this merely confirms the view that the Jews—all 15 million of them in a world of seven billion humans—are joined in a conspiracy to dominate the world. The paradox is that while there exist dangers for intellectuals, middle-class leaders, Jews and others, they are now indispensable in making the world work.

The Moral Vision

> One who loves gold will not be justified; one who pursues money will be led astray by it. Many have come to ruin because of gold, and their destruction has met them face to face.... Blessed is the rich person who is found blameless, and who does not go after gold (gold = *mamon*—Heb/Aramaic). Who is he that we may praise him? For he has done wonders among his people. {Ben Sira (Sirach) 31:5–9}.[6]

In the 2008–2012 international economic crisis, brought on by the financial institutions, almost dissolving the international system, it was the governments of the world that saved them. Governments themselves, and worldwide, were initially culpable. In the United States an irrational attempt to create bogus mortgage value bloated our economy. The financiers were quick to seize the opportunity. The ingenious abstract gambling instruments that were created made many super-wealthy before the energy crunch brought down this house of cards. Even then these clever parasites walked away with billions of dollars in bonuses.

The interesting outcome was that the banks and their financiers went unscathed, subsequently once more immersed in vast government transmitted wealth, the steep interest-rate curve. Yet they still were indispensable to the functioning of the system, thus becoming a metaphysically corrupt part of the social equation. The same universal process of power centralization and political/oligarchic partnerships are occurring in the communist world, yes, in Russia and also in China. Here nations wish to modernize their political-military-technological system. Mostly the intent is to empower the political system, perhaps as an ancillary benefit a boost to the long-downtrodden masses.

All nations recognize their need for some free enterprise for the business classes to function, as well as to modestly free the intellectual power of the professions, from medicine to computers to missile launchers. But the demand to all, and tacitly agreed to by the beneficiaries of such political dispensations is for these elect to lobotomize part of their brain function. Everywhere in the world there is a process of power centralization in which the educated and essential minds are now in bed intellectually and philosophically with the party in power. In the United States it may only be academic tenure, or government science grants. Perhaps it will turn out well for the masses. Perhaps the openness and creativity of our civilizational sense of progress will survive the 10 billion humans who are on the way to inhabiting our planet.

The injunction for the Jews corporately and as individuals is clear. It cannot have been altered from the time of the Mosaic laws. To be *chosen* is not to be materialistically or socially privileged. It is to be holy in the largest sense of that word, to be a moral human being living as part of a moral community. But to be moral requires thought and self-imposed disciplines. And these laws must be more than regulations for the preparation of food, or the program of synagogue attendance on the Sabbath. And here is where Judaism will be tested in forthcoming decades. It can continue as it has for the past several hundred years, generations of rabbis attempting to adapt the Talmudic tradition to a new generation of ever smaller numbers of participating Synagogue Jews, finding new ways to attempt to plug the dyke. It cannot be done. This Judaic setting is for yesterday, a marginal memory of the past.

To rescue Judaism to make it congruent with its political mirror in Israel requires a wholly different vision. This would require the maintenance of the moral commitments of the past, with teeth, as Moses and the prophets demanded of its people. It would also shape this moral center with regard to the evolution of the human race into the 21st century and beyond. Rabbi Ben Zakkai so compromised with regard to Roman power, as did the writers of Mishnah, the polygamous gaons of Muslim Babylonia, even Rabbi Gershom of Mainz with his Christian neighbors.

Moses Mendelssohn saw the need in his day in Berlin. The disintegration of the Ashkenazi rabbinic tradition was quick and convulsive. In our time the growth of wealth and power of the Europeans allowed the Jews to move out of the ghetto as entrepreneurs in the Christian world, or as converts to Christianity attempting to move upward rapidly in social status. The subsequent hatred of the Jews for their rapid intellectual and social advance set off a thunder cloud of anti-Semitism, eventually the mad horror of the *Holocaust* and the destruction of European Jewry.

But in this almost three-hundred-year period many Christians also participated in this rise to power and wealth. The millions that were destroyed in the *Holocaust* were mainly the poor Jews of Eastern Europe. Most of the Jews that Hitler raved on about in Germany and in Vienna were able to escape. Today the larger world within which the Jews live is not advancing in wealth. With each year, rational analysis argues that the economic/social situation will become worse. The Jews are now middle class and above throughout the world. Once they too thought that they were needed, then for the survival of Germany, even as the Nazis arose to power. Their presumption was probably accurate. But madness easily erases reality, and Hitler almost took down European civilization and the Jews before his atrocity was destroyed.

The Jews must become a balancing weight in the reshaping of civilization as it goes through forthcoming centuries of turmoil and reconstruction. Our planet will never be able to support the many billions now and in the future arriving on its surface. The injustice, the cruelty, the barbarism, the totalitarianism which may lurk and explode at various moments as the human race attempts to find its adaptive center for sustained and pluralistic progress in its civilizational career, cannot be catalogued in advance. But the Jews will once more be vulnerable as even now the increasing anti-Semitism in the advanced nations of the world expresses this hatred in ever more tangible form. Look at the State of Israel, and the profound danger that surrounds it by self-proclaimed enemies as well as its supposed founders and former supporters in the international community.

The hope for true Jewish reconstruction and progress lies in the expansion in numbers and activity of Jewish organizations, diverse and pluralistic. Hopefully the synagogue could lead in this restoration of Jewish influence by becoming a more intellectually and culturally adventurous institution. Once, it was such a magnet for the Gentiles. Other more secular forms of Judaic social and study groupings should be formed. What would be exhilarating and defensive of Judaism would be the identification of minds such as Einstein, Freud, even a Marx, lecturing as Jewish creative intellectuals to the world at large. Sadly, this can no longer take place from the standpoint of Talmudic Judaism.

All the post-Enlightenment synagogue transmutations of the ancient faith no longer resonate meaningfully except for those few ultra fundamentalists who live in another world, sadly supported by the taxes of the real world. In the nexus of events today and tomorrow, it will not be enough for a rabbi or a political leader of Israel to speak for the Jews. There must be another vision that will naturally flower into reality by the in-depth probings of a new generation of Jews studying their Judaic inheritance and its potencies for the future.

A Strong and Modest People

"Ah you who join house to house, who add field to field, until there is room for no one but you, and you are left to live alone in the midst of the land! The Lord of hosts has sworn in my hearing: Surely so many houses shall be desolate, large and beautiful homes without inhabitants" {Isaiah 5: 8–9, c. 730 BCE}. This is but a small sampling of the prophetic hatred of unjustly acquired and consumed wealth and privilege, at the expense of the worthy and guileless poor. But it is applicable at all times. And for the Jews who have the present abilities and the historic commitment for the highest levels of moral behavior the issue of leadership, personal sobriety is critical. Otherwise our privileges will be fatal to Jews and Judaism.

New Jewish groups will naturally form themselves within and without the synagogue when the barriers for entrance into Judaism are lifted. The new "God fearers" will be the rational and the morally committed. They will join in with the gusty sense of uniting at the great old festivals, a heritage of commemoration and celebration, as with the Yiddishites. They may want to come together as do the ethical culturists in serious discussion of important human and ethical questions. Eventually all these groupings of Jews will swell the agenda of survival in reason and science and our sense of justice.

But as Jews they should not be personally wealthy. They should not as a matter of necessity have to eschew those professions, businesses in which they may gain much material wealth. Wealth is power. And the importance of wealth is the power to do good and thus remain human and accessible to one's confreres. To remain a Jew there must be an ethical injunction. Be "classless," stay in the middle. Give your wealth away for high civilizational purposes, the intellectual fine and performing arts, museums, universities, medical research and hospitals, for all that is good, Judaic in nature or not. Teach your children to labor and not be separated from this middle. Live with modesty and togetherness in the community of Jews and aspiring humankind.

How can we consider rabbis to be true Jews in their invitations for the supposed conversion of the rich and famous, Hollywood and media stars with histories yet uncured of questionable if not degenerate ethical behaviors. Did these supposed converts surrender their wealth, and enter onto a new road of personal moral salvation? One does not ask for Jews to be celibates or puritans, hardly. But every Jewish congregation, synagogue or other, must establish standards by which its members will be judged. Do we want wealthy Jews who are thieves in the market place, convicted or no, to sit or stand among us?

The Jews today are leaders in all the walks of life. Now they must become moral and intellectual defenders of the substance of civilized life, protectors of the law, a democratic people who fight against irrational ideologies from the left or the right. Much is made of Karl Marx's anti-Semitism, his defining of the Jews as lustful for wealth. Part of his critique was a self-hating rationalization for becoming a *converso*. But part of his bilge was stimulated by the reality that within a few decades of the emancipation, the Jewish tradition of banking (usury?), as we have noted earlier, did produce a great number of wealthy Jewish banking and merchant families. They had the hidden knowledge of such matters, and made use of these talents in the wider world when they could. But these Jewish financiers did work within the lawful structure of their nationalities. Their wealth was part of the great expansion in wealth for all the European and North American nations. And of course Marx lived in church-mouse poverty, happily receiving handouts from a wealthy capitalist, still a Jew, Engels.

What kind of criteria can Jewish congregations hold their members to? As the saying goes with regard to pornography, you will know it when you see it. The Jews can be unique in the world of the 21st century and beyond, because their fellowship of belief and behavior will rest on an ancient and rich written and unwritten tradition in the search for a chosen-ness that seeks to place their own self-discipline onto a higher vision of human life, one without graven images, saints, gods, monks, today even without angels, the anticipation of the coming of the Messiah. We do not today need all the vestments and paraphernalia that decorate the religions of today. We need to cleanse ourselves of the robes, the beards, the trinket symbols of supposed holiness and affiliation. Ordinary humans choosing a leadership, a membership structure which allows them to speak for humanity and civilization, this is what Judaism ought to become. This leadership, not professional, not reimbursed, not necessarily trained in seminaries or rabbinical academies, so as to earn their living; merely secular humans using their minds and hearts to approach the most complex and difficult questions that have and will face humanity, now in intimate face-to-face contexts. And if they need to hire a rabbi or "teacher" to officiate at the high holy days, at a wedding or funeral, they can find him/her.

The *Holocaust* in Memory

The literature of Judaism gives poignant emphasis to past losses of their homeland, Jerusalem and its Temple. The heart throbbed as those elite groups of Jews were taken off as exiles to Babylon. Along the Euphrates, given the freedom to work, practice their religion, they prospered, but yearned. In less than three generations they were allowed to return by a new governance. Some did, to remember and rebuild.

While Israel is a testament to a new world governance that remembered the *Holocaust*, it is but several generations old. The *Holocaust* seared the lives and memories of all Jews throughout the world. Nevermore, say the Israelis, and indeed the Jews of the world do assent. But can *you* be so sure? There has to be an ongoing and perennial teaching mission here in regard to this event. That teaching does not necessarily lie in the political support for Israel, or to the synagogue cult which now symbolizes Judaism to the outside world. It must be rooted deep within the behavior and psyche of all Jews.

The Jews were singled out not merely for their religious practices, a minority in a larger demography of Christians. Most of those initially targeted by the fascists throughout Europe were largely assimilated, often secularized. That is why the Nuremburg laws went into such specificity as to who could be first excluded from society and then butchered.

That is why when we argue for a Judaism to be renewed as a defensive creed, in all behavioral respects, moral, social, political, economic, and intellectual, we argue for the disciplines of the Mosaic commandments. Naturally, the challenge is to reinterpret for our time and for our survival. Modesty, intellectuality, creativity, and a deep skepticism in being pulled in surreptitiously or overtly for momentary seductions by the powers that be. If there be emoluments to be obtained by Jews, then these should be returned to civilization for the protection of the millennial values that Jews claim to follow.

Modern Judaism: The Essence

1. Principles: There are limits to human knowledge. Ultimately we are as with our more ignorant ancestors, products of natural processes beyond our ken, even given

the powers of scientific reason. The danger is that we extrapolate this ignorance into an arrogance of unreason, ideology. Humans are susceptible and emotional. Thus we need science to help guide us tentatively and defensively in our behavior, personal as well as communitarian. Scientific method should be the modulating discipline for what should be tried, deemed successful or not. Beware of systems of belief that demand that humans bow down to human authority pretending to exert power in the name of ultimate, demanding gods.

2. Organization: The new Judaism will consist of congregations in study, reflection, celebration and mourning. Leadership will be by the wisest. Rabbis may be called upon for cultish traditions, readings in the ancient languages, officiating, if necessary. The study of the literature of Judaism should be undertaken by all Jews, not merely the professional rabbinate. Humanism lies in the application of reason to moral, political, and social problems. Sensitivity to natural, social, and human change and progress are absorbed in the definition of humanism as well as liberalism. Congregations of Jews can call themselves synagogues or not, here without the pomp, conspicuous consumption, or pseudoreligious ritual.

3. Political Association: Should Jews, qua Jews be part of the political establishment? Should Judaism become a religion of values, a congregation of the educated, an external (*perushim*) moral and intellectual community devoted to the critique of political power and privilege? How integrated into the power structure Jews will decide to become, is an important moral and intellectual question that needs to be debated, studied, then decided.

4. Jews and Wealth: Today Jews are overwhelmingly middle class. To survive in a world of want they will have to represent in their life behavior civilizational discipline, exemplars to the world as to how humans should live. Every congregation, synagogue or not, should make the necessary judgments about the character of their membership Wealth should be earned in order to be gifted for worthy high civilizational causes. No hereditary or unearned wealth should corrupt the generations. Educate your Jewish children to study, work, and become worthy.

5. Theological Judaism: Supernaturalism should remain a metaphor of our historic experience. Supernaturalism should not be a crutch for our experimental sojourn through life. Rationality, discipline, defensive living, the use of naturalistic canons of thought and social policy should become the anvil for our productive contributions to humankind. The survival of Judaism depends upon a modern vision of the moral depths of what it means to be a Jew.

6. Social Responsibility: The Jews have practiced social responsibility to their own for centuries. The basis for Jewish philanthropy within the community and at a distance to Jewish communities in danger, has always been based on the test of behavior in the face of circumstance. When individuals, families and communities, disintegrate morally and thus socially, parting from their obligations, Mosaic or

Talmudic, Jewish tradition has been to allow individuals, families and communities to suffer the consequences of their misbehavior. Here Judaism in essence argues that individual responsibility is the key to the larger issue of social obligation and responsibility, this, at the very least, for the survival of the community.

7. The *Holocaust*: This tragedy of the European Jews is the overriding lesson, for all time, and for all Jews. It is also a symbol of the irrationality and weakness of human beings in the face of ideology. Other genocides of the 20th century and into the 21st reveal the vulnerability of achieving humans, vulnerable minorities in the face of jealousy, ethnic, religious, and social-class hatred. Every Jew must remember the *Shoah*, and take stock of their own lives, never to become weak, defenseless targets for the irrational. This event will for long be a challenge for the future of the Jewish community, beyond the ancient Synagogue.

8. Leadership Education: There are in many nondenominational and even in ostensibly Christian American colleges and universities, Jewish Studies areas of learning. But these are not necessarily training grounds for the secular leadership of a growing Jewish community. Important Jewish institutions of higher education, especially those which train rabbis, Hebrew Union College, Yeshiva University, The Jewish Theological Seminary, and others, would seem to be paradigmatic institutions for the training of a non-rabbinate leadership class, supremely versed in Jewish biblical, Talmudic learning and history, Jewish philosophical and ethical traditions, those values which Jews must take to the outside world to show the non-Jew an entrance way into Judaism.

9a. Who Should Be a Jew? The door to being a Jew should be open for those educated or wanting, to be educated, to infuse the difficult problems of morality and values with reason, especially important in these very straightened times. The ancient heritage, the sacred writings and experiences, the Talmudic tradition, even only taking into account their historicity have nevertheless revealed hidden truths that have allowed Judaism to evolve so as to produce a creative, rational, progressive people. The Roman/Mishnaic intermarriage restrictions, the current rabbinic barriers to becoming a Jew are artificial reflections of the theocratic controls still maintained by the traditional rabbinate. These should be dissolved. Every Jewish community/congregation/synagogue should be able to establish its own criteria for what it means to become and be a Jew, only requiring circumcision, now a universally valued scientific medical heritage of the Semites and Hamites.

9b. "The consideration given by our legislator {Moses} to the equitable treatment of aliens also merits attention. It will be seen that he took the best of all possible measures at once to secure our customs from corruption, and to throw them open ungrudgingly to any who elect to share them. To all who desire to come and live under the same laws with us, he gives a gracious welcome holding that it is not family ties alone which constitute relationship, but agreement in the principles of conduct."[7]

Notes

Chapter two: Sources for the Religious

1. Finkelstein, L. 1955. "Jewish Religion: Its Beliefs and Practices," in *The Jews: Their History, Culture and Religion*, ed., L. Finkelstein, New York: Harper & Bros., pp. 1386–1387.
2. Itzkoff, S. W. 2000. *The Inevitable Domination by Man: An Evolutionary Detective Story*, Ashfield, MA: Paideia.
3. Marshack, A. 1972. *The Roots of Civilization*, London: Weidenfield and Nicolson.
4. Cassirer, E. 1929/1957. *The Philosophy of Symbolic Forms*, Vol. III, New Haven, CT: Yale Univ. Press, p. 90.
5. Charvat, P. 2002. *Mesopotamia before History*, New York: Routledge, pp. 158–159.
6. Bottero, J. 1992. *Mesopotamia*. Chicago: Univ. of Chicago Press, p. 193.
7. Postgate, J. N. 1992. *Early Mesopotamia*, London: Routledge, p. 299.

Chapter three: Torah/Law

1. Urbach, E. E. 1989. "Torah," *Judaism: A People and Its History*, ed., by R. Seltzer, New York: Macmillan, p. 85.
2. Urbach, *op. cit.*, p. 86.
3. Two excellent sources with which to identify the various strands of biblical tradition, i.e., who wrote what with regard to which group of writers wrote what: Gottwald, Norman. 1985. *The Hebrew Bible, A Socio-Literary Introduction*, Philadelphia: Fortress Press; Friedman, R. E. 1987/1997. *Who Wrote the Bible?* San Francisco: Summit/Harper.

4. Cowley, Arthur E. "Hebrew Literature," in *Encyclopedia Britannica, op. cit.*, 11th ed., Vol. 13, p. 169; Gordis, Robert, in Finkelstein, Louis, ed., 1955. *The Jews: Their History, Culture, and Religion*, 2 vols., New York: Harper and Bros.,Vol. 1, p. 482.
5. Campbell, Edward F. 1998. "A Land Divided," in Coogan, M. D., ed., *The Oxford History of the Biblical World*, New York: Oxford, p. 276; Cogan, M. 1998. "Into Exile," in Coogan, M. D., ed., *op. cit.*, p. 347; Halpern, B. 1981. "Sacred History and Ideology: Chronicles 'Thematic Structure—Indications of an Earlier Source'" in Friedman, R. E., ed., 1981. *The Creation of Sacred Literature*. Berkeley: Univ. of California.
6. *see passim;* Friedman, R. E., 1997. *Who Wrote the Bible?* New York: HarperCollins; Itzkoff, S. W. 2004. *Soul of the Israelites (Who Are the Jews?* Vol. 1), Ashfield, MA: Paideia.
7. 2 Kings 22:8; 2; Chronicles 34: 14–15.
8. Stenning J. F. 1910. "Bible: Old Testament Texts," *Encyclopedia Britannica 11th Edition*, Vol. III, p. 856.
9. Weber, M. 1921/1952. *Ancient Judaism*, New York: Free Press, p. 210.
10. Weber, M. *op cit*, p. 450.
11. Weber, M., *op cit.*, pp. 159, 161.
12. Weinfeld, M. 1989. "Israelite Religion," in *Judaism: A People and Its History*, ed., by R. Seltzer, New York: Macmillan, pp. 36–61.
13. McBride, S. D., Jr. 1989. "Deuteronomy: Introduction," *Harper/Collins Study Bible*. New York: Harper Collins, p. 268.
14. Weinfeld, *op cit.*, pp. 45–51.
15. Albright, W. F., 1955 "The Biblical Period," in Finkelstein, L., ed., *The Jews*, Vol. I, New York: Harper & Bros., p. 47.
16. Albright, *op. cit.* pp. 52–53.
17. Meyers, E. 1987. *Haggai, Zechariah 1–8: A New translation, Introduction and Commentary*. Anchor Bible 25B, Garden City New York: Doubleday, pp. 10–11.
18. Clines, David J. A. 1993. "Notes to Nehemiah," *Harper/Collins Study Bible*, New Standard Edition, New York: Harper/Collins, Notes, p. 734.
19. Leith, M. J. W. 1999. "Israel among the Nations," in Coogan, M., ed., 1998. *The Oxford History of the Biblical World, op. cit.*, p. 375.
20. Bickerman, Elias J. 1955. "The Historical Foundations of Postbiblical Judaism," in Finkelstein, Louis, ed., 1955. *The Jews, Their History, Culture, and Religion*, Vol. 1, N.Y.: Harper and Bros, pp. 86–88, p. 98.
21. Levine, L. 1999. "The Age of Hellenism," in H. Shanks, ed., *Ancient Israel*, Washington DC: Biblical Archaeological Society, p. 479.
22. Cogan, M. . . . Purvis pp. 205–207.
23. Clines, David J. A. 1993. "Notes to Nehemiah," *Harper/Collins Study Bible*, New Standard Edition, New York: Harper/Collins, Notes, p. 734.
24. Albright, W. F., "The Biblical Period," in Finkelstein, L., ed., *The Jews, op. cit.*, p. 49, estimates that the population was about 20,000; Finkelstein, I., and Silberman, N. A., in *The Bible Unearthed, op. cit.*, p. 308, estimate the population at 30,000.
25. Finkelstein, I., and Silberman, N. 2001. *The Bible Unearthed*. New York: The Free Press, p. 269.
26. Leith, *op. cit.*, p. 375.
27. Leith, *op cit*.
28. Meyers, E. 1987 *op. cit.*, pp. 10–11.

Chapter four: Scriptures

1. Clines, David J. A. 1993. "Introduction to 1 Esdras," *Harper/Collins Study Bible*, New Standard Edition, New York: Harper/Collins, p. 1723.
2. Leith, M. J. W. 1998. "Israel among the Nations," in Coogan, M., ed., 1998. *The Oxford History of the Biblical World, op. cit.*, p. 371; Myers, J. M. 1996. "Nehemiah," *Encyclopedia Judaica*, Vol. 12, Jerusalem: Ketev Publishing House, pp. 1114–1117.
3. Bickerman, Elias J. 1955. "The Historical Foundations of Postbiblical Judaism," in Finkelstein, Louis, ed., 1955. *The Jews, Their History, Culture, and Religion*, 2 vols., New York: Harper and Bros., Vol. 1, pp. 81–82.
4. Levine, Lee. 1999. "The Age of Hellenism," in Shanks, H., ed., 1999. *Ancient Israel*, Washington, D.C: Biblical Archaeological Society, p. 254.
5. Towner, W. Sibley. 1993. "Introduction to Malachi," in *Harper/Collins Study Bible*, New York: Harper/Collins, pp. 1428–1429.
6. Bickerman, Elias J. 1955. "The Historical Foundations of Postbiblical Judaism," in Finkelstein, Louis, ed., 1955. *The Jews, Their History, Culture, and Religion*, Vol. 1, New York: Harper and Bros., p. 98.
7. *Ibid.*, p. 76.
8. *Ibid.*, p. 75.
9. *Ibid.*, p. 77.
10. *Ibid.*, p. 79.
11. *Ibid.*, pp. 81–82.
12. *Ibid.*, pp. 97–99.
13. *Ibid.*, pp. 100–101.
14. Gottwald, N. K. 1985. *The Hebrew Bible, A Socio-Literary Introduction*, Philadelphia: Fortress Press. pp. 121–122.
15. Bickerman, *op cit*, p. 100.
16. Bickerman, *op. cit.*, p. 88; Jaeger, W. "Greeks and Jews: The First Greek Records of Jewish Religion and Civilization," *Journal of Religion*, XVIII, 38.
17. Bickerman, *op. cit.*, p. 102.
18. Bickerman, *op. cit.*, p. 88; Jaeger, *op. cit.*, 38.
19. Gruen, Erich S. 2001. "Jewish Perspectives on Greek Culture in Hellenism," in Collins, John J., and Sterling, Gregory E., eds. 2001. *Hellenism in the Land of Israel*, Note 101; Notre Dame, IN: Univ. of Notre Dame Press p. 83, Bickerman, *op. cit.*, pp. 88–89.
20. Bickerman, *op. cit.*, pp. 88–91.
21. Finkelstein, I., and Silberman, N. S. 2001. *The Bible Unearthed*, New York: The Free Press, pp. 315–316.
22. Bickerman, *op. cit.*, p. 100.
23. Rivkin, E. 1978. *A Hidden Revolution*, Nashville, TN: Abingdon, pp. 215 *ff*.
24. Levine, Lee I. 1999. "The Age of Hellenism," in Shanks, H., ed., 1999. *Ancient Israel*, Washington, DC: Biblical Archaeological Society, pp. 246–248.
25. *Ibid.*, p. 341, Note 40.
26. *Ibid.*, p. 249.

27. Bickerman *op. cit.*, p. *106ff.*
28. Greenspoon, L. J. 1998. "Between Alexandria and Antioch," in Coogan, M., ed., 1998. *Oxford History of the Biblical World, op. cit.*, pp. 455–457.
29. Levine, Lee I. 1999. "The Age of Hellenism," in Shanks, H., ed., 1999. *Ancient Israel, op. cit.*, pp. 246–248.
30. Vanderkam, J. C. 2001. "Greek at Qumran," in Collins, John J., and Sterling, Gregory E., eds. 2001. *Hellenism in the Land of Israel, op. cit.*, pp. 175–181.
31. Levine, Lee I. 1999. "The Age of Hellenism," in Shanks, H., ed., 1999. *Ancient Israel, op. cit.*, pp. 259–261.
32. *Ibid.*, p. 250.
33. Rivkin, E. 1989. "Pharisees," in R. Seltzer, ed., *Judaism: A People and Its History*. New York: Macmillan, pp. 65–71.
34. Rivkin, 1989. *Op. cit.*, p. 66.
35. Rivkin, *Ibid.*, p. 67
36. Rivkin, E. 1978. *A Hidden Revolution*, Nashville, TN: Abingdon.
37. Schiffman, I. 1985. *Who Was a Jew?* Hoboken, NJ: Ktav, pp. 44, 91.
38. Levine, Lee I. 1999. "The Age of Hellenism," in Shanks, H., ed., 1999. *Ancient Israel, op. cit.*, p. 263; Levine, Amy-Jill. 1998. "Visions of Kingdoms, From Pompeii to the First Jewish Revolt," in Coogan, M., ed., 1998. *The Oxford History of the Biblical World, op. cit.*, pp. 486, 512.
39. Goldin, Judah. 1955. "The Period of the Talmud (135 B.C.E.–1035 C.E.)," in Finkelstein, Louis, ed., 1955. *The Jews, Their History, Culture, and Religion, op. cit.*, Vol. 1, p. 148.
40. Goldin, J. 1955, *op cit*, pp. 130–132.
41. Gottwald, N. K. 1985. *The Hebrew Bible, A Socio-Literary Introduction, op. cit.*, p. 413.
42. Levine, Lee I. 2000. *The Ancient Synagogue*, New Haven, CT: Yale Univ. Press, p. 357.
43. Gaventa, B. R. 1993. "Notes to Acts," *Harper/Collins Study Bible, op. cit.*, p. 2090; Levine, Amy-Jill. 1998. "Visions of Kingdoms: From Pompeii to the First Jewish Revolt," in Coogan, M., ed., 1998. *The Oxford History of the Biblical World, op. cit.*, p. 477.
44. Gaventa, B. R. 1993. "Notes to Acts," *Harper Collins Study Bible, op. cit.*, p. 2068.
45. Noss, J. B. 1949. *Man's Religions*, New York: Macmillan, p. 576.
46. Noss, 1949, *op cit*, pp. 576–577.
47. Gottwald, N. K. 1985. *The Hebrew Bible, A Socio-Literary Introduction, op. cit.*, p. 6.
48. Goldin, J. "The Period of the Talmud" in Finkelstein ed., The Jews, Their History, Culture and Religion, *op. cit.*, p. 123.
49. Marcus, R. 1955. "Hellenistic Jewish Literature," in Finkelstein, Louis, ed., 1955. *The Jews, Their History, Culture, and Religion*, 2nd ed., Vol. 2, N.Y.: Harper and Bros., p. 746.
50. *Ibid.*
51. Goldin, Judah. 1955. "The Period of the Talmud (135 B.C.E.–1035 C.E.)," in Finkelstein, Louis, ed., 1955. *The Jews, Their History, Culture, and Religion, op. cit*, Vol. 1, p. 152; Lieberman, S. 1965. *Greek in Jewish Palestine*, New York: Feldheim Publishers, pp. 1, 20.

Chapter five: Talmudic Republic

1. Seland, T. 1995. "Establishment Violence in Philo and Luke," Biblical Interpretation Series, Leiden: Brill.

2. Johnson, Paul. 1987. *A History of the Jews*, New York: Harper and Row, p. 148.
3. Bigg, Charles, and Schurer, Emil. 1911. "Philo," *Encyclopaedia Britannica*, 11th ed., Vol. 21, New York: Cambridge Univ. Press, p. 411.
4. Gruen, Erich S. 2001. "Jewish Perspective on Greek Culture in Hellenism," in Collins, John J., and Sterling, Gregory E., eds., *Hellenism in the Land of Israel, op. cit.*, pp. 76–77.
5. Ruppin, A. 1973. *Jews in the Modern World*, New York: Arno Press, p. 22.
6. Juster, Jean. *Les Juifs dans l'Empire Romain*, 1, 209f, cited in Baron, S. W. *Social and Religious History of the Jews* 1, 132f; Goldin, Judah. 1955. "The Period of the Talmud (135 B.C.E.–1035 C.E.)," in Finkelstein, Louis, ed., 1955. *The Jews, Their History, Culture, and Religion, op. cit.*, Vol. 1, Note 49, p. 203.
7. Sterling, Gregory E. 2001. "Judaism between Jerusalem and Alexandria," in "Hellenism," in Collins, John J., and Sterling, Gregory E., eds. 2001. *Hellenism in the Land of Israel, op. cit.*, pp. 267–269.
8. Avi Yonah, M. 1945. *Byeme Roma Ubizantiyon*, Jerusalem: Magnes Press, p. 175f., Goldin, Judah. 1955. "The Period of the Talmud (135 B.C.E.-1035 C.E.)," in Finkelstein, Louis, ed., 1955. *The Jews, Their History, Culture, and Religion, op. cit.*, Vol. 1, Note 28, p. 212
9. Levine, L. 1999. "The Age of Hellenism," in *Ancient Israel*, ed., by H. Shanks, *op. cit.*, pp. 257–258.
10. Danby, H. 1933. *The Mishnah*, C. 220 CE, tr., with Introduction, Oxford: Oxford Univ. Press, p. xv.
11. Danby, H. 1933. *op. cit.*
12. Goldin, J. 1955. "The Period of the Talmud" in Finkelstein, L. ed., *The Jews, Their History, Culture, and Religion, op. cit.*, Vol. I, p. 152.
13. Urbach, E. 1989. "Torah," in *Judaism: A People and its History*, ed., by R. Seltzer, New York: Macmillan, p. 97.
14. Baron, S. W. 1942. *The Jewish Community*, Vol. 1, Philadelphia: The Jewish Publication Society of America, p. 141.
15. Bader, G. 1988. *Jewish Spiritual Heroes*, Northdale, NJ: Jason Aronson, pp. 411–436.
16. Rosner, F. 1975. *Moses Maimonides, Commentary on the Mishnah*, New York: Feldheim Publishers, p. 136.
17. Goldin, Judah. 1955. "The Period of the Talmud (135 B.C.E.–1035 C.E.)," in Finkelstein, Louis, ed., 1955. *The Jews, Their History, Culture, and Religion, op. cit*, Vol. 1, pp. 165–166.
18. Goldin, "The Period of the Talmud," in Finkelstein, ed., Vol. 1, p. 163; also fn. Levine, Lee I. 1999. "The Age of Hellenism," in Shanks, H., ed., 1999. *Ancient Israel, op. cit*, pp. 210, 263.
19. Cook, S. A. 1911. "Midrash," *Encyclopaedia Britannica*, 11th ed., *op. cit.*, Vol. 18, pp. 419–423.
20. Cook, S. A. 1911. "Talmud," *Encyclopaedia Britannica*, 11th ed., *op. cit.*, Vol. 26, pp. 380–386.
21. Neusner, Jacob. 1989. "Rabbinic Judaism in Late Antiquity," in Seltzer, Robert M., ed., 1989. *Judaism, A People and Its History, op. cit.*, pp. 75–76; Johnson, Paul. 1987. *A History of the Jews, op. cit.*, p. 157.
22. Baron, S. W. 1942. *The Jewish Community, op. cit.*, Vol. 1, p. 123.
23. Neusner, Jacob. 1989. "Rabbinic Judaism in Late Antiquity," in Seltzer, Robert M., ed., 1989. *Judaism, A People and Its History, op. cit.*, p. 77.
24. *Ibid.*, p. 78.
25. Steinsaltz A. 1989. *The Talmud,* New York: Random House, pp. 1–7.
26. Baron, S. W. 1942, *op. cit.* p. 109.

27. Steinsaltz, A. 1989. *op. cit.*, pp. 1–7.
28. Goldin, Judah. 1989. "Midrash and Aggadah," in Seltzer, Robert M., ed., 1989. *Judaism, A People and Its History, op. cit.*, p. 109.
29. Cook, S. A. 1911. "Talmud," in *Encyclopaedia Britannica*, 11th ed., *op. cit.*, Vol. 26, p. 384.
30. *Ibid.*
31. Noss, J. B. 1949. *Man's Religions*, New York: Macmillan, pp. 551–553; Goldenberg, R. 1989. "Talmud," in Seltzer, Robert M., ed., 1989. *Judaism, A People and Its History, op. cit.*, pp. 102–103.
32. Goldin, Judah. 1989. "Midrash and Aggadah," in Seltzer, Robert M., ed., 1989. *Judaism, A People and Its History, op. cit.*, p. 108.
33. Goldin, Judah. 1955. "The Period of the Talmud (135 B.C.E.–1035 C.E.)," in Finkelstein, Louis, ed., 1955. *The Jews, Their History, Culture, and Religion*, 2 vols., *op. cit.*, Vol. 1, p. 148.
34. Avi Yonah, M. 1945. *Byeme Roma Ubizantiyon*, Jerusalem, p. 175f; Goldin, Judah. 1955. "The Period of the Talmud (135 B.C.E.-1035 C.E.)," in Finkelstein, Louis, ed., 1955. *The Jews, Their History, Culture, and Religion*, 2 vols., *op. cit.*, Vol. 1, Note 28, p. 212.
35. Novak, D. 1989. "The Structure of Halakah," in Seltzer, Robert M., ed., 1989. *Judaism, A People and Its History, op. cit.*, p. 224.
36. Abrahams, Israel. 1910. "Circumcision," in *Encyclopaedia Britannica*, 11th ed., New York: Cambridge Univ. Press, Vol. VI, p. 404.
37. Goldin, Judah. 1955. "The Period of the Talmud (135 B.C.E.–1035 C.E.)," in Finkelstein, Louis, ed., 1955. *The Jews, Their History, Culture, and Religion*, 2 vols., *op. cit.*, Vol. 1, p. 177.
38. Maimonides, M. 1927. *Iggeret Teman* Warsaw, quoted in Goldin, J. 1955 "The Period of the Talmud (135 BCE-1035 CE), in Finkelstein, L. *The Jews* . . . Vol. 1, *op. cit.*, p. 197.
39. Goldin, Judah. 1955. "The Period of the Talmud (135 B.C.E.-1035 C.E.)," in Finkelstein, Louis, ed., 1955. *The Jews, Their History, Culture, and Religion*, 2 vols., *op. cit.*, Vol. 1, p. 177.
40. Singer, C. 1955. "Science and Judaism," in Finkelstein, Louis, ed., 1955. *The Jews, Their History, Culture, and Religion*, 2 vol., Vol. II, *op. cit.*, p. 1048.
41. Altmann, A. 1955. "Judaism and World Philosophy," in Finkelstein, Louis, ed., 1955. *The Jews, Their History, Culture, and Religion*, 2 vol., Vol 1, *op. cit.*, pp. 640–641; Cowley, A. C. 1911. "Saadiah," *Encyclopaedia Britannica*, 11th ed., *op cit*, Vol. 24, pp. 531–533.
42. Singer, C. 1955. "Science and Judaism," in Finkelstein, Louis, ed., 1955. *The Jews, Their History, Culture, and Religion*, 2 vol., Vol. II, *op. cit.*, p. 1054.
43. Baron, S. W. 1942. *The Jewish Community, op. cit.*, Vol. 1, p. 194; Maller, J. B. "The Role of Education in Jewish History," in Finkelstein, Louis, ed., 1955. *The Jews, Their History, Culture, and Religion*, 2 vol., Vol. II, *op. cit.*, pp. 907–908; Singer, C. 1955. "Science and Judaism," in Finkelstein, Louis, ed., 1955. *The Jews, Their History, Culture, and Religion*, 2 vol., Vol. II, *op. cit.*, p. 1055.
44. Rosner, F. 1975. *Moses Maimonides, Commentary on the Mishnah, op. cit.*, p. 136.
45. Patai, R. 1977. *The Jewish Mind*, New York: Scribner, p. 125.
46. Singer, C. 1955. "Science and Judaism," in Finkelstein, Louis, ed., 1955. *The Jews, Their History, Culture, and Religion*, 2 vol., Vol. II, *op. cit.*, pp. 1053–1054.
47. Novak, D. 1989. "The Structure of Halakah," in Seltzer, Robert M., ed., 1989. *Judaism, A People and Its History, op. cit.*, pp. 224–225.

48. Goldin, Judah. 1955. "The Period of the Talmud (135 B.C.E.-1035 C.E.)," in Finkelstein, Louis, ed., 1955. *The Jews, Their History, Culture, and Religion*, 2 vols., *op. cit.*, Vol. 1, p. 181.
49. Neusner, Jacob. 1989. "Rabbinic Judaism in Late Antiquity," in Seltzer, Robert M., ed., 1989. *Judaism, A People and Its History*, *op. cit.*, p. 79.
50. Goldenberg, R. 1989. "Talmud," in Seltzer, Robert M., ed., 1989. *Judaism, A People and Its History*, *op. cit.*, p. 106.
51. Neusner, Jacob. 1989. "Rabbinic Judaism in Late Antiquity," in Seltzer, Robert M., ed., 1989. *Judaism, A People and Its History*, *op. cit.*, p. 79.
52. Levine, Lee I. 2000. *The Ancient Synagogue, The First Thousand Years*, New Haven, CT: Yale Univ. Press, p. 360.
53. Levine, L. 2000, *op. cit.*, p. 359.
54. Levine, L. 2000, *op. cit.*, p. 375.
55. Neusner, Jacob. 1989. "Rabbinic Judaism in Late Antiquity," in Seltzer, Robert M., ed., 1989. *Judaism, A People and Its History*, *op. cit.*, p. 79.
56. Goldenberg, R. 1989. "Talmud," in Seltzer, Robert M., ed., 1989. *Judaism, A People and Its History*, *op. cit.*, pp. 104–1056.
57. Baron, S. W. 1942. *The Jewish Community*, *op. cit.*, Vol. 1, p. 124.
58. Itzkoff, S. W. 2006. *Fatal Gift*. Ashfield, MA: Paideia Publishers, p. 99.
59. Hilberg, R. 1985. *The Destruction of the European Jews*, Vol. I, 3rd ed., New Haven, CT: Yale Univ. Press, p. 22.
60. Graetz, H. (1817–1891). *History of the Jews*, Philadelphia: Jewish Publication Society, 5:292–301.
61. Patai, R. 1977. *The Jewish Mind*, New York: Scribner, p. 468.
62. Patai, *op. cit.*, quote of H. Graetz, *History of the Jews.*, *op. cit.*, pp. 469–470.

Chapter six: Haskalah: Crisis

1. Graetz, Heinrich. *History of the Jews*, Reprint, Philadelphia: Jewish Publication Society, 5:83–84, 167.
2. Bodian, M. 1997. *Hebrews of the Portuguese Nation*, Bloomington: Indiana Univ. Press.
3. Patai, R. 1977. *The Jewish Mind*, *op. cit.*, p. 166.
4. Luther, Martin. 1543. *Wittenberg, Von der Jueden und ihren Luegen*, p. Aiii, in Hilberg, R. 1985. *The Destruction of the European Jews*, Vol. II, 3rd ed., *op. cit.*, p. 409; also quoted in Hilberg, 1985. *The Destruction of the European* Jews, Vol. 1, 2nd ed., *op. cit.*, p. 16.
5. Sorkin, D. 1994. "Jews, the Enlightenment, and Religious Toleration—Some Reflections, in *The Jews in European History*. Cincinnati: Hebrew Union College Press, pp. 39–56.
6. Patai, *The Jewish Mind*, *op. cit.*, p. 236*ff.*
7. *Ibid.*, p. 251.
8. *Ibid.*
9. Montesquieu, Works I: 218–219.
10. Patai, *The Jewish Mind*, *op. cit.*, p. 252; Sorkin, "Jews, the Enlightenment, and Religious Toleration—Some Reflections," *op. cit.*, pp. 39–56.

11. Gilman, S. L. 1996. *Smart Jews*, Lincoln: Univ. of Nebraska Press, p. 15; Kant, I. *Anthropology from a Pragmatic Point of View*, tr. by V. L. Dowdell (1978), Carbondale: Southern Illinois Univ. Press, pp. 101–102.
12. Patai, *op. cit.*, p. 445; Kant, I. 1789 *Anthropologie*, Part 1, Bk. 1, Par. 29.
13. Kant, I. (1798) 1838. "Der Streit der Facultäten," in *Sämtlicher Werke*, 10, Leipzig, p. 338; Meyer, M. 1994. "Should and Can an 'Antiquated' Religion Become Modern?" in *The Jews in European History*, ed., by Wolfgang Beck, Cincinnati: Hebrew Union College Press, pp. 62–63.
14. Tr. by R. Patai, 1977. *The Jewish Mind*, *op. cit.*, p. 244.
15. Abraham, Israel. 1911. "Moses Mendelssohn," in *Encyclopedia Britannica*, 11th ed., *op. cit.*, Vol. XVIII, p. 121.
16. Altman, Alexander. 1955. "Judaism and World Philosophy," in Finkelstein, Louis, ed., 1955. *The Jews, Their History, Culture, and Religion*, *op. cit.*, 2 vols., Vol. 1, p. 660.
17. Sorkin, D. 1944."Jews, the Enlightenment, and Religious Toleration—Some Reflections," *op. cit.*, pp. 48–49.
18. Salo Baron, quoted by Patai, *The Jewish Mind*, *op. cit.*, p. 253.
19. Dawidowicz, L. S. 1975. *The War against the Jews, 1933–1945*, New York: Holt, Rinehart and Winston, pp. 26–27; Johann Gottlieb Fichte, *Reden an die deutsche Nation* (1808).
20. Finkelstein, L. 1955. "Jewish Religion: Its Beliefs and Practices," in *The Jews: Their History, Culture and Religion*, ed., L. Finkelstein, 2 vols., *op. cit.*, Vol. 1, p. 1347.
21. Meyer, M. 1989. "Reform Judaism," in Seltzer, R., ed., *Judaism: A. People and Its History*. *op. cit.*, pp. 307–320.
22. Meyer, M., 1955, *op. cit.*
23. Rosenblum, H. 1989. "Conservative Judaism." in *Judaism, A People and Its History*, ed., R. Seltzer. *op. cit.*, pp. 290–300; Liebman, C. 1989. "Orthodox Judaism," in Seltzer, R. ed., *Judaism: A People and Its History*, *op. cit.*, pp. 275–289.
24. Davis, M. 1955. "Jewish Religious Life and Institutions in America," in *The Jews: Their History, Culture and Religion*, ed., L. Finkelstein, *op. cit.*, pp. 354–453.
25. Davis, M. 1955, *op. cit.*
26. Davis, M. 1955, *op. cit.*, pp. 381–383.
27. Davis, M. 1955, *op. cit.*
28. Borowitz, E. 1989 "Judaism: An Overview, in *"Judaism, A People and Its History*, ed., R. Seltzer, *op. cit.*, p. 25.
29. Kaplan, Mordecai. 1934. Judaism as a Civilization. New York: Macmillan.
30. Ibid., p. 391.
31. Schulweis, H. 1989. "Reconstructionist Judaism," in R. Seltzer, ed., *Judaism: A People and its History*, *op. cit.*, pp. 304–305
32. Davis, M. 1955. "Jewish Religious Life and Institutions in America," in *The Jews: Their History, Culture and Religion*, ed., L. Finkelstein, *op. cit.*, p. 419.
33. Dan, J. 1989. "Hasidism," in *Judaism, A People and Its History*, R. Seltzer, ed., *op. cit.*, pp. 263–274.
34. Patai, *The Jewish Mind*, *op. cit.*, pp. 180–181.
35. Dubnow, S. 1931. *Geschichte des Chassidismus*, tr. Patai, Berlin: Judischer Verlag, I-67–68.
36. Zipperstein, S. 1989. "Judaism in Northern and Eastern Europe Since 1500," in *Judaism, A People and Its History*, ed., R. Seltzer, *op. cit.*, p. 188.
37. Hartman, D. 2007. "The real threat to Judaism's renewal," *Haaretz.com*, May 23.

Chapter seven: Our Judaic Heritage

1. Cook, S. 1911. "Talmud," in *Encyclopaedia Britannica, 11th ed.*, Vol 26, *op. cit.*, p. 284.
2. Smalley, B. 1952. *The Study of the Bible in the Middle Ages*, New York: Oxford Univ. Press, p. 78.
3. Pipes, D. 2005. "The Future of Judaism," *New York Sun*, January 25; Pipes, D. 2006. "More About the Future of Judaism," www.danielpipes.or/blog/2006. April 27.

Chapter eight: *Holocaust:* A Message for the Jews

1. Marcus, J. R. 1934. *The Rise and Destiny of the German Jew*, Cincinnati: Union of American Hebrew Congregations, pp. 26–36.
2. Fritsch, Theodor. 1896. Anti-Semitism. Leipzig: Hammer Verlag.
3. Fritsch, Theodore. 1923, 1927. *The Riddle of Jewish Success,* Leipzig; Patai, p. 457; also see Weiss, J. 1996. *Ideology of Death,* Chicago: Ivan Dee.
4. Gilman, S. 1996. *Smart Jews: The construction of the image of Jewish superior intelligence,* Lincoln, Univ. of Nebraska Press, p. 46; Woltmann, L. 1904. "Rassenpsychologie und Kulturgeschichte," *Politisch-Anthropologische Revue* 3:350–357.
5. Berkley, G. 1988. *Vienna and Its Jews: The tragedy of success,* Cambridge, MA: Abt Books, p. 108.
6. Gilman, *op. cit.*, pp. 47–48.
7. Weyl, N. 1989. *The Geography of American Achievement,* Washington, D.C.: Scott-Townsend, pp. 242–243.
8. Berkley, *op. cit.*, p. 159.
9. Comas, J. 1951. *Racial Myths*, Paris: UNESCO, pp. 27–32.
10. Hitler, A. *Mein Kampf*; Gilman, *op. cit.*, pp. 48–49.
11. Patai, R. 1977. *The Jewish Mind, op. cit.*
12. Patai tr., p. 476.
13. Patai, *op. cit.*, p. 471*ff.*
14. Patai, *op. cit.*, p. 463; Abrahamsen, D. 1946. *The Mind and Death of a Genius,* New York: Columbia Univ. Press, p. 183*ff.*
15. Berkley, *op. cit.*, p. 48.
16. Comas, *op. cit.*, pp. 27–32.
17. Quoted in Gilman, p. 45.
18. Kretschmer, E. 1919. *Geniale Menschen,* Berlin: Julius Springer, 1929, p. 79; Gilman, pp. 53–54; see also a contemporary Jewish analysis: Fishberg, M. 1918. "Rassenlichtung der Juden," in *Statistik der Juden,* Berlin: Judischer Verlag, pp. 70–86.
19. Guenther, H. F. K. 1930. *Rassenkunde des judischen Volke,* Munich: J. F. Lehmann, pp. 202–203, cited in Patai, pp. 304–305.
20. Lenz, F., Bauer, E., Fischer, E. 1931. *Human Heredity,* Ch. by Fritz Lenz, "The Inheritance of Intellectual Gifts," New York: Macmillan, pp. 674–677; Patai, p. 327*ff*; Gilman, pp. 53–54.
21. Leroy-Beaulieu, A. 1893. *Israel among the Nations: A Study of Jews and Anti-Semitism,* Paris: Levy, p. 226.

22. Gilman, *op. cit.*, p. 4*ff.*
23. Galton, F. 1869. *Hereditary Genius: An Inquiry into its Laws and Consequences*, London: Macmillan, Ch. 23 on Race, Ch. 4 on Jews and Italians; Gilman, *op. cit.*, quotes, pp. 33–34; C. Russell writing in 1900 states of the Jewish East End school children: "The foreign children in the East End are universally allowed to be sharper and more intelligent than the English and they carry off a large percentage of the prizes and scholarships." In Weyl, N., and Possony, S. T. 1963. *The Geography of Intellect*, Chicago: Regnery, p. 162.
24. Davidowicz, L. 1975. *The War Against the Jews, 1933–1945*, N.Y. Holt Rinehart and Winston, p. 47.
25. Hitler, A., *Mein Kampf*, quoted in Gilman S., *op. cit.*, pp. 48–49; all quotes from: Hitler, A. 1943 (1927). *Mein Kampf* 3 vols., rev. ed., Boston: Houghton Mifflin, Total of 1312 pp.
26. Zweig, A. 1983. "Ruckblick auf Barberei und Buchverbrennung," in *Das Vorspiel Die Buchverbrennung am 10 Mai 1933*, ed., by T. Friedrich Berlin: LitPol, pp. 43–45.
27. Joseph Goebbels, Hitler's Minister of "National Enlightenment and Propaganda," in a September 29, 1933, statement published in *New York Times*, quoted in, Marcus, J. 1934. *The Rise and Destiny of the German Jew*, Cincinnati: Union of Hebrew Congregations, p. 43.
28. Goldin, Judah. 1955. "The Period of the Talmud (135 B.C.E.–1035 C.E.)," in Finkelstein, Louis, ed., 1955. *The Jews, Their History, Culture, and Religion, op. cit.*, Vol. 1, p. 152; Lieberman, S. 1965. *Greek in Jewish Palestine*, New York: p. Feldheim, pp. 1, 20.
29. Medawer, J., and Pyke, D. 2001. *Hitler's Gift*, New York: Arcade.
30. Vincent, p. 1966. "The Measured Intelligence of Glasgow Jewish School Children," *Jewish Journal of Sociology*, 8:92–108; Eysenck, H. and Kamin, L. 1981. *The Intelligence Controversy*, New York: J. Wiley.
31. Page, E. 1976. "A Historical Step beyond Terman," in Keating, D. ed., *Intellectual Talent*, Baltimore: Johns Hopkins Press, pp. 305–306; Itzkoff, S. 2005. *Rebuilding Western Civilization*, Ch. 4, "Civilizational Intelligence," pp. 59–84, Ashfield, MA: Paideia.
32. Werner Heisenberg, a noted Gentile physicist who could have led the Nazi atomic program, stayed behind in Germany, an ambivalent recruit to the Nazi war machine. Werner von Braun, an enthusiastic rocket scientist for Hitler's B-2 war against England, became an eager turncoat working for the American program after 1945.

Chapter nine: Israel, Judaism: Our Contemporary World Malaise

1. Chang, J. & Halliday, J. 2005 *Mao, the Unknown Story*, New York: Knopf.
2. Itzkoff, S. 2008. *The World Energy Crisis and the Task of Retrenchment* Lewiston, New York: Mellen.
3. Brooks, D. 2010. "The Tel Aviv Cluster," *New York Times*, 12 Jan.
4. Lombroso, C. (1835–1909) 1889. *The Mind of Genius.*
5. Laski, H. 1910. "The Scope of Eugenics," *Westminster Review*, July.
6. Hart, M. 2007. *The Healthy Jew: The Symbiosis of Judaism and Medicine*, New York: Cambridge Univ. Press; Hashiloni-Dolev, Y. 2006. "Between Mothers, Fetuses and

Society: Reproductive Genetics in the Israeli-Jewish Context," *NASHIM*; Hashiloni-Dolev, Y. 2007. *What Is a Life (un)Worthy of Living*, Dordrecht: Springer/Kluwer.
7. Kolata, G. 2003. "Using Genetic Tests Ashkenazi Jews Vanquish a Disease," *New York Times*, 18 Feb; Goddard, L. 2003. "Genetic Tests Offered," *South Florida Sun Sentinel*, 21 Feb.
8. Joseph Chamie (former Head, UN Population Division). 2008. Center for Migration Studies, New York: *The World Almanac, 2008*; *The CIA World Fact Book*.
9. "Arab Human Development Report-2002." *New York Times*, 2 July '02.
10. Arab 2003. Human Development Report.
11. Brooks, D. *op. cit.*
12. Brooks, D. *op. cit.*

Chapter ten: Understanding Historical Judaism

1. Weber, M. 1919/1952. *Ancient Judaism*, New York: The Free Press, p. 138.
2. Greenstein, Edward L. in *HarperCollins Study Bible, op. cit.*, Notes, p. 81.
3. Abrahams, Israel. 1910. "Circumcision," *Encyclopedia Britannica, Brit., op. cit.*, 11th ed., Vol. VI, pp. 389–390; Gottwald, N. K., *op. cit.*, p. 218.
4. Weber, M., *op. cit.*, p. 34.
5. Weber, M., *op. cit.*, p. 336*ff.*
6. See Notes in New Standard Bible—Harpers, on Mesopotamian lunar calendar prohibitions—fear of godly retribution transferred to Israelites. E. Greenstein. p. 116.
7. Weber, M., *op. cit.*, p. 149*ff.*
8. Weber, M. *op. cit.*, pp. 47–49.
9. Fourth Commandment, Masoretic text.
10. *Ibid.*
11. Milgrom, J. 1989. Notes, *The New Revised Standard Bible, op. cit.*, pp. 167–168.
12. Kaplan, M. 1934. *Judaism as a Civilization*, pp. 440–443; Weber, M., *op. cit.*, p. 351*ff.*
13. Friedman R. 1997. *Who Wrote the Bible?* San Francisco: Harper, p. 96.
14. Rivkin, E. 1978. *A Hidden Revolution, op. cit.*
15. Weber, M. *op. cit.*, pp. 385–389.
16. Kaplan, M. 1958. *Judaism without Supernaturalism*, New York: Reconstructionist Press, pp. 66–67.
17. Kaplan, M. 1934. *op. cit.*
18. Weber, M. *op. cit,*. pp. 139–146.
19. Cohen, S. 1999. *The Beginnings of Jewishness*, Berkeley: Univ of California, pp. 263–307, esp. p. 273.
20. Weber, M., *op. cit.*, pp. 350–351.
21. Cohen, S., *op. cit.*, p. 273.
22. Cohen, S., *op. cit.*, pp. 293–298
23. Epstein, L. 1942. *Marriage Laws in the Bible and the Talmud*, Cambridge, MA: Harvard Univ. Press.
24. Cohen, S., *op. cit.*, p. 296.

25. *Ibid.*, pp. 290–291.
26. Hilberg, R. 1985. *The Destruction of the European Jews,* Vol. I, 3rd ed., New Haven, CT: Yale Univ. Press, p. 22.
27. Abrahams, I. 1934. *Jewish Life in the Middle Ages,* 2nd ed., Chs. XIX, XX, London: Edward Goldstone.

Chapter eleven: Judaism Reconstituted

1. Neusner, J. 1989. "Rabbinic Judaism in Late Antiquity," in *Judaism: A People and its History,* ed., by R. Seltzer, *op. cit.*
2. Kaplan, M. 1934. *Judaism as a Civilization, op cit.,* pp. 513–514.
3. Wine, S. 1995. *Judaism beyond God,* Farmington Hills, MI: Society for Humanistic Judaism-KTAV Publishing House, p. 221.

Chapter twelve: Values and the Future

1. Rivkin, E. 1978. *The Hidden Revolution, op cit.,* p. 255.
2. Levine, L. 2000 *The Ancient Synagogue. op cit.*
3. Wine, S. 1997. *Judaism beyond God,* Farmington Hills, MI: Society for Humanistic Judaism-KTAV Publishing House, pp. 259–260.
4. Harrington, Edward. 1989, in *Harper Collins Study Bible, op cit.,* pp. 1601–1602.
5. Milne, Pamela. 1989, in *Harper Collins Study Bible, op. cit,* p. 1303.
6. Mack, B. 1989. "Sirach," in *Harper Collins Study Bible, op. cit.,* pp. 1530–1532. c. 180 BCE—Jerusalem.
7. Josephus, c. 90 CE. *Against Apion* II, pp. 209–210.

Index

A
Abba, Rabbi, 73
abortion, 138, 139
Abraham, Israel, 89
Adath Jeshurun, 92
Adler, Felix, 24, 95, 180
Ahab, King, 35
Ahlwardt, Herman, 120
Altman, Alexander, 89
American Hebrew College, 95
am ha arez, xii, 35, 36, 48, 106, 156, 193
ammei ha arets, 56
Amon, 34
amoraim, 71, 72
anti-Semitism, 118–21, 195
Aquinas, Thomas, 170
Arabs, 141
Arafat, Yasser, 140
Aristotle, 148
Armenia, 132
Ashkenazi Jews, 4, 139, 166, 169
Ashkenazim, 76–78, 85

Aufklärung, 86–88
Averroes, 170

B
Babylonia, 40
Bamberger, Seligman Ber, 94
Baron, S.W., 65
Beginnings of Jewishness, The, xiv
Bet Din, 52, 68
Bickerman, E.J., 39
Boeckel, Otto, 120
Book of Beliefs and Convictions, 74
Buddhism, 4, 24

C
Cambodia, 133
Cassirer, Ernst, 20
Catholicism, 181
Centralverein deutscher Staatsburger judischer Glaubens, 121
Chabad, 8
Chamberlain, Houston Stewart, 120

China, 183
Christianity, 2, 4
    abortion and, 138
    Papal, 8
    right wing of, 138
    rise to power, 195
    scholasticism and, 71, 113
    South Korea and, 5
    as an underground religion, 70
Cincinnati movement, 179
circumcision, 149–51, 176–177
Codex Theodosius, 77
Cohen, Shaye, xiv, 162
Communism, 189
Confusionism, 24
Conservative movement, 181
Contra Apion, 108
Copernicus, Nicholas, 83
Costa, Uriel da, 84
Cro-Magnon man, 14–16, 17, 18, 21

D
Darwin, Charles, 124
Delmedigo, Joseph, 89
Deutsche Volksage, Die, 120
Diaspora, 56
Discourse on the Status of the Jews, 83, 87

E
economic crisis, 194
Edomites, 41
Einhorn, David, 94
Eliezer, Israel ben, 98
Elion, 158
Elohim, 67
Encyclopedia Britannica, 28
Enlightenment, xv
Epstein, Louis, 162
Essenes, 53, 55, 59
Ethical Culture Society, 24, 180
Eugenics, 138

F
Fascism, 189
Fichte, Johann Gottlieb, 92

Finkelstein, Louis, 11, 25, 97
Foundations of the Nineteenth Century, 120
Frankel, Zacharias, 93, 95
Friedlander, David, 87
Friedman, Richard, 30, 31
Fritsch, Theodore, 119

G
Gabirol, Solomon Ibn, 74
Galton, Francis, 124
Gaon, Saadia, 190
Gedaliah, 38
Geiger, Abraham, 93
Gemara, 70–72
Gemeinde, 92
genocide, 133
Goebbels, Joseph, 125, 126
Goldin, Judah, 77
Graetz, H., 81, 93
Guide of the Perplexed, 87

H
Haggadah, 67
ha golah, 96
Hahn, Otto, 129
Halakhah, 67, 70, 72, 79, 113, 176
Handbook of Anti-Semitism, 119
Haredim, x, xiii, 8, 179, 181
Hasidism, 98–99
Haskala, 80, 83–86
Hasmoneans, 52, 53
haverim, 56
Hebrew Union College, xiv
Herzl, Theodore, 122
Hezekiah, 30, 103
Hinduism, 23
Hirsch, Samuel Raphael, 93, 94
Hitler, Adolf, 124–27, 132–33, 195
Hobbes, Thomas, 28
Holdheim, Samuel, 93
Holocaust, xiii, xv, xvi, 1, 4, 6, 7, 95, 98,
    116, 117–18, 127–30, 167, 198, 200
Holy Scriptures, xi, 59–61
holy scrolls, 105
Human, All Too Human, 123

human behavior, 12, 16
human sacrifice, 23
Humanist Synagogue movement, 180
hypertropism, 13
Hyrcanus, John, 52, 53

I

Introduction to Commentary on Tractate Aboth, Mishnah, 75
Islam, 2
Israel, 46, 117, 178, 182, 184
    destiny of, 136–38
    Hamas and, 142
    as the "Jewish state," 188–89
    socio/scientific exemplar of, 138–40
    survival of, 140–42
Israel, Mennasseh ben, 84, 88

J

Jerusalem, Or, On Ecclesiastical Authority and Judaism, 89
Jew and modern Capitalism, The, 120
Jew Bill, 87
Jewish Humanism, 3
Jewish State, The, 122
Jewish Theological Seminary, xiv, 3, 11, 96, 97
Jews/Judaism
    19th-century American leadership, 94
    abortion and, 138, 139
    accommodation with modernity, 95–98
    accomplishments of, 14243
    American, 24
    apogee of, 108
    Ashkenazi, 4, 139, 166, 169
    assimilation in 19th-century Paris, 90–92
    Babylonian, 73–74
    case for, 3–6
    Catholic Church and, 7
    celibacy, 182
    challenge in 21st century, 144
    child molestation, 182
    Christianity and, 8, 66, 113
    circumcision and, 149–51, 176–77
    as a classless society, 184, 196
    community in Spain, 74
    Conservative movement, 11
    contemporary dilemmas, 177–80
    conversion to Christianity, 114
    crisis of, 115
    decline of, x
    Diaspora, 56, 58, 63, 117
    dietary laws, 153–54
    Dionysian form of, 79
    disintegration of Temple, 51–55
    education and, ix–x
    entering the Germanies, 86
    European reform and, 92–94
    expansion of organizations, 195–96
    expulsion from Poland, 85
    expulsion from Portugal, 85
    expulsion from Spain, 76, 85
    fifth revolution, xv–xvi
    first religious revolution, 45
    four revolutionary stages of, xiv–xv, 109–11
    future of, 133–36, 185, 190
    Greeks and, 65
    Hasidism, 98–99
    Hellenization of, 48–51
    historic challenge of, 169–71
    historical, 147–49
    Holy Land, 58
    intellectual values of, 127–28, 129
    intermarriage, 98
    internationalization of, 178
    leadership education, 200
    leadership of, 101, 185, 188–90, 190–92, 193, 197–98
    literacy and, 46–48
    Mainz and, 165
    marriage and, 4, 160, 161
    model for the secular, 187
    modern, 198–200
    modern significance of, xvii, 1
    monotheism and, 64, 147–49, 174, 181
    moral vision for, 193–96
    Muslims and, 5, 113
    national defense of, 102–5
    Oral Torah and, 155–59
    organization of, 199
    pacifism and, 46

Palestinian War, 8
pogroms and, 77
political realm and, 188, 199
population statistics, 1, 65, 99, 135
portable literary heritage of, 111
potential of, 181–83
principles of, 198–99
Protestantism and, 7
rabbinic, 73–74
rationality, 166–67
recognition of, 123–24
reconstructionist movement, 96
Reform, 24, 118
Roman Empire and, 109, 162
Sabbath and, 151–53, 174
Sadducees and, 156
Samaria and, 39
science and, 75
scholarly classes and, 103
secular analysis, 8–9
self-hatred, 121–22
social responsibility and, 199–200
supernaturalism and, 181
survival of, 101–2
Talmudic, 80, 165, 171
Temple cult, 102–5
theological, 199
ultraorthodox, 9
in the United States, 2, 5, 94, 191
wealth and, 199
worldly need for, 183–85
writings of, 105–9
Josefowitz, Herschel, 91
Joseph, Saadia ben, 164
Josephus, 55, 58, 64, 65, 66, 108, 111, 128, 170
Josiah, 34
Judah, 104, 105
Judaism as a Civilization, 97
Justin, Jean, 65

K

Kant, Immanuel, 88
Kaplan, Mordicai, 3, 4, 5, 8, 97, 115, 172, 179
kashruth law, 153, 175–76

Kibbutzim, 136
Knesset ha Gedolah, 52
Kohut, Alexander, 95
Kraemer, Joel, xiv
Kretchmer, Ernst, 123

L

Landau, Ezekiel, 91
Laski, Harold, 138
Leeser, Isaac, 95
Lenz, Fritz, 123
Leroy-Beaulieu, Anatole, 124
Letter Concerning Toleration, 87
Lettres Juives, 87
Lettres Persanes, 88
literacy, 78–82
Locke, John, 87
Lombroso, Cesare, 138
Luther, Martin, 83, 119
Luzzatto, Simeone, 83

M

Maccabean revolt, 157
Maimon, Solomon, 90, 143
Maimonides, xiv
Maimonides, Moses, 75, 76, 87, 89, 112, 128, 143, 170, 187
Marr, Wilhelm, 119
Marshack, Alexander, 18
Marx, Karl, 124, 170–71, 197
matrilineal principle, 159–63
Mein Kampf, 125, 132
Meitner, Lise, 129
Mendelssohn, Felix, 91
Mendelssohn, Moses, xiii, 86–87, 88–90, 91, 134, 143, 170, 195
Mesopotamia, 106
Meyer, Karl, 124
Meyer, Michael, 88
Mishnah, xiv, 61, 66, 67–70, 160
modernity, 173
Mohammed, Muthathir, 133
monotheism, 64, 147–49, 173, 181
Montesquieu, 88

Morias, Sabato, 95
Mu'tazilah, 74

N
Nabonidas, King, 37
Nasi, Judah Ha, 69
Neanderthals, 14
Nehushtan, 33
Neue Freie Presse, 122
Newton, Isaac, 88
Nietzsche, Friedrich, 123
Nineveh, 37

O
Oral Law, 56, 66, 71, 106, 107, 115, 160
Oral Torah, xii, 50, 56–57, 61, 155–59
Orientalism, 156

P
Patai, Raphael, 85, 121
Pentateuch, 24, 103
Pericles, 106
Pharisees, 53, 55–59, 157, 158, 159
  process of development, 32
  Samaritan version of, 31
  translation into Greek, 49
Philo, 64, 66, 108, 128, 143, 163, 170
polytheism, 23
Preacher of Morals, 87
Proseuch, 107

Q
Qumran, 53, 54, 59

R
Rabbi Isaac Elchanan Theological Seminary, 95
rabbinism, xi–xii, xiv, 73–74, 188
Rabshakeh, 34
rationality, 166–67
Reasons for Naturalizing the Jews of Great Britain and Ireland, 87
Reconstructionism, 3, 179
Redactor, 30

Reform movement, 181
religiosity, 19–23
  evolution of, 23–24
  Judaism and, 24–25
religious symbols, 19
Revel, Bernard, 95
Riddle of the Jewish Success, The, 119
Rivkin, Ellis, 51, 56

S
Saadia, 73–74, 143
Sabbath, 151–53, 174
Sadducees, 54, 107, 156
Samaria, 21–23, 24, 39
Sanhedrin, 49, 52
Sarton, George, 76
Schecter, Solomon, 95
Schneerson, Isaac, 99
scribes, 41
Shabattu, 152
Shasu Bedouins, 148
Shintoism, 5
Singer, C., 74
Smith, William Robertson, 28
Society for Ethical Culture, 95
Society for the Culture and Science of Judaism, 93
Soferim, 106, 107, 157
Sofer, Moses, 91, 93
Sombart, Werner, 120
Spinoza, Baruch, 28, 84, 114, 128, 143
Spinoza, Benedict, 170
Stalin, Joseph, 126, 132
Steinhardt, Mendel, 92
Streicher, Julius, 121
supernaturalism, 181
Synagogue, 58, 107, 172, 188

T
Talmud, xi, 71, 77
  Ashkenazic, 80
  gift of, 111–14
  new, 192
  republic, 63–65

ritual and moral behavior, 170
Sabbath violations, 175
scientific revolution and, 170
study, 81
survival and, 163–66
Tannaim and, 68
TaNaK, xii
Tanakh, 71
Tannaitic writings, 51
Taoism, 24
Tel Aviv, 137
Temple, destruction of, 59, 63
Ten Commandments, 35, 104
Third Reich, 123
Tolland, John, 83–84, 87
Torah, xi, 27–28, 42–43
    completion of, 37
    Greek philosophers and, 65
    Halakhah, 67
    historical Judaism, 43
    as an intellectual process, 78
    introduction of, 41
    J and E versions of, 22
    myth of, 173
    as *nomos*, 108
    Pericles and, 106
    prelude to, 25–26
    reinterpretation of, 58
    in Samaria, 38–40
    translation into Greek, 49, 107
totem and taboo, 21

U
Union of Orthodox Rabbis, 97

V
Veit, Philip, 91
Victory of the Jews over the Germans, The, 119
Vindiciae Judaeorum, 88
Voltaire, 87, 88

W
Wellhausen, Julius, 28, 30
Wessely, Naphtali Herz, 87, 89
Wine, Sherwin, 3, 4, 5, 8, 172, 180, 190, 191
Wise, Isaac Meyer, 94
Woltmann, L., 120
Words of Peace and Truth, 89
Workmen's Circle, 182
Workmen's movement, 181
Written Law, 56, 71

X

Y
Yahweh, 50
Yavneh, 68
Yehud, 46, 47
yeshiva, 77
Yeshivoth, 79

Z
Zalman, Eliyyahu ben, 91
Zionism, 98, 118, 121–22, 131, 136
Zoroastrianism, 1, 3, 106, 156
Zunz, Leopold, 93